The Guitar Cookbook

by Jesse Gress

Backbeat Books

San Francisco

Published by Backbeat Books
600 Harrison Street, San Francisco, CA 94107
www.backbeatbooks.com
Email: books@musicplayer.com
An imprint of the Music Player Network
United Entertainment Media, Inc.
Publishers of *Guitar Player* and musicplayer.com

Distributed to the book trade in the U.S and Canada by
Publishers Group West, 1700 Fourth Street, Berkeley, CA 94710

Distributed to the music trade in the U.S. and Canada by
Hal Leonard Publishing P.O. Box 13819, Milwaukee, WI 53213

Cover Design by Richard Leeds
Cover Illustration by Mary Fleener
Text Design and Composition by Chris Ledgerwood

Library of Congress Cataloging-in-Publication Data
Gress, Jesse
      The guitar cookbook / by Jesse Gress
            p. cm.
      Cover title: Guitar player presents The guitar cookbook.
      ISBN 0-87930-633-5 (alk. paper)
      1. Guitar—Instruction and study. I. Title: Guitar player presents The guitar cookbook.
II. Guitar player. III. Title

MT580 .G722 2001
787.87'193—dc21

                                                             2001035133

Printed in the United States of America

01 02 03 04 05   5 4 3 2 1

Table of Contents

Dedication

Dedicated to Doc and Ginnie, who enabled me to study and play music,
and to Mary Lou and Deidre, who inspire me to continue.

In memory of Howard Roberts, Tommy Tedesco, and Mary Gress.

Introduction

All music is born of the same three basic elements: rhythm, melody, and harmony. All melodies and harmonies are derived from only twelve different notes. But with ingredients this minimal, how can we categorize music into such diverse genres as classical, jazz, blues, rock, metal, fusion, R&B, country, and hip hop? The question may as well be, "How can you use lumber, nails, and a hammer to build such diverse objects as buildings, bridges, and furniture?" Rhythms, notes, and instruments are simply raw materials and tools for skilled hands and creative minds.

Rhythm—which you can define as any event measured by the division of time—is music's primal element. Rhythm can exist without melody, but melody cannot exist without rhythm. For instance, it's easy to tap a rhythm on a tabletop or door, but without melody notes it's hard to tell "shave and a haircut" from "Who Let the Dogs Out." Stripped of its melody notes, "Mary Had a Little Lamb" could be interpreted as "London Bridge," "Twinkle Twinkle," or "In the Hall of the Mountain King."

Rhythm is the bonding agent that allows musical pitches to be organized in time. A melody is simply an organized group of single pitches superimposed over a specific rhythm. "Mary Had a Little Lamb" glues three different pitches—E, D, and C—to the preceding rhythm.

Harmony—two or more pitches sounding simultaneously—thickens a melody or creates its harmonic environment. You can drastically alter how a melody is perceived by changing its harmonic "climate." When a melody touches listeners' emotions, they might describe it as happy, sad, comical, or scary. This is rarely the result of the melody alone. Different pitches played below a melody suggest different harmonies, which in turn provoke this variety of emotional responses.

In the key of *C*, the first six notes of "Mary Had a Little Lamb" are traditionally played over a *C* bass note. This is how we are used to hearing it:

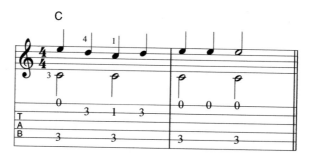

Replace the *Cs* with these bass notes and observe the harmonic mood swing.

Now play the same melody over *E, D, F,* or *B.* Dramatic, isn't it? The melody interacts differently with each bass note. Illuminating physical objects with colored lights to alter the viewer's perception is a common concept in theater, film, and still photography. In music, the melody is the object and the harmony is the coloration. Check out any film score and notice how the music fits the action. Imagine a thrilling car chase scored inappropriately with a quiet section from a Mozart piano sonata and you'll begin to understand how music can manipulate human emotions and make us laugh, cry, or stand up and cheer. Think of each note as a talented ensemble actor, ready to switch harmonic roles at any time.

Timbre—tonal quality—also plays a role in the emotional perception of a melody. Each musical genre is equipped with its own arsenal of instruments, and specific timbres are expected in certain styles of music. You probably won't find a banjo a in chamber music group, a French horn in a country band, or a guitar in a marching band, though more and more cross-pollination is occurring as music follows its evolutionary path.

Dynamics—changes in relative volume—provide contrast between musical events. Music without dynamic contrast quickly becomes dull (too soft) or obnoxious (too loud). A balance of dynamics—shifting from soft to loud, with many subtle, in-between levels—makes a musical performance come to life.

What does all this have to do with playing guitar? *Everything.* In the big picture, being a musician is about much more than playing songs on the guitar. It's about discovering, understanding, and becoming conversant in music's hidden language. I've designed *The Guitar Cookbook* for guitarists who want to become better musicians.

If you are just beginning to play the guitar, applying an understanding of basic music theory to the fingerboard will provide a solid foundation and answers to many questions about rhythm, melody, and harmony before they pop up in practice. If you are an "ear player" and already have a large, stylized musical vocabulary, studying harmony and theory will help you to manipulate already familiar sounds by understanding their inner mechanisms. In the mechanics of music, all melodic and harmonic ideas are fashioned from the same fabric. With increased harmonic awareness, you can transform melodies from major, minor, or blues licks that only "work" over certain chords, to interchangeable melodic-line forms you can manipulate to fit *any* chord.

I suspect a large percentage of guitarists—myself included—were initially lured to our instrument by its *sound* as much as the music people played on it. Once hooked, we encountered the formal-vs.-self-study controversy, which leads to a shocking realization: Unless we choose the classical route, there is no standardized method for guitarists! This seems to put us at a disadvantage compared to the well-worn early training regimens forced on students of piano, violin, and school-band instruments. Or does it? Some of the greatest guitar music has come from self-taught players. But can we assume they rejected music theory outright? Maybe they just never had access to it in the first place.

Fortunately, there has never been a better time to study music on the guitar. New playing techniques are surfacing, and dozens of experienced performers and teachers are sharing their insights in academic institutions and via print, audio, video, and electronic media. Students can now learn in two to five years what once took ten to twenty.

The chapters in this book are logically sequenced, but you shouldn't approach the material only in its presented order. Generally, the first half of each chapter is the hunting-and-gathering stage. You go to the market and collect ingredients, then head for the kitchen to cook up something tasty. You may find it helpful to skip around and find detailed explanations and examples of various points and concepts according to your needs. Don't hesitate to work on any section of the book for weeks or even months. Think of it as a legitimate "cookbook"—a collection of conceptual recipes designed to satisfy your musical appetite with an infinite variety of tastes and textures. I've explained each concept thoroughly, but its application is left up to you—as it should be. With this approach, you play what you want, not what I want. (In the back of the book, I've provided blank music paper for you to write your own melodic ideas, chords, and fretboard maps.)

The goal is to develop a personalized musical vocabulary based on the illustrated concepts and examples, and learn to recognize their applications in *all* music. Once you clearly understand these concepts and achieve the level of technique necessary to execute them, endless musical ideas will flow readily.

This book is not meant to be a one-stop guitar method. It focuses on learning *how* to learn as much as *what* to learn. Add its contents to the growing storehouse of knowledge that comprises your musical vocabulary. If you study with a teacher, bring it to your lessons and ask questions. Refer to it in conjunction with all other study materials, especially recordings. I can't stress enough the importance of listening to music. You are what you hear. If you listen to and analyze enough good music, it will rub off. The elements of music are interconnected, and you can never know too much, so if each new discovery raises a dozen new questions, don't worry—you're definitely on the right track!

The bottom line? You are your own teacher. Teach yourself well, and your music will be without limitations.

CHAPTER ONE

Musical Notation

To fully comprehend the material in this book, you should have a basic understanding of standard music notation as well as specialized guitar notation systems, such as tablature and fingerboard grids.

RHYTHMIC NOTATION

Rhythm may be defined as accented divisions of time. It is measured by a steady basic pulse, or beat. The rate of that pulse is called the tempo and is measured in beats-per-minute, or bpm. For example, one beat per second is equal to 60 bpm.

Rhythms are notated using symbols called notes. Each type of note has a specified length, or duration, relative to the tempo. Each note also has a corresponding rest symbol, which indicates a period of silence equal to the duration of the note.

Example 1.1 (on the following page) shows the most common note types, their names, durations, and corresponding rests. Note that a dot increases the duration of a note by half of its original value. (A dotted quarter-note, for example, lasts for one-and-a-half beats.)

The musical staff consists of five parallel, horizontal lines which are read from left to right to represent the linear flow of music on paper.

To notate rhythms, the staff is divided into units of time called measures or bars. Each measure is divided by a bar line. A double bar line indicates the end of a section or entire piece. Repeat signs (‖: :‖) designate a section of the staff to be repeated.

A time signature resembling a fraction placed on the staff following the clef sign designates the meter—how many of which kind of note each measure will contain. The

Ex. 1.1

Note Symbol	Name of Note	Duration	Rest Symbol
𝅝·	Dotted whole-note	6 beats	▬·
𝅝	Whole-note	4 beats	▬
𝅗𝅥·	Dotted half-note	3 beats	▬·
𝅗𝅥	Half-note	2 beats	▬
♩·	Dotted quarter-note	1 1/2 beats	𝄽·
♩	Quarter-note	1 beat	𝄽
♪·	Dotted eighth-note	3/4 beat	𝄾·
♪	Eighth-note	1/2 beat	𝄾
𝅘𝅥𝅯·	Dotted 16th-note	3/8 beat	𝄿·
𝅘𝅥𝅯	16th-note	1/4 beat	𝄿
𝅘𝅥𝅰·	Dotted 32nd-note	3/16 beat	𝅀·
𝅘𝅥𝅰	32nd-note	1/8 beat	𝅀

top number (numerator) indicates the number of beats-per-bar and the bottom number (denominator) indicates which type of note receives one beat. Within any given tempo, this provides a basic, repetitive pulse that may be subdivided to produce endless rhythmic variations.

$\frac{4}{4}$ = four per bar / quarter-notes $\frac{3}{4}$ = three per bar / quarter-notes $\frac{6}{8}$ = six per bar / eighth-notes $\frac{7}{8}$ = seven per bar / eighth-notes

Ex. 1.2 illustrates the staff, treble clef, metronome mark, measures, bar lines, and repeat signs using the basic pulse of the above time signatures. (Note how the flagged notes are beamed into groups.)

Ex. 1.2

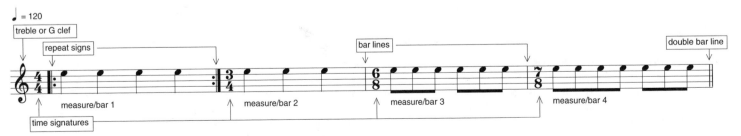

PITCH NOTATION

Musical pitches are written on or between the lines of the staff using notes to indicate both pitch and duration. The range of the staff can be extended in either direction using ledger lines. Guitar music is notated in the treble clef, or *G* clef, and is written one octave (the equivalent of 12 frets) higher than it actually sounds. If the guitar was notated at its true pitch, most of its notes would fall into the bass clef or extend far below the treble-clef staff, requiring many hard-to-read ledger lines. All sheet music not specifically arranged for guitar should be played an octave higher than written.

The musical alphabet contains seven natural notes—*A, B, C, D, E, F, G*. The distance between all adjacent natural notes is a whole-step (two frets) except for *B* to *C* and *E* to *F* which are a half-step (one fret) apart. This corresponds to the missing black keys between *B* and *C*, and *E* and *F*, on keyboard instruments. The natural notes repeat in different octaves throughout the full range of the guitar.

In standard tuning, the range of an instrument is determined by the distance between its lowest and highest notes. The range of natural notes on a 22-fret guitar fingerboard is one whole-step shy of four octaves. **Ex. 1.3** shows the range of the guitar on the treble-clef staff.

Ex. 1.3

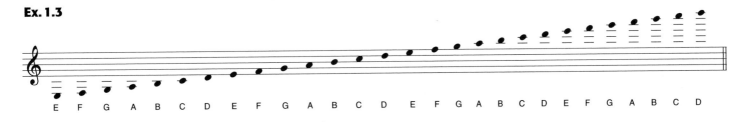

Excessive ledger lines may be eliminated by writing music an octave lower than intended and notating *8va* above the staff, as shown in **Ex. 1.4**. An *8va* symbol and its dotted bracket indicate that all designated notes are to be played one octave higher than written. *15ma* raises pitches two octaves. The term "loco" cancels a previous *8va* or *15ma* indicator.

Ex. 1.4

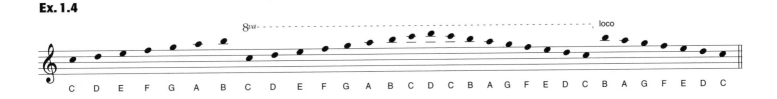

Each octave contains a total of 12 half-steps, or 12 different-named pitches. Besides the seven natural notes, the five remaining notes are indicated using symbols called "accidentals," which raise or lower natural notes by one half-step. A sharp sign (♯) before a note raises the note one half-step, while a flat sign (♭) lowers it one half-step. Bar lines automatically wipe out any accidentals not in the key signature. (We'll get to key signatures soon.) At times it's necessary to use double sharp (𝄪) and double flat (♭♭) symbols. A natural sign (♮) preceding a note cancels any previously indicated accidental for the remainder of that measure.

Some identical pitches are spelled two different ways (**Ex. 1.5**). These are called "enharmonic" equivalents.

Ex. 1.5

Notes are stemmed according to their location on the staff. The middle *B* line serves as the dividing point. Single notes written on or above the *B* line are downstemmed while notes written below it receive upstems. For intervals and chords, the note farthest from the *B* line determines stem direction.

FINGERBOARD GRIDS

Grids diagram a section of the guitar fingerboard and are useful for graphic depictions of chords and scales. A chord grid (**Ex. 1.6**) provides instant visualization of the shape a chord produces on the fingerboard. Any chord can be illustrated on a grid.

Ex. 1.6

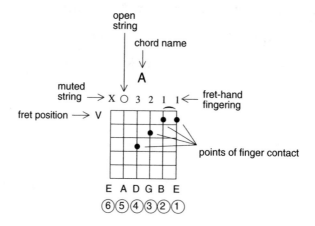

Grids are also handy for diagramming scales (**Ex. 1.7**). Any scale can be illustrated on a grid.

Ex. 1.7

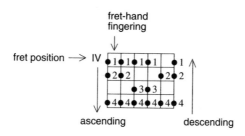

A grid can display the entire fingerboard horizontally or vertically. Dots, scale degree numbers, or note names on the grid can be connected to illustrate chord and arpeggio shapes or the order in which notes are to be played (**Ex. 1.8**).

Ex. 1.8

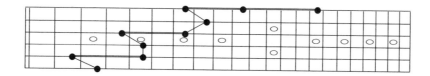

TABLATURE

Tablature—or "tab"—adds a sixth line to the staff, creating a pictorial representation of the six guitar strings. Fret numbers are written directly on the string or strings to be played, and indicate a corresponding note's exact position on the fingerboard.

The tab staff is aligned directly below the standard notation, forming a two-stave system. Each fret number is aligned with the note or notes it represents in the standard notation. **Ex. 1.9** illustrates single notes, harmonic intervals, and chords using tab.

Ex. 1.9

Rhythms are derived from the standard notation only. Special left- and right-hand techniques may be symbolized in both staves. These are examined in the upcoming chapter on technique, which includes detailed explanations of string bending, hammer-ons, pull-offs, slides, and slurs, as well as their written symbols.

There is no set standard for tab notation. Transcription folios, books, and other study materials that use tab will almost always include a key to the publisher's particular style of notation. It must be stressed that tab should be used as an educational tool, not a crutch. If your goal is to become a session player, you'll be expected to read standard notation. You'll never see tab on a studio chart!

PICK AND FINGER NOTATION

Notes may be picked using downstrokes (⊓) and upstrokes (V). These symbols are usually placed above or below the standard notation staff.

Fret-hand fingering is notated with small Arabic numerals next to or above noteheads: 1=1st finger (index), 2=2nd finger (middle), 3=3rd finger (ring), and 4=4th finger (pinky).

The following abbreviations are used to notate pick-hand fingering:

p=thumb, *i*=index finger, *m*=middle finger, *a*=ring finger, and *c*=pinky.

READING MUSIC ON THE GUITAR

Reading standard music notation on the guitar can be quite confusing. Identically written notes may be played in up to five different locations on the fingerboard. With so many choices, the main dilemma is where to play a written note. The answer depends on where you played the previous note as well as the location of the following note. Any single note is usually part of a longer phrase, and you'll always have a choice of several fingerings for the same phrase in different positions on the fingerboard. Phrases that are extremely difficult to play in one position often turn out to be relatively simple in another position. Explore several possibilities when deciding where to play a phrase and choose the position that feels and sounds best to you.

Another consideration: The shorter the length of string being sounded, the darker the note will sound. Compare the timbre of the five *Es* in **Ex. 1.10**.

Ex. 1.10

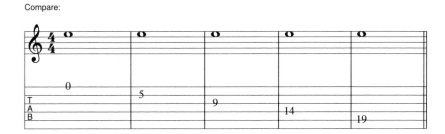

The only notes not duplicated on a guitar in standard tuning are found at the extreme low and high registers of the fingerboard (**Ex. 1.11**).

Ex. 1.11

The range of the guitar can be extended via manual or mechanical methods. You can play notes above the highest fretted note on the first string (that's *D* on a twenty-two-fret guitar) by bending the string. You can go even higher with harmonics, a slide bar, or by fretting directly on your pickups. A guitar equipped with a vibrato bar can bend down to pitches below low *E* without retuning.

In standard tuning, you'll find identical pitches located 2½ steps/5 frets apart on adjacent strings, except between the *B* (2nd) and *G* (3rd) strings where the distance is reduced to 2 steps/4 frets (**Ex. 1.12**).

Ex. 1.12

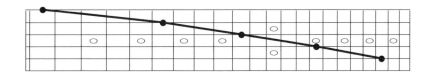

Ex. 1.13

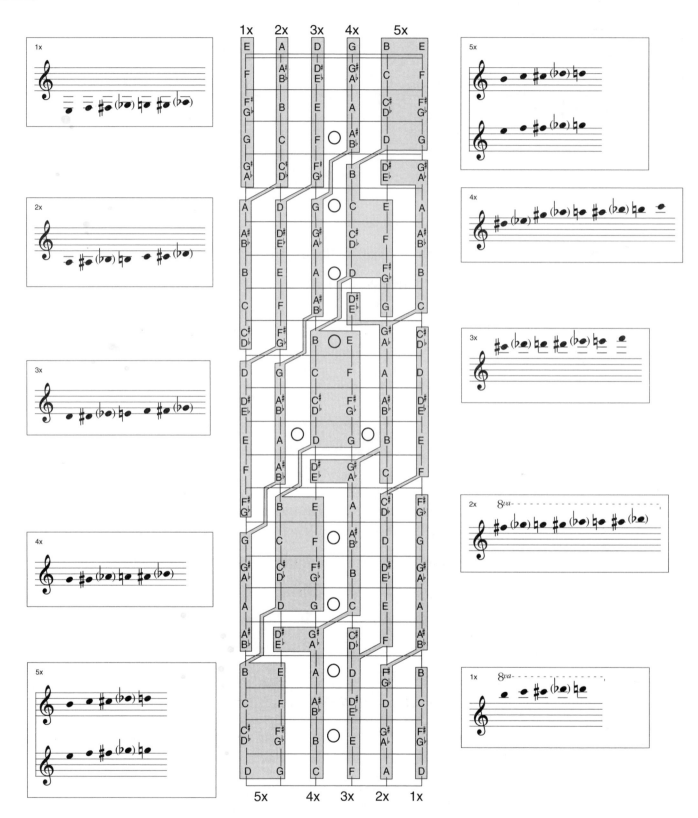

The full-fingerboard grid in **Ex. 1.13** illustrates all note repetitions on the guitar, and groups them by the number of times they appear. Notice how the fingerboard repeats one octave higher beginning at the twelfth fret.

Your objective is to memorize the name and location of every note on every string. Notes can be memorized by their numbered fret positions on the fingerboard. Use the fret-position markers—usually dots or inlaid designs at the third, fifth, seventh, ninth, twelfth, fifteenth, seventeenth, nineteenth, and twenty-first frets—to keep your bearings.

Start with both open-*E* strings and learn to equate the natural notes with their fret or dot positions: *F*=first fret (no dot), *G*=third fret (1st dot), *A*=fifth fret (2nd dot), *B*=seventh fret (3rd dot), *C*=eighth fret (no dot), *D*=tenth fret (no dot), *E*=twelfth fret (double dot). Once you can visualize the positions of the natural notes, the sharped and flatted notes will be easy to find. Write out your own chart for each string and compose your own exercises using only the notes on that string. Next, write exercises for two-string combinations, then three, and so on. Remember—unless you alter your guitar's tuning, the notes will always be found in the same places on the fretboard.

MELODIC MOTION

Generally, you will encounter three types of motion when reading single-note melodies:

• SCALEWISE MOTION (**Ex. 1.14**). Notes moving from one scale tone to the next in ascending or descending order.

Ex. 1.14

Scalewise motion

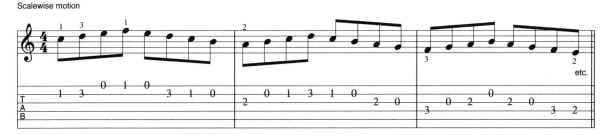

- INTERVAL SKIPS (**Ex. 1.15**). Notes that move greater or lesser distances than in scalewise motion, or scale tones moving to non-scale tones.

Ex. 1.15

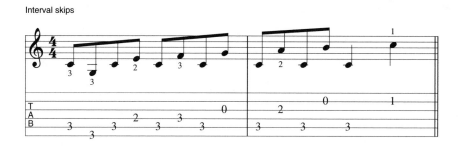

Interval skips

- CHORD ARPEGGIATION (**Ex. 1.16**). A series of interval skips that spell out chord voicings one note at a time.

Ex. 1.16

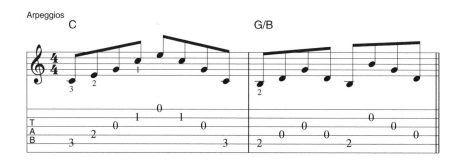

Arpeggios

As you learn about intervals, scales, and chords in the upcoming chapters, it will become apparent that the above holds true for almost any written music. Learning to recognize these three types of melodic motion will measurably improve your reading skills.

SIGHT-READING

Sight-reading is the ability to play a piece of written music correctly and musically on sight, without previous practice. But take note: "without practice" does not mean "without preparation." Great sight-readers can mentally scan a piece of written music and recognize all forms of melodic and rhythmic motion almost instantly. The process appears effortless because these readers are so familiar with the materials of music.

Shortcuts may be helpful, but there is no substitute for the hours of practice it takes to develop great sight-reading facility. If you want to hone your sight-reading skills, make an effort to read any music you can get your hands on—and not just music written for the guitar. Flute, clarinet, and violin studies are particularly well suited to guitar.

It's important to bear in mind that written music is an abstraction of the actual *sound* of music. The map is not the territory, in other words, and a musician *can* have a functional knowledge of written music without being a great sight-reader. So if you honestly don't care about reading music, then don't bother practicing this skill. If you want to read just enough to be able to understand written music, fine. If your goal is to be a monster sight-reader, then go for it! Set realistic goals and don't expect miraculous results without a lot of hard work.

CHAPTER TWO

Tuning and Intonation

It takes practice to master tuning the guitar. If you become frustrated, don't worry—it will come with time. Put the guitar down for a while, relax, and try again later. Do this several times every day and, slowly but surely, you will improve.

Of course, using an electronic tuner simplifies and takes the pain out of the tuning process, but the following "ear" methods have a more beneficial effect on a person's overall musicality. Tuners are great time-savers on gigs or in the studio, but they don't nurture the ability to *hear* whether your guitar is in or out of tune.

THE BASICS

Standard 6-string guitar tuning uses the following pitches from low (sixth string) to high (first string): *E, A, D, G, B,* and *E*. The adjacent string-pairs are tuned in ascending fourth intervals, except for the third and second strings, which are a major third apart (see *Chapter 4*, "Melodic Intervals," Ex. 4.2). This interrupts fingerboard symmetry, but gives us two open *E*s. (Alternate tunings are both numerous and widespread, but exploring each one could fill a book of its own.)

When playing alone, it is only essential to get the guitar in tune relative to itself—not necessarily to concert pitch, or A=440Hz. Playing with other instruments, however, does require being tuned to this standard reference pitch. A guitar will also be more accurately intonated—that is, play in tune all over the fingerboard—when tuned to concert pitch. Use a tuning fork for reference.

THE MECHANICS

Tightening a string raises its pitch, while loosening lowers it. Many standard headstocks features three tuning machines per side. Holding the guitar in playing position, turn the pegs counter-clockwise to tighten the sixth, fifth, and fourth strings, and clockwise to tighten the third, second, and first strings. Reversing these directions loosens the strings. When a headstock has six tuners on the top side, turn all of them counter-clockwise to tighten the strings or clockwise to loosen them. (Helpful hint: A string will be less likely to slip and go flat when the final tuning adjustment is a tightening action.)

Most players favor tuning from low to high, regardless of which tuning method they use. Step one is to tune to a reference pitch. When tuning to a fixed-pitch instrument such as piano or organ, begin by tuning the open fifth string to the second *A* below middle *C*. Why *A* and not low *E*? Because *A* is easier to hum—*E* is just too low for most people's voices. When tuning to another guitar, use its open *A* as your reference. Either way, while both notes ring—your *A* and the *A* from the other instrument—listen for pulsating "beats" or "waves" in the sound. As the notes approach unison, the beating becomes slower. When the notes are in tune with each other, they are vibrating at the same rate and the beating stops.

THE OLD-FASHIONED METHOD
Once the fifth string is tuned, follow these steps:

- Play the fifth string at the 5th fret, and let it ring while sounding the open fourth string (**Ex. 2.1a**).
- Determine whether the fourth string must be raised or lowered to achieve unison. Try humming the note from your fifth string (5th fret) for reference—internally or externally—while playing the open fourth string.
- Adjust the open fourth string until it sounds exactly the same as the note at the 5th fret of your fifth string. Again, listen to how the two notes create beats when they are not quite in tune. Since both notes must ring together in order to hear the beats, try keeping the fifth string fretted with one hand while reaching over to turn the pegs with the other.

- Double-check by comparing the open fifth string with its octave on the fourth string at the 7th fret (**Ex. 2.1b**).

- Next, play the fourth string at the 5th fret—your new reference pitch—and tune the open third string to that note using the method described above, as shown in **Ex. 2.1c**. Double-check by comparing the open fourth string to its octave on the third string at the 7th fret (**Ex. 2.1d**).

- Now, play the third string at the 4th fret and tune the open second string to it, as shown in **Ex. 2.1e**. (Note: The third strings is the only string on which we use the note at the 4th fret to tune the next string.) Again, listen for the beats and double-check by comparing the open third string to its octave on the second string at the 8th fret. That's one fret higher than the other octave references we've used so far (**Ex. 2.1f**).

- Next, tune the open first string to the note on the second string at the 5th fret (**Ex. 2.1g**). Double-check the open second string against its octave on the first string at the 7th fret (**Ex. 2.1h**).

- Finally, tune the open sixth string to the open 1st string (**Ex. 2.1i**). Both notes are *Es*, but they are two octaves apart, making the beats more difficult to hear. Double-check by comparing the note on the sixth string at the 5th fret to the open fifth string (**Ex. 2.1j**), then compare the open sixth string with its octave on the fifth string at the 7th fret (**Ex. 2.1k**).

Ex. 2.1

Check octaves and unisons using any of the chord forms in **Ex. 2.2**.

Ex. 2.2

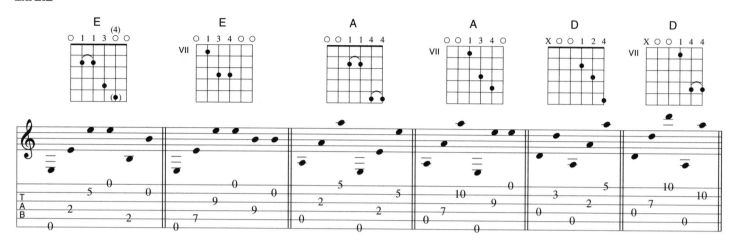

TUNING WITH HARMONICS

To sound a natural—or open-string—harmonic, touch a string directly over the indicated fretwire without pressing it to the fingerboard. Pluck the string and simultaneously lift your finger from the string. The ringing note you'll hear—higher in pitch than the open string itself—is called a "harmonic." Using harmonics to tune frees the fretting hand to make adjustments while both notes ring. The beating of out-of-tune pitches is also more apparent between harmonics than between fretted and open strings.

Begin by tuning the *A* harmonic on the fifth string at the 5th fret to a 440Hz reference source such as a tuning fork or the *A* above middle *C* on a fixed-pitch keyboard instrument (**Ex. 2.3a**; the diamond-shaped note heads indicate harmonics).

Play, in close succession, the harmonic on the fifth string at the 5th fret and the harmonic on the fourth string at the 7th fret (**Ex. 2.3b**). While both are ringing, adjust the fourth string until the beats slow and disappear. Repeat this process on the fourth and third strings (**Ex. 2.3c**).

Since the third and second strings are tuned a half-step closer than all other adjacent string groups, harmonics at the 5th and 7th frets are a half-step apart instead of in unison. You can resort to the old-fashioned method to tune this string, or use the harmonic on the third string at the 12th fret as a reference for the fretted note on the second string at the 8th fret (**Ex. 2.3d**).

Revert to the previous process to tune the first string to the second string (**Ex. 2.3e**), and then reverse the process to tune the low *E* string to the fifth string (**Ex. 2.3f**).

Ex. 2.3

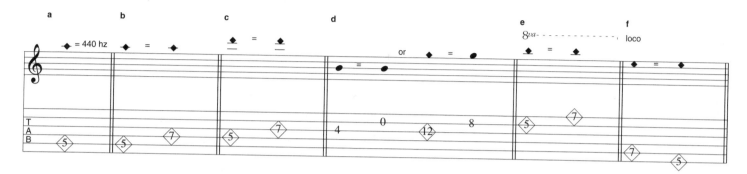

You can also use harmonics one octave apart to tune—except between the third and second strings—as shown in **Examples 2.4a–2.4e**.

Ex. 2.4

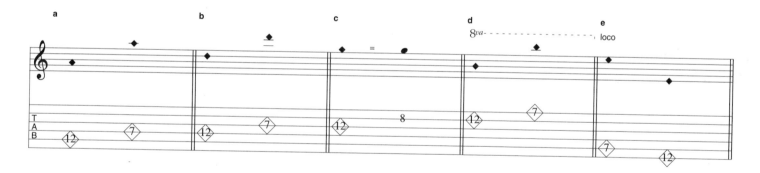

INTONATION

String gauge, the age of a string, minute changes in finger pressure, temperature, and humidity are just a few of the many factors that affect a guitar's "intonation"—the ability to play in tune with itself anywhere on the fretboard. For a guitar to be properly intonated, it is crucial that the length of each string from the nut to the 12th fret be equal to the distance between the 12th fret and the bridge saddle.

To check your guitar's intonation, compare any 12th-fret harmonic to the fretted note at the same location. Assuming that your guitar has no serious neck or fret problems, the harmonic will provide an in-tune reference for the note at the 12th fret. The fretted note may be fine-tuned by moving the bridge (or bridge saddle) towards or away from the neck. The highest degree of accuracy can be attained on guitars with individually adjustable bridge saddles. On such guitars, each string may be shortened or lengthened to raise or lower the pitch of the note at the 12th fret, so the harmonic can be matched exactly.

If the note at the 12th fret sounds flat—or lower than the harmonic—the string must be shortened to raise its pitch. To shorten a string, move the saddle towards the neck. If the note at the 12th fret sounds sharp—or higher than the harmonic—the string must be lengthened. To lengthen a string, move the saddle away from the neck.

Take your time and make very minute adjustments, checking each one carefully. Repeat this procedure on each string, as shown in **Examples 2.5a–2.5f**.

Ex. 2.5

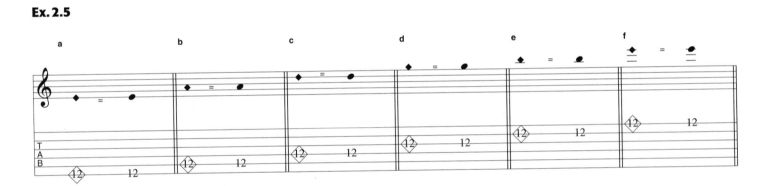

An electronic tuner is definitely recommended for setting intonation accurately, but try an ear-check first and see how well you fare. A guitar will stay properly intonated for months, as long as any broken strings are replaced with exactly the same gauge and brand. But take note: Old strings cause lots of intonation problems. So, the next time you can't seem to get in tune, ask yourself the magic question: "How long has it been since I changed those *#@% things?"

CHAPTER THREE

Rhythm

Rhythm is arguably the most important element of music because it remains intact when separated from melody and harmony. A rhythm may be notated without a melody, but a melody cannot be notated accurately without rhythm. Rhythm is the glue that binds the other musical elements and prevents them from dissolving. It is the force that unites ensembles.

Rhythm is linear—it flows with time. On paper, it flows from left to right. Reading and writing rhythms is a matter of memorizing how each common rhythm sounds and being able to identify it instantly. When you hear a rhythm, try to visualize how it looks on paper; when you see a written rhythm, imagine how it sounds.

Internalize the rhythms in this chapter so that you can recognize them by sight or sound. Remember that the subdivisions of beats will always look and sound the same, regardless of musical context. Because these divisions can be combined in so many different ways, there is a nearly endless number of rhythmic possibilities. But regardless of their relative complexity or simplicity, all rhythms happen one beat at a time.

BASIC DIVISIONS

There are two basic types of rhythmic groupings: "simple" and "compound." In simple time, each beat is divided by two. Dividing a note in half produces a strong downbeat followed by a weaker upbeat. Simple time signatures include 2/4, 3/4, 4/4, 5/4, 6/4, and 7/4.

In compound time, beats are initially divided by three. Dividing a note into thirds produces a strong downbeat followed by two weaker upbeats. Compound time signatures include 3/8, 6/8, 9/8, 12/8, and 15/8. All other groupings of time are derived from various combinations of two and three beats.

Ex. 3.1a illustrates the equal subdivisions of a quarter-note, from two to eight events per beat.

Ex. 3.1a

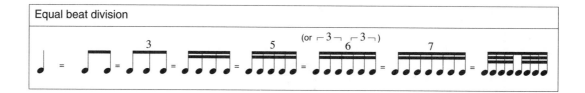

The ratio of these divisions can be altered to produce many variations. Eighth-notes split a beat precisely in half (50/50), while "shuffle" and "swing" rhythms generally use a 66.6/33.3 ratio (♩♪) or a 75/25 ratio (♪♪). These values may be stretched slightly, resulting in subtle "ahead of the beat" or "behind the beat" feels.

Ex. 3.1b depicts some common rhythms, mixing note types within a single beat. The rhythms are grouped by the number of events per beat.

Ex. 3.1b

(Unequal beat division — rhythm chart grouped by Two events per beat, Three events per beat, Four events per beat, and Five events per beat.)

Ex. 3.2a shows basic beat divisions applied to five common meters.

Ex. 3.2a

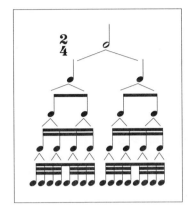

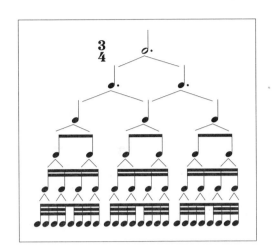

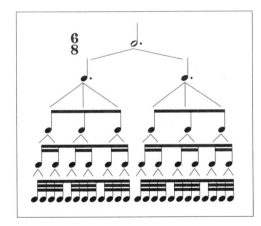

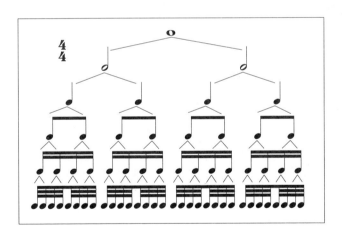

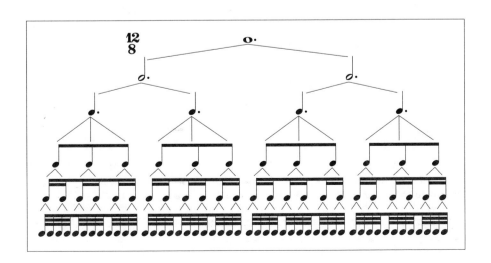

Theoretically, any note is divisible by any number. **Ex. 3.2b** extrapolates simple and compound divisions from a single whole-note.

Ex. 3.2b

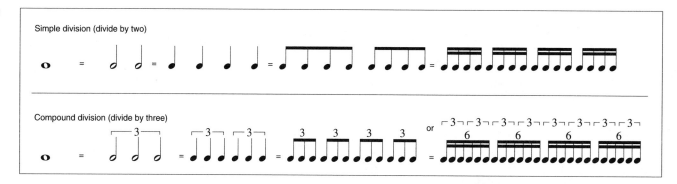

COUNTING TIME

If you've already got a flawless sense of rhythm, you may skip this bit. But if your playing suffers from a certain "timeless" quality, this section is for you.

In order to play time, you have to *feel* time. Time is not something you hop on and ride—*you* have to generate it. Begin by learning to synchronize your internal clock to any tempo. This can be accomplished by tapping a foot (heel or toe), bobbing your head or rocking your entire body, vocalizing clicks or grunts, or counting out loud—whatever locks you to the tempo. Concentrate on the downbeats and use the silent upbeat occurring halfway through each beat as a point of reference. This will decrease the tendency to rush or lag behind the tempo. Keep it clock-steady.

Next, you must feel the meter designated by the time signature. Written as fractions, time signatures divide a constant flow of metronomic beats into equal or unequal groupings called "measures" or "bars." The numerator assigns which type of note receives one beat and the denominator designates how many beats are in each measure. A measure of time can contain either an even or odd number of beats. For example, 4/4—or "common time" (**c**)—designates four beats per bar and the quarter-note as the basic unit of beat measurement. 2/4 and 3/4 use the same quarter-note pulse, but with two and three beats to the bar, respectively. These meters can be combined to produce 5/4, 6/4, 7/4, and so on. When 2, 8, or 16 is the denominator, the only thing that changes is which type of note receives a beat. Catching on?

Using a metronome or drum machine, establish a comfortable tempo within the indicated bpm range and simultaneously tap, clap, and count (yes, out loud) the 2/4, 3/4, and 4/4 rhythms in **Ex. 3.3a**. Repeat each rhythm at least four times before moving on. Accenting the downbeats—especially the almighty "one"—will help you to keep your groove steady as each example subdivides. Repeat all the examples, gradually increasing the tempo each time.

Ex. 3.3a

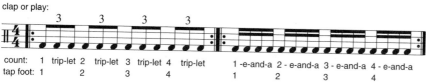

After you can tap, clap, and count the divisions of each meter at a reasonable tempo, pick up the guitar and replace the claps with muted-string *chicks*. You can use single or multiple strings. Lock in the groove on your "guit-drum" by keeping your foot taps, head bobs, or whatnot in sync with your picking or strumming motion. Pick down for downbeats and up for upbeats. You can probably pick much faster than you can clap, so feel free to raise up the tempo.

Ex. 3.3b illustrates how to count in various meters with eighth-note denominators. Stay within the indicated tempos and repeat the tap/clap/count routine before picking up your instrument.

Ex. 3.3b

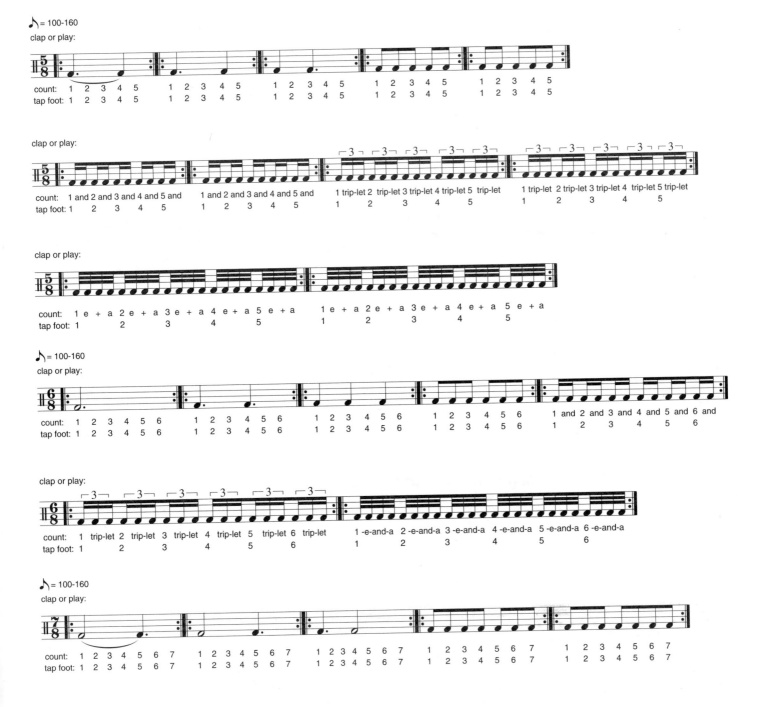

Ex. 3.3b (continued)

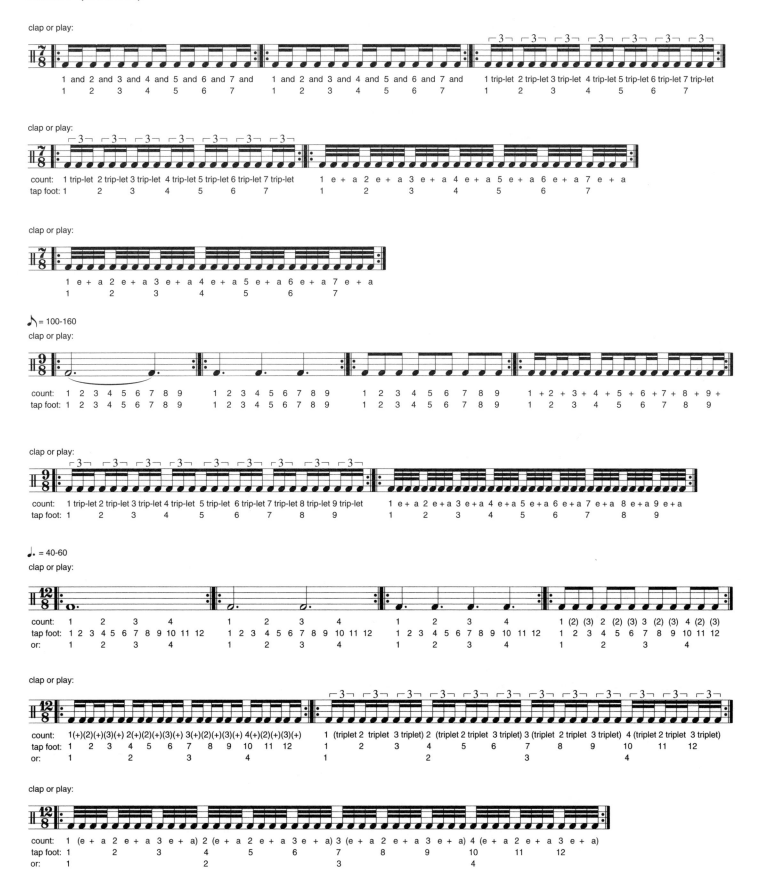

Foot-tapping at faster tempos—in the 140-240 bpm range for 4/4 or 6/8—may necessitate dividing the denominator in half, just to keep up the tempo. This is called "cut time" and is designated by a vertical slash through the common time symbol (₵).

Tap, clap, and count the rhythms in **Ex. 3.3c** and notice how the frequency of foot taps has been cut in half. When the beat divisions become too fast to clap, switch to alternate-picked muted strings.

Ex. 3.3c

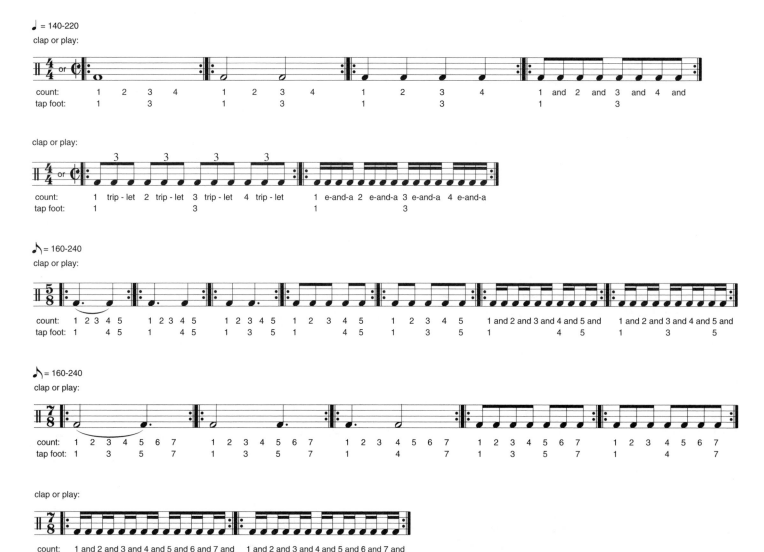

Do all you can to improve your ability to count and feel time. Take up bongos, learn to conduct, study the mathematics of rhythm—whatever works for you. You can practice playing and feeling time just about anywhere. If you're someplace where clapping or counting aloud is inappropriate, just tap your knee quietly instead.

TIED RHYTHMS

A rhythmic tie (⌢ ⌣) is a slur symbol drawn between the heads of two or more notes of the same pitch. Such symbols are used to indicate that the first note should sustain for the duration of the notes' sum total value. Here are some ground rules for ties:

- Ties can be used within a single measure or across bar lines.
- Unnecessary ties should be avoided.
- Rest symbols are never tied.
- For sixteenth-notes, ties are used only across each downbeat—rarely within the same beat.
- In 4/4, always use ties to sustain notes across the third beat. In other words, beat three should always be clearly visible—regardless of whether it is played or tied. This beat acts as a mid-measure landmark and makes rhythms much easier to read.

RHYTHMIC MOTIFS

A "rhythmic motif" is a short, repetitive rhythm figure onto which any melody notes may be grafted. The one-bar motifs in **Ex. 3.4a** consist of half-, quarter-, and eighth-note groupings. Repeat each one at least four times.

Ex. 3.4a

Ex. 3.4b

Ex. 3.4b introduces ties, "syncopations" (emphasized upbeats), and dotted notes. Each rhythm can be played using straight or swing eighth-notes. Clap, tap, or play each rhythm on muted strings before attempting to assign pitches or chords to it. Knowing *when* to play is just as important as knowing *what* to play, so don't take rhythm for granted. Work with each new rhythm you encounter until it becomes a natural part of your vocabulary.

All of these motifs can be turned into sixteenth-note rhythms by converting them to double-time. To convert a rhythm to double-time, simply halve the value of each note. This turns a two-bar motif into a one-bar motif, cuts a one-bar motif down to a half-bar, and so on. Conversely, any rhythm can be half-timed by doubling the duration of each note. In half-time, a one-bar motif expands to two bars, a two-bar

Ex. 3.4b
(continued)

motif becomes four bars, and so on. Read the chart in **Ex. 3.4c** from right to left for
double-time conversion and left to right for half-time.

Ex. 3.4c

Ex. 3.4d shows a two-bar double-time conversion.

Ex. 3.4d

Ex. 3.5a shows a slew of 3/4 motifs featuring mixed half-note, quarter-note, dotted-quarter, and eighth-note rhythms.

Ex. 3.5a

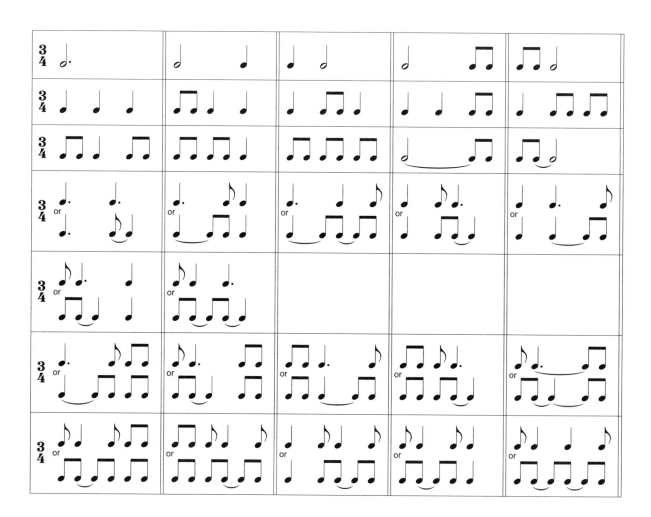

Each 6/8 motif in **Ex. 3.5b** can be thought of as two double-timed 3/4 motifs. Since the unit of beat measurement is eighth-notes, upbeats are notated as sixteenth-notes. For 12/8 motifs, just connect two bars of 6/8.

Ex. 3.5b

Ex. 3.5b (continued)

Supplement your rhythmic awareness by listening for the previous motifs on recordings and recognizing them in print. Study rhythms in sheet music, transcription folios, classical and film scores, or drum methods. (While you're at it, buy a pair of drumsticks!)

RHYTHMIC DISPLACEMENT

Any rhythmic motif can start either on a downbeat or an upbeat, and we can displace any motif by starting it on any other downbeat or upbeat in a measure of time. Displacing a motif by eighth-notes produces eight rhythmic variations, or permutations—one starting on each eighth-note of the measure.

Ex. 3.6a and **Ex. 3.6b** illustrate the sequential eighth-note displacement of a two-note and a six-note motif.

Ex. 3.6a

Ex. 3.6b

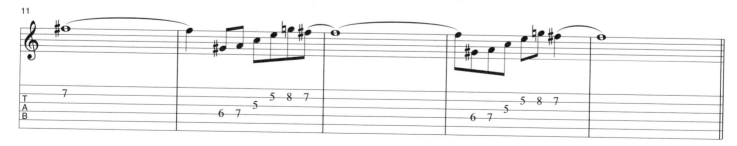

RHYTHMIC EAR-TRAINING

The first step in learning or transcribing any musical phrase by ear is to internalize its rhythm. Once the correct rhythm is determined, it becomes much easier to hear pitched notes because you know *where* they occur and *when* to listen for them.

To improve your rhythmic ear, ask a drummer or other rhythmically inclined musician pal to record a few dozen separate one-bar rhythms similar to those in Examples 3.4a–b and 3.5a–b, then get to work transcribing them. Listen to the entire measure, then immediately stop the recording and try to replay the rhythm in your head or sing it out loud. If you have trouble retaining the whole rhythm, zero in on one beat at a time until you've memorized the entire measure. Get any book on orchestration and learn the conducting patterns for a variety of time signatures. Waving your hand in front of your face while vocalizing a rhythm will give you a visual indication of where the rhythm falls in relation to the pulse. When you think you've got it, *write it down*. This helps your recognition the next time you encounter the rhythm. Eventually, you'll find yourself retaining and recalling much longer rhythms.

If you can't enlist a partner, record the previous motifs in random order—you can assign notes to them if you wish—and re-transcribe them. Make several different recordings so you can't memorize their order, and keep a key in order to check your results. These recordings can also double as melodic ear-training studies.

For a sight-reading project, copy each rhythm motif from the previous examples—including their double- and half-time conversions—to individual index cards and use them as rhythmic flash cards. Set the metronome, flash on a rhythm card on beat "one," scan the rhythm for the remainder of that bar, then clap, tap, or play it on the downbeat ("one") of the following measure. Construct a Rhythm Rolodex™!

Pick random phrases from your favorite recordings and notate their rhythms. Don't limit yourself to guitar music. Transcribing rhythms from drum kits, vocals (sung or, for the terminally ambitious, *spoken*), horns, and other instruments will only have a positive effect on your ears. And, as with all aspects of music, the more you do it, the better you get.

CHAPTER FOUR

Melody

To measure physical distance, a foot is divided into 12 inches. Similarly, an octave is divided into 12 half-steps. On the guitar, an octave can be divided into 12 frets (one half-step each) along a single string. The half-step is the unit of measurement used to define musical intervals—the distance between any two notes. In other words, any two notes can be said to be a specific number of half-steps apart.

INTERVALS

Intervals are the building blocks of melody and harmony. A melodic interval measures the distance between two separate notes, while a harmonic interval measures the distance between two notes played simultaneously. Chords contain three or more notes, so there are compound intervals within chords. When one chord moves to another chord, the root motion—the distance between the two chords' roots—can be measured in intervals. Intervals provide a way to measure and communicate the relative distances within music. Thus, any melodic or harmonic structure can be described in terms of its intervallic shape.

Before learning to play the intervals on the guitar, see how many you can recognize by ear. You have already heard most of them used in music thousands of times, and must simply learn to identify them by name. This is most easily accomplished by equating the sound of an interval with an already familiar melody.

Unless noted otherwise, the ascending and descending intervals in **Ex. 4.1** are used to play the first movement between notes in the following popular melodies. Sing or hum them without your guitar, before looking for them on the fingerboard. Continue each melody as far as you can, then analyze its intervallic structure.

Ex. 4.1

	Ascending Intervals		Descending Intervals	
Minor seconds (1/2 step)	"White Christmas" "Strawberry Fields Forever" "Raindrops Keep Falling on My Head" "With a Little Help from My Friends" "Caravan"	"Stormy Weather" "Baby You're a Rich Man" "Michelle" "Stardust" "My Romance" "Jaws" (shark theme)	"Heart and Soul" "Puff the Magic Dragon" "Beautiful Dreamer" "Never Never Land" "Lucy in the Sky with Diamonds" (chorus) "Pomp and Circumstance" "Stella by Starlight"	"Mexican Hat Dance" "Mame" "I Am the Walrus" "God Bless America" "Fly Me to the Moon" "O Little Town of Bethlehem" "Sabre Dance"
Major seconds (1 step)	"America" "Happy Birthday" "Do-Re-Mi" "Oh! Susanna" "Rock of Ages" "In My Life" "Yankee Doodle" "Freres Jacques" "Theme from the Addams Family" "You are the Sunshine of My Life"	"Autumn Leaves" "Goin' Out of My Head" "Norwegian Wood" "Eleanor Rigby" "I've Just Seen a Face" "Tenderly" "Tobacco Road" "Close Encounters of the Third Kind" (theme) "My Funny Valentine" "Stairway to Heaven" "You Really Got Me" (chorus)	"Swanee River" "Three Blind Mice" "We Three Kings" "Deck the Halls" "The First Noel" "She's Leaving Home" "If I Were a Rich Man" "Sunshine of Your Love" (instrumental riff)	"Alfie" "Yesterday" "Satin Doll" "Ob-La-Di, Ob-La-Da" "Don't Get Around Much Anymore"
Minor thirds (1 1/2 steps)	"Hello Dolly" "Hawaii Five-O" "The Impossible Dream" "Greensleeves" "Close to You" "O Holy Night" "Turkey in the Straw" (chorus) "Proud Mary"	"Davy Crockett (chorus)" "On a Clear Day" "(I Can't Get No) Satisfaction" "Blue Jay Way" "A Day in the Life" "Light My Fire"	"Star Spangled Banner" "Dixie" "Caissons Go Rolling Along" "Misty"	"Girl from Ipanema" "Hey Jude" "Good Day Sunshine" "Light My Fire" (2nd and 3rd notes)
Major thirds (2 steps)	"When the Saints Go Marching In" "On Top of Old Smokey" "The Impossible Dream" "I Feel Pretty"	"Can't Buy Me Love" "Here, There and Everywhere" "Limbo Rock" "Baby Elephant Walk"	"Summertime" "Bad Moon Rising" "Light My Fire" (instrumental riff)	"Sentimental Journey" Big Ben Chimes
Perfect fourths (2 1/2 steps)	"Auld Lang Syne" "Amazing Grace" "When Johnny Comes Marching Home" "Someday My Prince Will Come" "All the Things You Are" "Home on the Range" "Man on the Flying Trapeze" "Never on Sunday" "Fiddler on the Roof" "Exodus" (theme)	"O Christmas Tree" "The Twelve Days of Christmas" "We Wish You a Merry Christmas" "Here Comes the Bride" "Tonight" (*West Side Story*) "How High the Moon" "La Cucaracha" "Tequila" "Bonanza" (theme) "Nowhere Man"	"Clementine" "O Come All Ye Faithful" "Walk Right In" "I've Been Working on the Railroad"	"King of the Road" "All of Me" "Goodnight" (Beatles) "Green Acres" (theme)
Flatted fifths (3 steps)	"Maria" (*West Side Story*) "Blue Jay Way" (1st and 3rd notes) "Purple Haze" (combined guitar and bass on opening riff)	"(I Can't Get No) Satisfaction" (1st and 3rd notes) "Angel Eyes" (1st and 3rd notes)	"Purple Haze" (2nd and 3rd notes of opening riff)"	

	Ascending Intervals		Descending Intervals	
Perfect fifths (3 ½ steps)	"My Favorite Things" "Chim-Chim-Cheree" "God Rest Ye Merry, Gentlemen" Palace guard chant from "Wizard of Oz"	"Angel Eyes" "Moon River" "Scarborough Fair" "Georgy Girl" "Goldfinger" "Star Wars" (theme)	"Feelings" "Watch What Happens" "Star Spangled Banner" (1st and 3rd notes)	"Pop Goes the Weasel" (title phrase) "Dixie" (1st and 3rd notes)
Minor sixths (4 steps)	"Because" "She's a Woman"	"To Life" (*Fiddler on the Roof*)	(Theme from *Love Story*) "Where Do I Begin?"	
Major sixths (4 ½ steps)	"It Came Upon a Midnight Clear" "When Sunny Gets Blue" "Take the 'A' Train" "Days of Wine and Roses" "On Broadway"	"Jingle Bells" "All Blues" "My Wild Irish Rose" "Short'nin' Bread" (chorus) NBC or doorbell chimes	"Nobody Knows the Trouble I've Seen"	"All Blues" (2nd and 3rd notes)
Minor sevenths (5 steps)	"Somewhere" (*West Side Story*) "Star Trek" (original TV series) "Close to You" (1st and 3rd notes)	"She Came In Though the Bathroom Window" "Edelweiss" (1st and 3rd notes) "On a Clear Day" (1st and 3rd notes)	"Willow Weep for Me" (1st and 3rd notes)	
Major sevenths (5 ½ steps)	"Over the Rainbow" (1st and 3rd notes) "Bali Ha'i" (1st and 3rd notes)	"Christmas Song" (1st and 3rd notes) "Sabre Dance" (1st note above tonic)	"I Love You" (Cole Porter)	
Octaves (6 steps)	"Over the Rainbow" "Christmas Song" "Bali Ha'i" (1st and 3rd notes) "When You Wish upon a Star" "The Immigrant Song"	"Swanee River" (2nd measure) "The Lonely Goatherd" "The Rain in Spain"	"You've Got to Hide Your Love Away" (chorus) "Willow Weep For Me"	

After acclimating your ear to the intervals used in these well-known melodies, it becomes apparent that these movements occur in all music and that endless combinations of rhythms, harmonies, timbres, and playing techniques are used to vary and disguise the same intervallic motion over and over. This perspective will improve your ability to recognize intervals in all music. As you learn more about scale construction and theory, be sure to explore these examples as part of your fingerboard ear-training. Also, try to determine how each melody functions in relation to its key center.

MELODIC INTERVALS APPLIED
TO THE FINGERBOARD

The chart in **Ex. 4.2** lists the name, distance, and shape of all intervals within one octave. The goal is to equate the sound of the intervals with their physical shapes on the fingerboard.

Ex. 4.2

Name of Interval	Distance in steps	Shape of interval on fingerboard		
		Anywhere	Except when top note is on *B* string	
Minor second	¹/₂ step			
Major second	1 step			
Minor third	1 ¹/₂ steps			
Major third	2 steps			
Perfect fourth	2 ¹/₂ steps			
Flatted fifth (sharp fourth)	2 steps			Except when top note is on *B* or *E* string
Perfect fifth	3 ¹/₂ steps			
Minor sixth (sharp fifth)	4 steps			
Major sixth	4 ¹/₂ steps			
Minor seventh	5 steps			
Major seventh	5 ¹/₂ steps			
Octave	6 steps			

EXTENDED INTERVALS

When the distance between two notes is greater than an octave, it is called an "extended interval." Think of extensions as smaller intervals plus one octave. The chart in **Ex. 4.3** lists the name, distance, and shape of all common intervals over one octave.

Ex. 4.3

Name of interval	Distance in steps	Shape of interval on fingerboard	
		Anywhere	Except when top note is on *B* or *E* string
Flatted ninth (minor second plus one octave)	6 ½ steps		
Ninth (major second plus one octave)	7 steps		
Sharp ninth (minor tenth) (minor third plus one octave)	7 ½ steps		
Tenth (major third plus one octave)	8 steps		
Eleventh (perfect fourth plus one octave)	8 ½ steps		
Thirteenth (major sixth plus one octave)	10 ½ steps		

INTERVAL INVERSIONS

To invert any interval within an octave, raise the bottom note or lower the top note by one octave. Extended intervals must be raised or lowered *two* octaves. The sum of any of the first 12 intervals plus its inversion equals one octave. The sum of any extended interval plus its inversion is two octaves.

An interval and its inversion both contain the same notes, but their qualities reverse: Inverted major intervals become minor and inverted minor intervals become major. Perfect intervals remain perfect, while a ♭5—being exactly half of an octave—inverts to itself. This simple formula computes all interval inversions within one octave: GIVEN INTERVAL+INVERSION=9. For example: Major second+?=9. (Answer: Minor seventh.)

Ex. 4.4 shows the first 12 interval inversions based on a *C* root.

Ex. 4.4

Inverted major and perfect intervals

| major 2nd = minor 7th | major 3rd = minor 6th | perfect 4th = perfect 5th | perfect 5th = perfect 4th | major 6th = minor 3rd | major 7th = minor 2nd | octave = unison |

Inverted minor and altered intervals

| minor 2nd = major 7th | minor 3rd = major 6th | flatted 5th = flatted 5th | minor 6th = major 3rd | minor 7th = major 2nd |

INTERVALLIC RELATIONSHIPS

When single notes, melodic lines, or chords are moved through a series of symmetric interval skips, they eventually return to their point of origin. These cycles include all the possibilities of motion between musical ideas. To build a strong musical vocabulary, play all new ideas through each cycle. This will help you to memorize the ideas in all keys. This is a lot of information to process, so select only one or two cycles per practice session. Create your own exercises based on the models in **Examples 4.5a–4.5e**.

Ex. 4.5a

Single notes
(major seconds)   (minor thirds)   (minor sevenths)

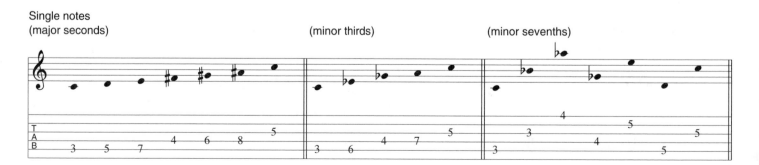

Ex. 4.5b

Lines/motifs
(minor thirds)

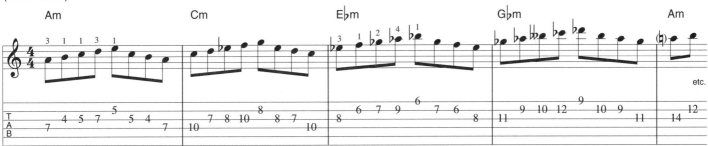

Ex. 4.5c

Arpeggios
(flatted fifths)

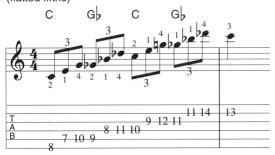

Ex. 4.5d

Chords
(major thirds)

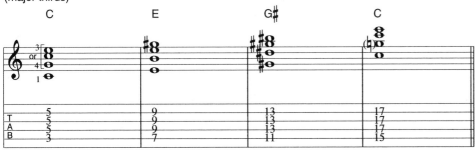

Ex. 4.5e

Chord progressions
(minor thirds)

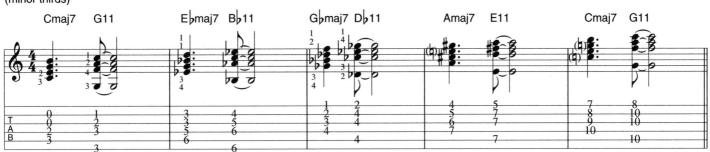

INTERVALLIC CYCLES

The chart in **Ex. 4.6** illustrates all intervallic cycles within one octave. Dig its perfect symmetry—flipped over, it reads exactly the same! Played in reverse, each cycle inverts in relation to its intervallic counterpart.

Ex. 4.6

Intervallic cycles	
Cycle of minor 2nds	C • C#(Db) • D • D#(Eb) • E • F • F#(Gb) • G • G#(Ab) • A • A#(Bb) • B • C
Cycle of major 2nds	C ——— D ——— E ——— F#(Gb) ——— G# ——— A# ——— C
Cycle of minor 3rds	C ——— Eb ——— F#(Gb) ——— A ——— C
Cycle of major 3rds	C ——— E ——— G# ——— C
Cycle of perfect 4ths	C • F • Bb • Eb • Ab • Db F#(Gb) • B • E • A • D • G • C
Cycle of flatted 5ths	C ——— F#(Gb) ——— C
Cycle of perfect 5ths	C • G • D • A • E • B • F#(Gb) • Db • Ab • Eb • Bb • F • C
Cycle of minor 6ths	C ——— Ab ——— E ——— C
Cycle of major 6ths	C ——— A ——— F#(Gb) ——— D#(Eb) ——— C
Cycle of minor 7ths	C ——— Bb ——— Ab ——— F#(Gb) ——— E ——— D ——— C
Cycle of major 7ths	C • B • A#(Bb) • A • G#(Ab) • G • F#(Gb) • F • E • D#(Eb) • D • C#(Db) • C

Traditionally depicted on the outer perimeter of a circle, the cycle of fourths and fifths (**Ex. 4.7**) is a common teaching aid because it includes all 12 notes. Revolve clockwise for ascending fifths and counter-clockwise for ascending fourths.

Ex. 4.7

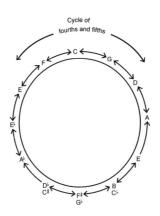

Cycle of fourths and fifths

To further illustrate their symmetry, all intervallic cycles may be drawn on the circle of fourths and fifths. Note how the amount of notes in a cycle corresponds with the amount of points on its related geometric shape.

- **Ex. 4.8a**: Minor seconds/major sevenths=12 points (12-point star).
- **Ex. 4.8b**: Major seconds/minor sevenths=6 points (hexagon).
- **Ex. 4.8c**: Minor thirds/major sixths=4 points (square).
- **Ex. 4.8d**: Major thirds/minor sixths=3 points (triangle).
- **Ex. 4.8e**: Flatted fifths=no points (lines bisect circle).

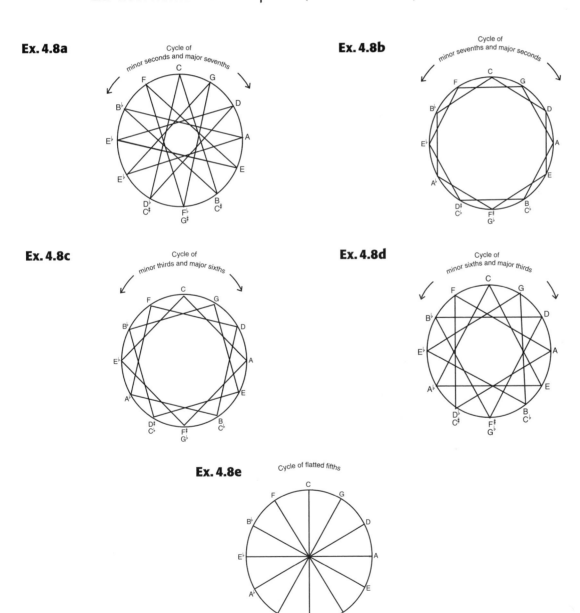

SCALES

The word "scale" comes from the Latin "scala" and "scalae," meaning ladder and stairs. In music, a scale is an ascending or descending group of five to 12 notes which span one octave and adhere to a predetermined interval structure. A given scale is defined by its root, or starting note, and its step formula, or the whole- and half-steps between each scale degree. The scale degrees are numbered according to their intervallic distance from the chosen root, using Arabic numerals—2 is the 2nd degree, 3 is the 3rd degree, and so on.

CHROMATIC SCALES

The chromatic scale is built entirely of half-steps and contains all 12 notes, making it the "mother of all other scales." There is really only one chromatic scale, and any note may be designated as its root. **Ex. 4.9** is a chromatic scale with a C root.

Ex. 4.9

Ex. 4.10 diagrams three chromatic scale fingerings.

Ex. 4.10

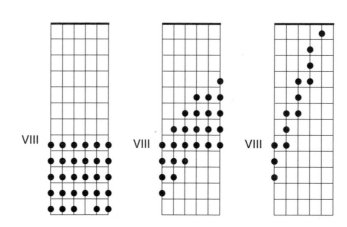

TETRACHORDS

A "tetrachord" is a group of four successive scale tones confined to half of an octave, or no greater than three whole-steps. Each tetrachord in **Ex. 4.11** has its own step formula. Most eight-note scales may be viewed as a coupling of two tetrachords.

Ex. 4.11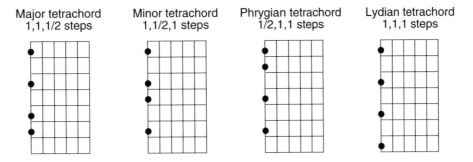

There are three fingering possibilities for any tetrachord played on adjacent strings. **Ex. 4.12** illustrates these using a major tetrachord. (Parenthetical fingerings show the same shapes on the *G* and *B* strings.)

Ex. 4.12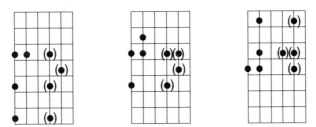

MAJOR SCALES

The major scale forms the basis for most music in the Western world. It consists of seven different notes (the eighth-note is one octave above the starting note) and uses a formula of whole-step, whole-step, half-step, whole-step, whole-step, whole-step, half-step. **Ex. 4.13** splits the major scale in half to reveal two major tetrachords spaced a whole-step apart.

All notes in the scale are in the key of—or "diatonic to"—the root note, which is also called the "tonic."

Ex. 4.13

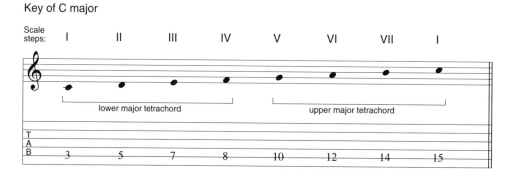

Since there are 12 different notes, or potential roots, there are 12 different-sounding keys—one starting on each note of the chromatic scale. The key of C uses all natural notes (the white piano keys). In major keys other than C, accidentals (black piano keys) must be added to conform to the major scale's step formula.

A key signature—placed on the staff between the clef sign and the time signature—identifies which notes are to be sharped or flatted throughout a given section of music. The key signature also identifies the tonic by indicating the number of sharps or flats in the scale. There are "sharp keys" (keys that have sharps in their signature) and "flat keys" (keys that have flats in their signature).

SHARP KEYS

Successive sharp keys are constructed using the cycle of fifths. The key with one sharp is built from the 5th scale degree of the key with no sharps, the key with two sharps is built from the 5th of the key with one sharp, and so on. This process is repeated through the cycle until all seven notes have been sharped, for a total of seven sharp keys. Notice how the upper major tetrachord of a key becomes the lower major tetra-chord of the following sharp key (**Ex. 4.14**).

Ex. 4.14

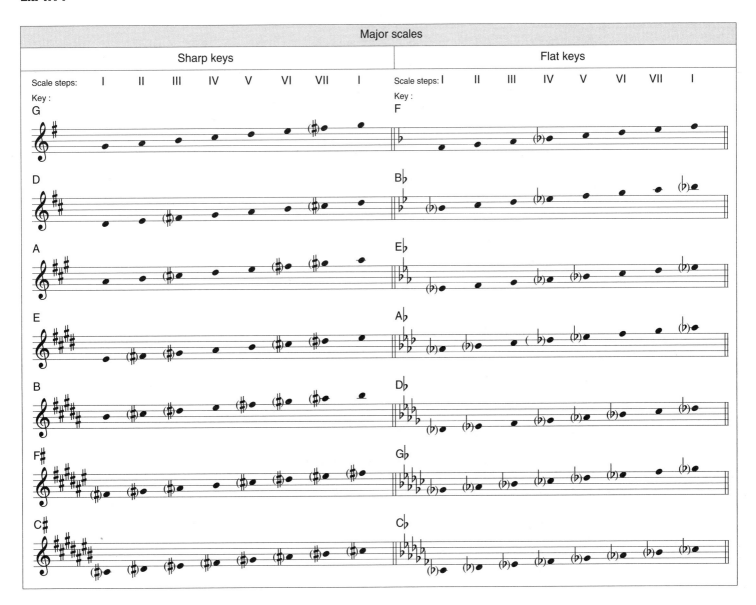

Each sharp is added to the key signature in successive order and all previous sharps are retained in the same order in each subsequent key. Because each new sharp always occurs on the 7th scale degree, the note one half-step above the last sharp in any key signature names that key. (The parenthetical accidentals are here to ease the learning process, but don't expect to see them outside of this book—that's the key signature's job!)

FLAT KEYS

Flat keys are constructed using the cycle of fourths. The key with one flat is built from the 4th scale degree of the key with no flats, the key with two flats is built from the 4th of the key with one flat, and so on. Continue until all seven notes have been flatted, for a total of seven flat keys (again, see Ex. 4.14).

The 4th degree of each successive flat key is flatted to maintain the correct major scale step formula. Each new flat, coincidentally, names the following key. In other words, the second-to-last flat in a major key signature names that key.

How can there be 15 keys when there are only 12 different notes? Three of these are enharmonically related keys which sound identical but are spelled differently—*B=C♭, C♯=D♭,* and *F♯=G♭.* Write out all 15 keys repeatedly, until you can do it without referring to this book for help.

RELATIVE MINOR KEYS

For each major key, there is a corresponding minor key that shares the same key signature. *A* minor, for example, has no sharps or flats, just like *C* major—its relative major key. Remember, the root of a major key's relative minor is always three half-steps below the root of the major key. Conversely, the root of a minor key's relative major is always three half-steps above the root of the minor key.

Relative major and minor keys at a glance:

Relative major and minor keys-at-a-glance												
	1♯	2♯	3♯	4♯	5♯/7♭	6♯/6♭	7♯/5♭	4♭	3♭	2♭	1♭
C	G	D	A	E	B/C♭	F♯/G♭	C♯/D♭	A♭	E♭	B♭	F
Am	Em	Bm	F♯m	C♯m	G♯m/A♭m	D♯m/E♭m	B♭m/A♯m	Fm	Cm	Gm	Dm

MAJOR SCALES APPLIED TO THE FINGERBOARD

There are many ways to approach playing major scales on the guitar. The repetition of notes on the fingerboard allows numerous fingering options. Except for the Segovia fingerings in classical guitar study, there is no set standard for scale fingerings. Most guitarists are left to devise their own fingering systems. Without a model, this can take years. Let's look at our options.

Ex. 4.15 illustrates how the major scale manifests on any single string.

Ex. 4.15

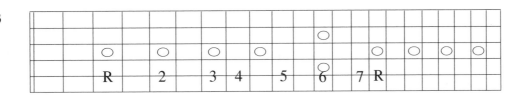

Since the major scale consists of two major tetrachords played a whole-step apart, any major tetrachord fingering may be repeated a whole-step higher on an adjacent string to form an entire major scale (**Ex. 4.16**). As with intervals, these tetrachords retain their shape anywhere on the fingerboard, except for the necessary *B*-string adjustments

Ex. 4.16

  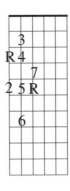 

Tetrachord shapes may be strung together to form memorable, repetitive patterns that span several octaves. The three-octave *G* major scale in **Ex. 4.17** combines two different major tetrachord fingerings which overlap every eight notes.

Ex. 4.17

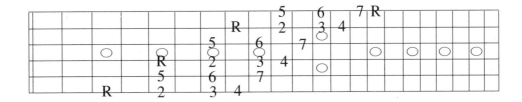

FIVE MAJOR SCALE FINGERING PATTERNS

Fingerboard position is determined by the fret location of the 1st finger. Momentarily limiting the fret hand to any given position on the fingerboard, a span of four frets is easily accessible by assigning one finger per fret. The fret hand may stay in one position and cover more than a two-octave range by playing across all six strings instead of along the length of one or two. If necessary, you may easily stretch a half-step out of position in either direction with your 1st or 4th finger.

It is possible to organize the major scale into five connecting fingering patterns. This serves two purposes: To break the fingerboard down into memorable "neighborhoods" via five individual patterns, and to create a movable, 12-fret template that unites the entire fingerboard in any key.

Ex. 4.18a illustrates all five patterns and their combined template in the key of C. You'll find most of the previously described interval and tetrachord shapes woven into these individual and combined fingering patterns.

These five patterns are related to the five basic, open-position major guitar chords— C, A, G, E, and D. (Retention hint: What's that spell? *CAGED*.) Learn to associate each scale pattern with its open chord shape. In any key, Pattern 1=C shape, Pattern 2=A shape, Pattern 3=G shape, Pattern 4=E shape, and Pattern 5=D shape. The patterns always connect in the same order: Pattern 1, followed by Patterns 2, 3, 4, and 5. The patterns overlap when they are assembled into the *CAGED* template. Since the chord shapes contain fewer notes than the scale patterns, it is easier to use them as guides. In fact, if you know these chords, you already know almost half of the notes in each scale pattern! The next chapter details the connection between scales and chords.

Each pattern uses either two or three notes on each string, and one of three fingerings will be used on each string: Whole-step/half-step, half-step/whole-step, or just a whole-step. Memorize the shapes of individual patterns by looking for duplications of these three fingerings within each pattern.

Once you can ascend and descend all five fingering patterns by heart, explore them in greater depth by applying melodic motifs, sequences, and permutations. Memorize the location of every root in each pattern. These form an easy-to-move, six-note "root

Ex. 4.18a

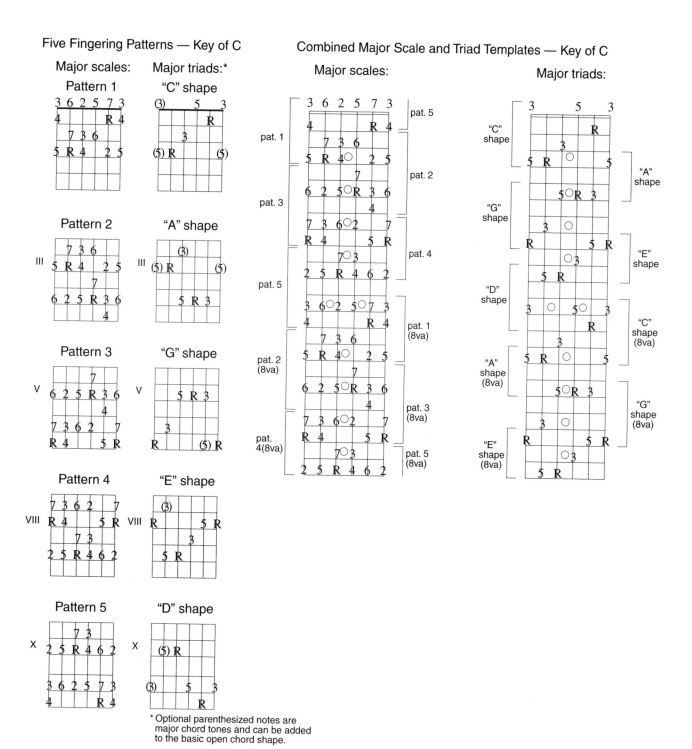

Five Fingering Patterns — Key of C

Major scales: Major triads:*

Combined Major Scale and Triad Templates — Key of C

Major scales: Major triads:

* Optional parenthesized notes are
major chord tones and can be added
to the basic open chord shape.

matrix" (**Ex. 4.18b**) which enables you to immediately locate any interval or transpose any pattern to any key.

Ex. 4.18b

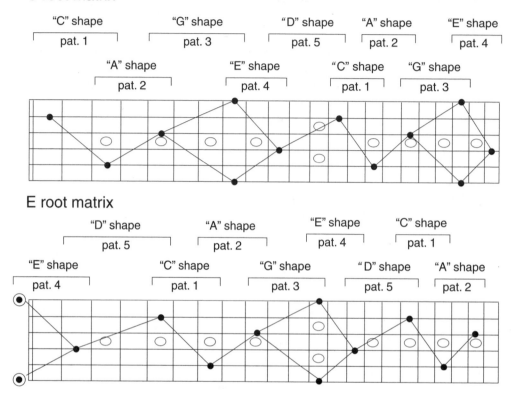

C root matrix

| "C" shape | "G" shape | "D" shape | "A" shape | "E" shape |
| pat. 1 | pat. 3 | pat. 5 | pat. 2 | pat. 4 |

"A" shape / pat. 2   "E" shape / pat. 4   "C" shape / pat. 1   "G" shape / pat. 3

E root matrix

"D" shape / pat. 5   "A" shape / pat. 2   "E" shape / pat. 4   "C" shape / pat. 1

"E" shape / pat. 4   "C" shape / pat. 1   "G" shape / pat. 3   "D" shape / pat. 5   "A" shape / pat. 2

TRANSPOSING THE FIVE
MAJOR SCALE FINGERING PATTERNS

For keys other than *C*, the entire *CAGED* template must be moved, or transposed. Transposing the fingerboard to any key is simply a matter of sliding the entire template to other fret positions. This provides a visual display of the correct notes in any major key. Some patterns, especially those that span five frets, will require fingering adjustments when played in open or first position.

The five fingering patterns always connect in the same order: Pattern 1, followed by Patterns 2, 3, 4, and 5, or *CAGED*. The entire *CAGED* template repeats one octave higher above the 12th fret. Moving the template towards the nut causes patterns that had vanished behind the nut to reappear one octave higher, below the 12th fret.

Ex. 4.19

Major scale in open position:	Major triad in open position:	Major scale raised 1/2-step:	Major triad raised 1/2-step:	Major scale raised whole-step:	Major triad raised whole-step:
pattern 1	C	C♯(D♭)	C♯(D♭)		
pattern 2	A	B♭(A♯)	B♭(A♯)	B	B
pattern 3	G	G♯(A♭)	G♯(A♭)		
pattern 4	E	F	F	F♯(G♭)	F♯(G♭)
pattern 5	D	D♯(E♭)	D♯(E♭)		

To play any major scale, move any fingering pattern up or down the fingerboard until the root matrix aligns with the chosen key. This transposes the entire fingerboard to that key and automatically aligns the five fingering patterns. Start on any root of any pattern and play ascending or descending scale degrees through the next octave(s).

For instance, to organize the fingerboard into the key of *F*, begin by locating the lowest-positioned *F* notes on the fingerboard (sixth and first strings, at the 1st fret). Determine which scale pattern or chord shape uses that root location (Pattern 4) and align it with the proper fret (first position) so the root positions overlap the *F*s. This shifts the *CAGED* template to *EDCAG*, and automatically aligns patterns 5, 1, 2, and 3 to correctly display the entire fingerboard in the key of *F*. Use this process to transpose any of the five major scale fingering patterns into any key (**Ex. 4.19**, previous page).

Practice all major scales through each intervallic cycle (see Ex. 4.6) while applying rhythmic and melodic motifs, sequences, and permutations (see Examples 4.41–4.45).

RELATIVE MINOR SCALES AND MODES

Music derived from the major scale doesn't always sound major. Modes provide alternative major and minor tonalities which are relative, or diatonic, to a given major key. They may be thought of as scales within scales, or inversions of a scale. Any scale contains as many relative modes as it has different notes—one starting on each scale degree. Since the major scale consists of seven different notes, it yields seven relative modes.

Modes can have two relationships to a tonic: relative or parallel. The seven relative modes are derived by designating each degree of the major scale as a root and playing through its octave. Though a relative mode uses the same notes as the original scale, the interval structure of the formula shifts, changing its sound. Parallel modes build each modal formula from a single tonic note. This requires a different major scale for each mode. The chart in **Ex. 4.20** shows the seven modes relative to and parallel to the key of *C*.

The following breakdown of modes is presented in order from least to most alterations in the original major scale formula. Their interval structures are numbered in scale degrees and the formulas are measured in whole- and half-steps. "Home Base" identifies which of the five major scale fingering patterns begins on—or closest to—the

Ex. 4.20

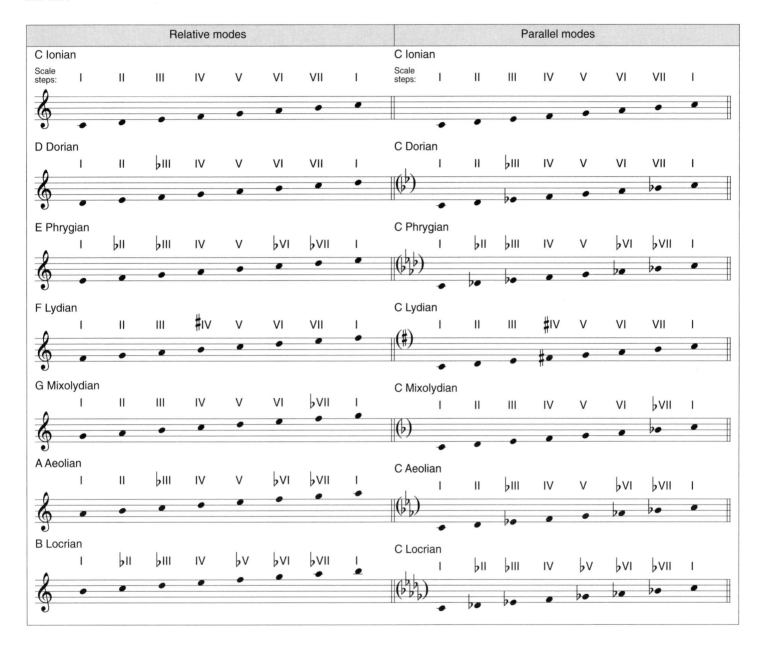

modal tonic. Remember that locating one pattern automatically sets up the entire *CAGED* template. Map out each diatonic and parallel mode on paper in all 15 keys using both standard and grid notation, then explore them in depth by applying melodic motifs, sequences, and permutations.

We've already been through the Ionian mode, which is the original Greek name for the major scale. But, since it is our point of reference, let's review.

IONIAN MODE

Degrees: Root, 2, 3, 4, 5, 6, 7, Root

Step Formula: 1, 1, 1/2, 1, 1, 1, 1/2

Home Base: Pattern 4

Play the Ionian mode (**Ex. 4.21**) by starting on the root of any major scale fingering pattern, or play two major tetrachords a whole-step apart.

Ex. 4.21

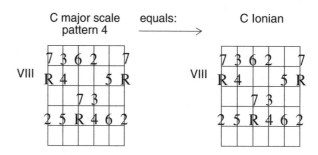

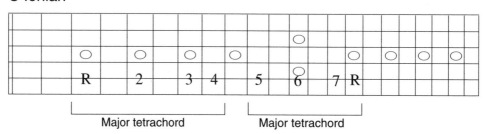

Major tetrachord   Major tetrachord

LYDIAN MODE

Degrees: Root, 2, 3, #4, 5, 6, 7, Root

Step Formula: 1, 1, 1, 1/2, 1, 1, 1/2

Home Base: Pattern 1

Think of the Lydian mode (**Ex. 4.22**) as a major scale with a #4. The diatonic mode that starts on the 4th degree of any major scale is that key's relative Lydian mode. Play the Lydian mode by starting on the 4th degree of any major scale fingering pattern, or play a major tetrachord a half-step above a Lydian tetrachord.

Ex. 4.22

C major scale
pattern 1

converted to:
——————→

F Lydian

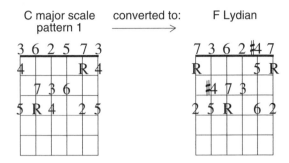

C Lydian

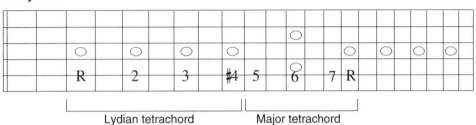

Lydian tetrachord   Major tetrachord

MIXOLYDIAN MODE

Degrees: Root, 2, 3, 4, 5, 6, ♭7, Root

Step Formula: 1, 1, 1/2, 1, 1, 1/2, 1

Home Base: Pattern 2

Think of the Mixolydian mode (**Ex. 4.23**) as a major scale with a ♭7. The diatonic mode that starts on the 5th degree of any major scale is that key's relative Mixolydian mode. Play the Mixolydian mode by starting on the 5th degree of any major scale fingering pattern, or play a minor tetrachord one whole-step above a major tetrachord.

Ex. 4.23

C major scale
pattern 2

converted to:
——————→

G
Mixolydian

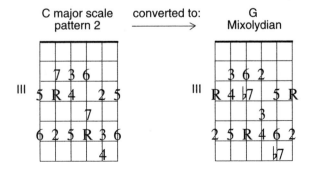

Ex. 4.23 (continued)

C Mixolydian

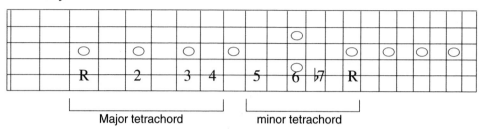

Major tetrachord   minor tetrachord

DORIAN MODE

Degrees: Root, 2, ♭3, 4, 5, 6, ♭7, Root

Step Formula: 1, 1/2, 1, 1, 1, 1/2, 1

Home Base: Pattern 5

The Dorian mode (**Ex. 4.24**) is the first of four minor modalities built from the major scale. Think of the Dorian mode as a major scale with a ♭3 and ♭7—or, more appropriately, as a minor scale with a ♮6. (More on this in a minute.) The diatonic mode built from the 2nd degree of any major scale is that key's relative Dorian mode. Play the Dorian mode by starting on the 2nd degree of any major scale fingering pattern, or play two minor tetrachords a whole-step apart.

Ex. 4.24

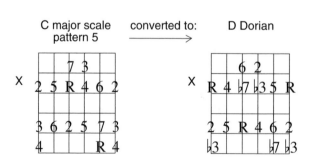

C Dorian

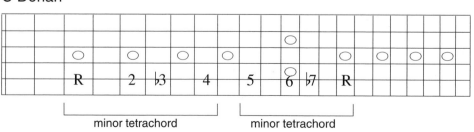

minor tetrachord   minor tetrachord

AEOLIAN MODE

Degrees: Root, 2, ♭3, 4, 5, ♭6, ♭7, Root

Step Formula: 1, 1/2, 1, 1, 1/2, 1, 1

Home Base: Pattern 3

While the Aeolian mode (**Ex. 4.25**) may be viewed as a major scale with a ♭3, ♭6, and ♭7, it should be considered on its own merits. We'll use the Aeolian mode as a reference for comparisons among the other three minor modes.

The diatonic mode built from the 6th degree of any major scale is that key's relative Aeolian mode. Play the Aeolian mode—hereafter referred to as the relative minor, natural minor, or minor scale—by starting on the 6th degree of any major scale fingering pattern, or play a Phrygian tetrachord a whole-step above a minor tetrachord.

Ex. 4.25

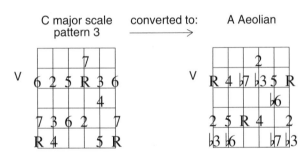

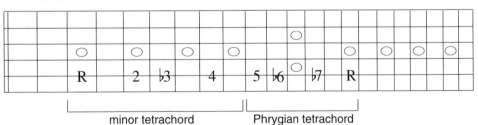

C Aeolian

minor tetrachord   Phrygian tetrachord

PHRYGIAN MODE

Degrees: Root, ♭2, ♭3, 4, 5, ♭6, ♭7, Root

Step Formula: 1/2, 1, 1, 1, 1/2, 1, 1

Home Base: Pattern 1

Note how each successive minor mode sounds darker than the last. Think of the Phrygian mode (**Ex. 4.26**) as a natural minor scale with a ♭2. The diatonic mode built from the 3rd degree of any major scale is that key's relative Phrygian mode. Play the Phrygian mode by starting on the 3rd degree of any major scale fingering pattern, or play two Phrygian tetrachords a whole-step apart.

Ex. 4.26

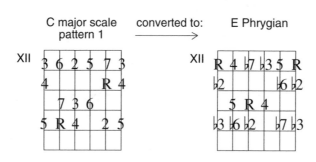

C Phrygian

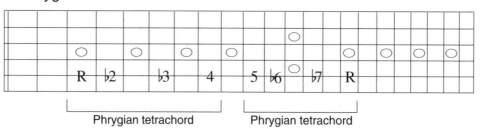

Phrygian tetrachord   Phrygian tetrachord

LOCRIAN MODE

Degrees: Root, ♭2, ♭3, 4, ♭5, ♭6, ♭7, Root

Step Formula: 1/2, 1, 1, 1/2, 1, 1, 1

Home Base: Pattern 4

Darkest of the lot, the Locrian mode (**Ex. 4.27**) is built from the 7th degree of any major scale. Play the Locrian mode by starting on the 7th degree of any major scale fingering pattern, or play a Lydian tetrachord a whole-step above a Phrygian tetrachord.

Ex. 4.27

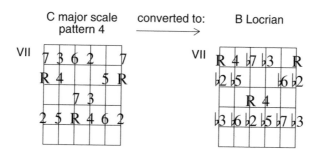

C major scale   converted to: B Locrian
pattern 4

C Locrian

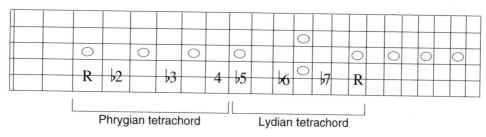

Practice all modes through each intervallic cycle (see Ex. 4.6) using rhythmic and melodic motifs, sequences, and permutations (see Examples 4.41–4.45).

HARMONIC MINOR AND MELODIC MINOR SCALES

There are two forms of the minor scale that are not diatonically related to the major scale and require alterations to that formula: harmonic minor and melodic minor.

HARMONIC MINOR SCALE

Degrees: Root, 2, ♭3, 4, 5, ♭6, 7, Root

Step Formula: 1, 1/2, 1, 1, 1/2, 1/2, 1

Home base: Revised Pattern 3

The harmonic minor scale (**Ex. 4.28**) may be viewed as a major scale with a ♭3 and ♭6, as a natural minor scale with a ♮7, or—best of all—a melodic minor scale with a ♭6. To form five connecting harmonic minor fingering patterns, flat all 3s and 6s in the parallel major scale patterns, or convert the neck to the parallel natural minor scale and raise all 7s one half-step. Harmonic minor key signatures are borrowed from their parallel natural minor key, and accidentals are added to each measure as needed. Another way to form the harmonic minor scale is to play a harmonic minor tetrachord a whole-step above a minor tetrachord.

Ex. 4.28

A Harmonic minor

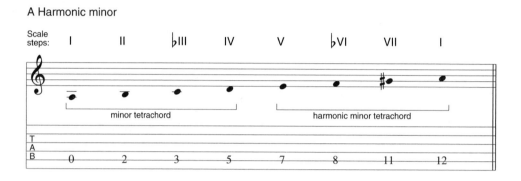

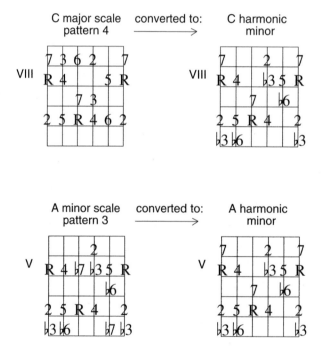

Ex. 4.29 illustrates the remaining 14 harmonic minor scales.

Practice all harmonic minor scales through each intervallic cycle (see Ex. 4.6) using adapted rhythmic and melodic motifs, sequences, and permutations (see Examples 4.41–4.45).

Ex. 4.29

MELODIC MINOR SCALE

Degrees: Root, 2, ♭3, 4, 5, 6, 7, Root

Step Formula: 1, 1/2, 1, 1, 1, 1, 1/2

Home Base: Revised Pattern 3

The melodic minor scale (**Ex. 4.30**)—also called the "jazz minor" scale—can be viewed as a major scale with a ♭3 or, more appropriately, a minor scale with a ♮6 and ♮7. To form five connecting melodic minor fingering patterns, simply flat all 3s in the parallel major scale patterns, or convert the neck to the parallel minor scale and raise all 6s and 7s by one half-step. You could also convert the neck to the parallel Dorian mode and raise all 7s one half-step. Melodic minor key signatures are borrowed from their parallel natural minor key. Extra accidentals are added to each measure as needed. Another way to form the melodic minor scale is to play a major tetrachord a whole-step above a minor tetrachord.

Ex. 4.30

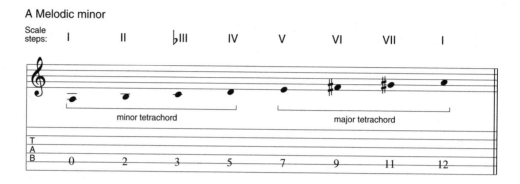

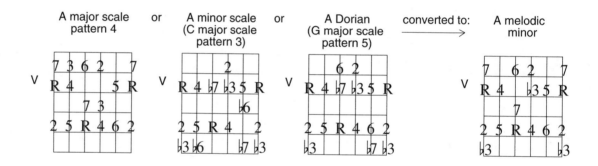

Ex. 4.31 illustrates the remaining 14 melodic minor scales.

Practice all melodic minor scales through each intervallic cycle (see Ex. 4.6) using rhythmic and melodic motifs, sequences, and permutations (see Examples 4.41–4.45).

The harmonic and melodic minor scales each contain seven modes (called "synthetic modes"), and present a potential embarrassment of melodic and harmonic riches. Practice them through each intervallic cycle as you did the major scales and modes. Explore each one in depth using motifs, sequences, and permutations.

Ex. 4.31

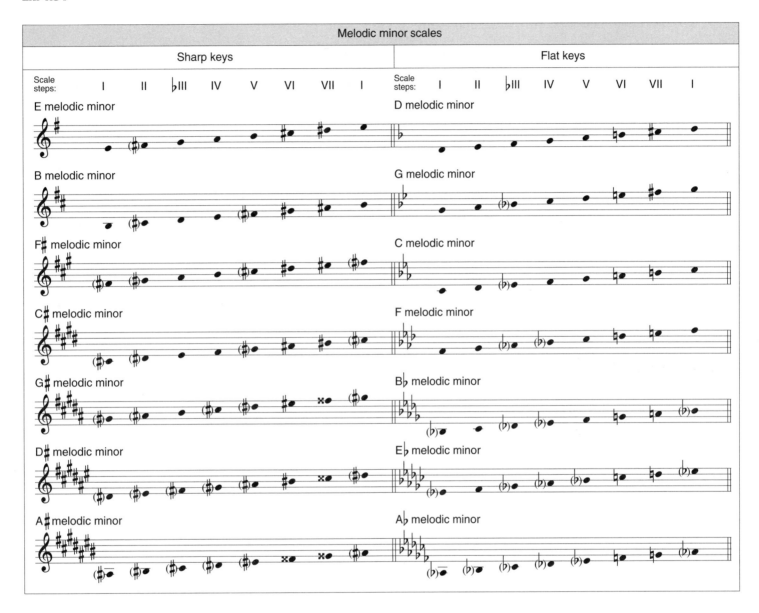

PENTATONIC, BLUES, DIMINISHED, WHOLE-TONE, AND EXOTIC SCALES

Not every scale contains the same number of notes. As its name implies, the pentatonic scale consists of five different notes per octave. The two diminished scales use eight notes apiece, while the whole-tone and blues scales are six-note (hexatonic) scales.

PENTATONIC MAJOR SCALE

Degrees: Root, 2, 3, 5, 6, Root

Step Formula: 1, 1, 1½, 1, 1½

Home Base: Revised Patterns 5, 1

The pentatonic scale is one of the earliest known scales and is widespread in both Western and non-Western cultures. It may have originated as a row of perfect-fifth intervals: *C, G, D, A, E.* The pentatonic major scale is identical to its parallel major scale with the 4th and 7th scale degrees omitted. These are the active tones in a major scale— the tones that produce natural melodic tension. The tendency of the 4 is to resolve down one half-step to the 3, while the 7 wants to resolve up one half-step to the tonic. Omit these notes from the scale and the need for resolution is eliminated. Unlike the major scale, any note of the pentatonic scale provides a satisfactory melodic target, or point of arrival.

Ex. 4.32 shows the construction of a *C* pentatonic major scale which shares a key signature with its parallel major scale. To form five connecting pentatonic major fingering patterns, remove all 4s and 7s from the five parallel major scale patterns.

Ex. 4.32

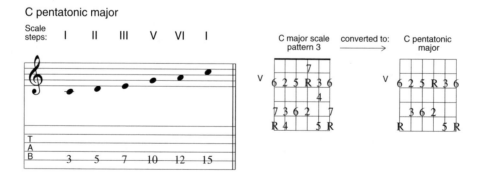

C pentatonic major

PENTATONIC MODES

Every pentatonic scale contains five modes (**Ex. 4.33**).

Ex. 4.33

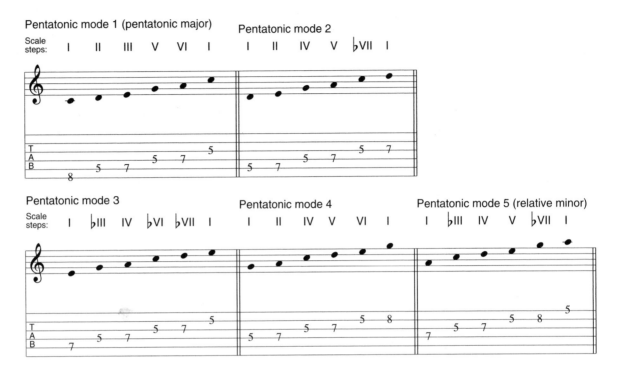

PENTATONIC MINOR SCALE

Degrees: Root, ♭3, 4, 5, ♭7, Root

Step Formula: 1½, 1, 1, 1½, 1

Home Base: Revised Pattern 5

Pentatonic mode 5 is the relative pentatonic minor scale. Again, the relative minor root lies a minor third—or three frets—below any major root. A pentatonic minor scale shares a key signature with its parallel natural minor scale. To form five connecting pentatonic minor fingering patterns, revise the pentatonic major patterns by rethinking all of its 6s as the roots of the relative pentatonic minor scale (**Ex. 4.34**, next page).

Ex. 4.34

A pentatonic minor (mode 5)

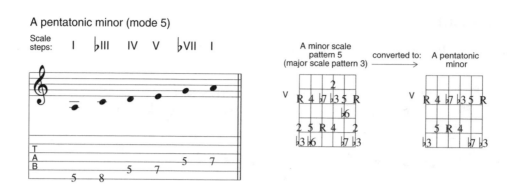

Write out and play all pentatonic scales and modes through each intervallic cycle (see Ex. 4.6), using rhythmic motifs and applicable melodic motifs, sequences, and permutations (see Examples 4.41–4.45).

THE BLUES SCALE

Degrees: Root, ♭3, 4, ♭5, 5, ♭7, Root

Step Formula: 1½, 1, 1/2, 1/2, 1½, 1

Home Base: Revised Pattern 5

The pentatonic minor scale is often mistakenly referred to as the blues scale. They are similar, but the blues scale adds a ♭5, forming a six-note scale which can no longer be called pentatonic (**Ex. 4.35**). To form five connecting blues scale fingering patterns, add ♭5s to the five pentatonic minor patterns.

Ex. 4.35

A blues scale

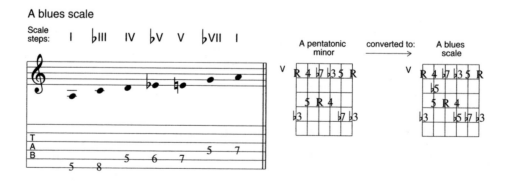

Practice all blues scales through each intervallic cycle (see Ex. 4.6), using rhythmic motifs and applicable melodic motifs, sequences, and permutations (see Examples 4.41–4.45).

HALF/WHOLE DIMINISHED SCALE

Degrees: Root, ♭2, ♭3, 3, ♯4, 5, 6, ♭7, Root

Step Formula: 1/2, 1, 1/2, 1, 1/2, 1, 1/2, 1

Home Base: Any half/whole diminished pattern

WHOLE/HALF DIMINISHED SCALE

Degrees: Root, 2, ♭3, 4, ♭5, ♭6, 6, 7, Root

Step Formula: 1, 1/2, 1, 1/2, 1, 1/2, 1, 1/2

Home Base: Any whole/half diminished pattern

There are two diminished scale formulas (**Ex. 4.36**). Both feature symmetrical construction of alternating half- and whole-steps and are modes of each other. The name of each scale describes its step formula: Half/whole diminished is built half-step/whole-step/half-step/whole-step and so on, while the whole/half diminished is built whole-step/half-step/whole-step/half-step and so on. Another way to form these scales is to play two diminished tetrachords one half-step apart (for half/whole) or two minor tetrachords one half-step apart (for whole/half).

Ex. 4.36

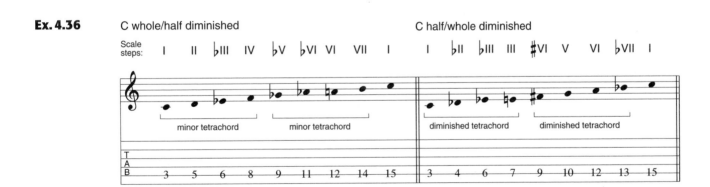

Converting the major scale fingering patterns to diminished scales is cumbersome and impractical. The symmetry of these scales generates the same shapes anywhere on the fingerboard (**Ex. 4.37**, next page). Be sure to make the necessary *B*-string revisions.

Ex. 4.37

G diminished (half/whole)

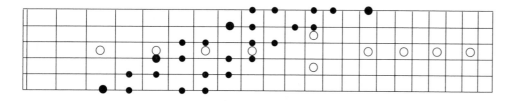

G diminished
(whole/half)

C diminished
(half/whole)

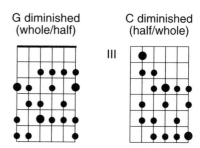

Melodically, the diminished scale can be used to play lines over altered dominant-7th chords (see *Major Scale Harmony*). Play the half/whole scale starting on the root of any altered dominant-7th chord, or the whole/half scale one half-step above the root of a dominant-7th chord.

Practice all diminished scales through each intervallic cycle (see Ex. 4.6), using rhythmic motifs and applicable melodic motifs, sequences, and permutations (see Examples 4.41–4.45).

WHOLE-TONE SCALE

Degrees: Root, 2, 3, #4, #5, ♭7, Root

Step Formula: 1, 1, 1, 1, 1, 1

Home Base: Any whole-tone pattern

The whole-tone scale (**Ex. 4.38**) is constructed of six whole-steps and corresponds intervallically with the cycle of major seconds. There are no whole-tone modes, only transposed whole-tone scales.

Ex. 4.38

C whole-tone

The symmetry of the whole-tone scale also makes converting the five major scale fingering patterns unnecessary. **Ex. 4.39** illustrates several movable whole-tone scale fingerings.

Ex. 4.39   C whole-tone

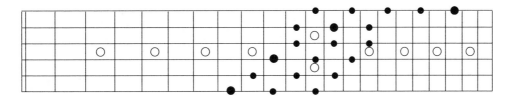

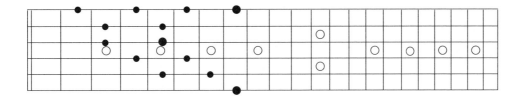

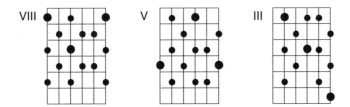

Melodic lines built from the *C* whole-tone scale may be played over parallel chords containing a raised 5—such as *Caug, C7♯5, C7♯5♯9,* and *Cmaj7♯5*—or those that contain an augmented triad—such as *Cm/maj7* (see "Chord Construction" in Chapter 5, Examples 5.2 and 5.3).

Practice all whole-tone scales through each intervallic cycle (see Ex. 4.6), using rhythmic motifs and applicable melodic motifs, sequences, and permutations (see Examples 4.41–4.45).

EXOTIC SCALES

There are many scales in use throughout the world, each with its own unique formula. As with major and pentatonic scales, these exotic scales yield as many modes as they have notes. Like any scale, they may be played through each intervallic cycle and adapted to all rhythmic and melodic motifs, sequences, and permutations.

The scales in **Ex. 4.40** come from various parts of the globe. They all contain either five or seven different notes and produce an equal amount of modes. Revise the five major scale fingering patterns to form a separate 12-fret template for each exotic scale and its modes. After you sequence, permute, and harmonize all of the major and minor scales, revisit these to unlock their melodic and harmonic treasures.

Ex. 4.40

Hungarian Gypsy minor

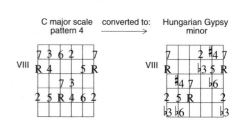

Javanese

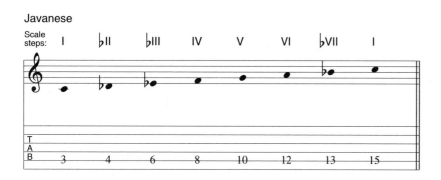
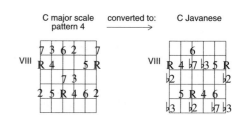

Ex. 4.40 (continued)

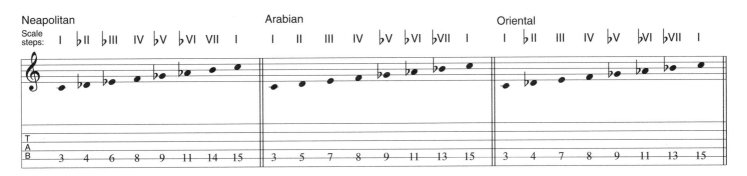

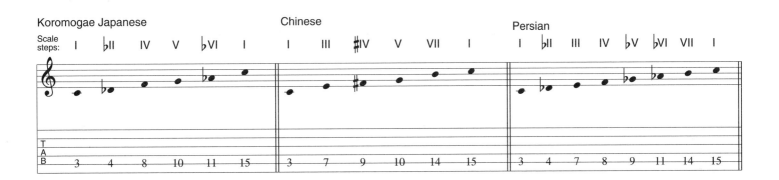

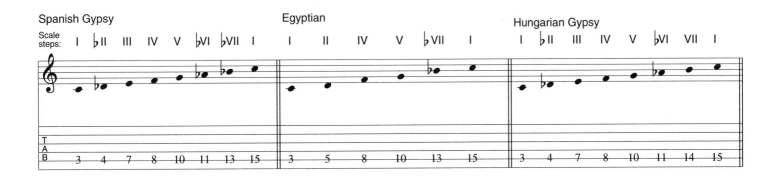

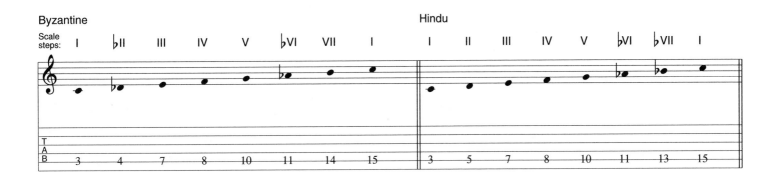

MELODIC MOTIFS, PERMUTATIONS, AND SEQUENCES

Great melodies do not happen by playing ascending and descending scales. They happen by putting scales to work and exploring their many melodic configurations.

MELODIC MOTIFS

Any melody can be represented numerically. A melodic motif is a short pattern of notes whose numerical interval structure has been adapted to a given scale. In the following examples, "1" represents the root, "2" represents the 2nd scale degree, "3" the 3rd, and so on.

Ex. 4.41a illustrates a 1-2-3-5 motif adapted to a C major scale. A melodic motif may be attached to any rhythmic motif as shown in **Ex. 4.41b**.

Ex. 4.41a

Ex. 4.41b

Each of the following three-, four-, and five-note melodic motifs in **Examples 4.42a–4.42c** is applicable to any seven-note scale. Apply them to the major scale and its modes first, then try them on other scales. (For pentatonic or hexatonic scales, omit the motifs that use inappropriate scale degrees.) Sharp or flat the numerical scale degrees to correspond with a given scale or mode. For instance, "1-2-3-4" translates to

"1-2-♭3-4" in a minor scale, or "1-2-3-♯4" in a whole-tone scale, but is not applicable to pentatonic scales. Use the rhythmic motifs in Chapter 3 to jump-start any melodic motif.

Ex. 4.42a

Three-note melodic motifs (6 permutations each)

Ex. 4.42b

Four-note melodic motifs (24 permutations each)

Ex. 4.42b (continued)

Ex. 4.42c

Five-note melodic motifs (120 permutations each)

MELODIC PERMUTATION

Permutation is a device used to determine all possible combinations of notes in a given melodic motif. Any four-note motif yields twenty-four (1x2x3x4) different fingering combinations, or permutations.

Ex. 4.43 illustrates all twenty-four permutations along with some suggested four-note melodic shapes. (There are six permutations beginning with each finger.) These are designed to improve your command of any combination of fret-hand fingers. (Note: *For this example only*, all numbers represent fingerings, not scale degrees.)

Ex. 4.43

24 Fingering Combinations			
1 2 3 4	2 1 3 4	3 1 2 4	4 1 2 3
1 2 4 3	2 1 4 3	3 1 4 2	4 1 3 2
1 3 2 4	2 3 1 4	3 2 1 4	4 2 1 3
1 3 4 2	2 3 4 1	3 2 4 1	4 2 3 1
1 4 2 3	2 4 1 3	3 4 1 2	4 3 1 2
1 4 3 2	2 4 3 1	3 4 2 1	4 3 2 1

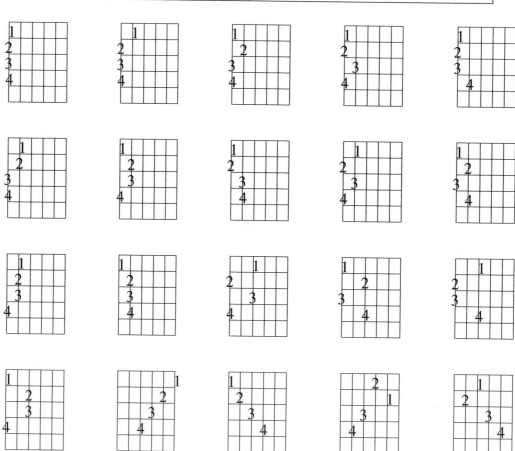

Ex. 4.43 (continued)

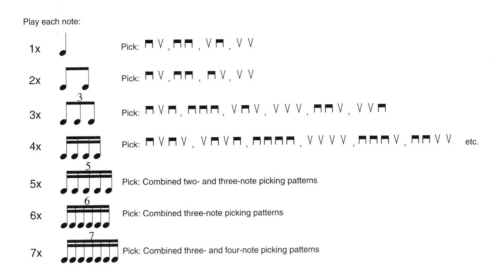

A three-note motif yields six (1x2x3) permutations while a five-note motif produces 120 (1x2x3x4x5)!

All previously illustrated motifs can be permuted. Think of them as short melodies. Find the ones you like, string them together to form longer lines, and incorporate these into your improvisations. As you study harmony, observe and memorize how they behave in different harmonic environments, that is, over different chords. Once you combine permutations with additional or repeated notes, rhythmic variations, and techniques—such as bends, hammer-ons, and pull-offs—the melodic possibilities become limitless.

Any motif may be altered to fit the sound of any chord. The ascending and descending "1-2-3-5" motifs in **Ex. 4.44a** have been adjusted to accommodate three different types of chords.

Ex. 4.44a

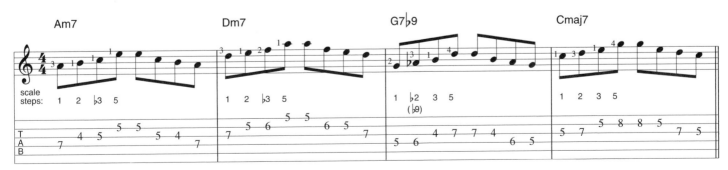

These motifs can be permuted to create a smoother transition between chord changes (**Ex. 4.44b**).

Ex. 4.44b

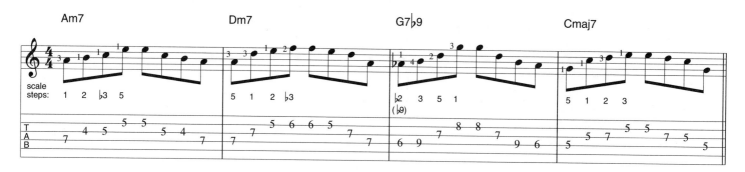

SEQUENCES

Since we are representing intervals and melodic motifs numerically, it is possible to adapt them to mathematical sequences. There are two types of sequences—"intervallic" and "motivic"—and two subdivisions of each: "diatonic," where each step of the sequence uses notes from a single scale, and "parallel," where each step of the sequence uses the same interval or motif without adjustment. Like the intervallic cycles we've seen, sequences and their permutations introduce all possibilities of melodic motion.

Ex. 4.45 shows seven diatonic interval sequences.

Ex. 4.45

Ex. 4.45 (continued)

Diatonic thirds

Diatonic fourths

Diatonic fifths

Ex. 4.45 (continued)

Diatonic sixths

Diatonic sevenths

Octaves

Ex. 4.45 (continued)

Try reversing the order of notes in every other interval:

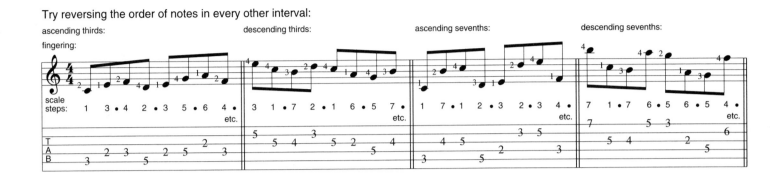

Any melodic motif and its permutations may be applied to any numerical sequence. There are six permutations of each three-note motivic sequence in **Ex. 4.46a** and twenty-four permutations of each four-note sequence in **Ex. 4.46b**.

Ex. 4.46a

Three-note motivic sequences (6 permutations each)

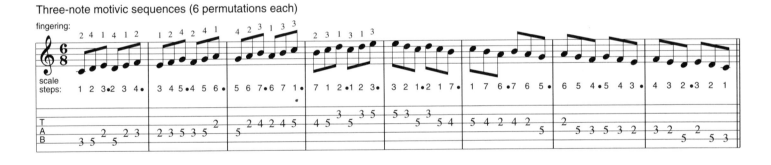

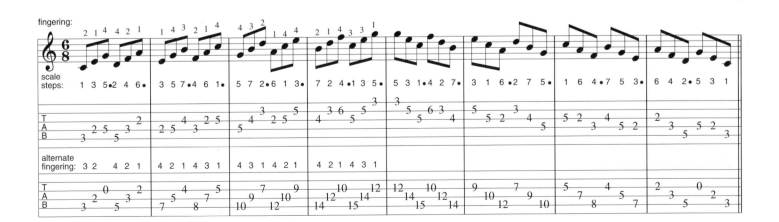

Ex. 4.46a (continued)

Ex. 4.46b

Four-note motivic sequences (24 permutations each)

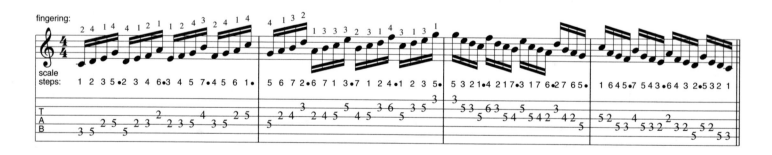

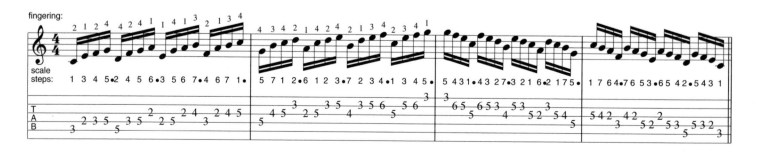

Ex. 4.46b continued

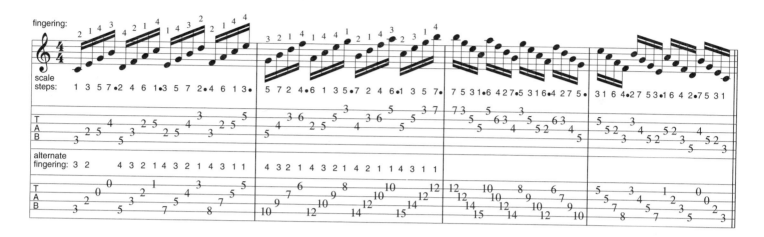

Play all sequences ascending and descending, applying the pick-hand techniques from Ex. 4.43. For extra credit, write out all motifs and sequences and their permutations in standard notation in all keys.

OCTAVE DISPLACEMENT

Any note or notes in any scale, melodic line, or chord may be displaced by one or more octaves in either direction. This can be used for subtle melodic alterations or to render a familiar melody unrecognizable. See if you can decode the octave-displaced chordal melody in **Ex. 4.47a**.

Ex. 4.47a

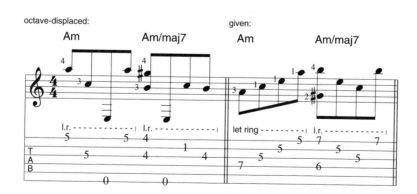

Start by displacing a few notes in short, familiar melodic lines. **Examples 4.47b** and **4.47c** use the *A* natural minor and pentatonic minor scales.

Ex. 4.47b

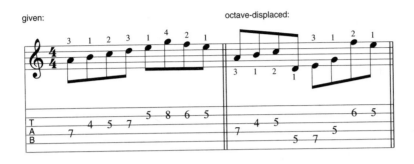

Ex. 4.47c

Ex. 4.47d twists a simple chromatic scale into an octave-displaced nightmare. To get a handle, group the notes into threes and check out the repetitive fingerings.

Ex. 4.47d

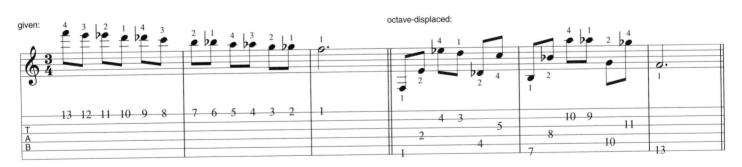

Octave displacement puts wide intervallic skips into your playing, making old ideas sound fresh. Once again, a simple concept yields thousands of new ideas. Catching on? Go displacement-crazy with all of your favorite lines and watch the heads turn.

MELODIC EAR-TRAINING

The ability to hear music correctly is an important prerequisite to playing music: To play music, you must first hear the correct notes and rhythms internally. Every time you play a melodic line, you should sing or hum it internally. If you don't do this already, start today. This alone can make your music much stronger. If you are vocally challenged, don't worry about singing perfectly in tune. Get as close as you can. If you can hear the correct notes internally, you are on the right track.

The next time you have trouble playing a phrase, try singing it out loud, slowly. If you are unsure about any of the notes, you will have a hard time playing the phrase correctly.

Great musicians have great ears. Your objective is to develop a keen sense of relative pitch, or the ability to recognize all of the musical intervals by ear. With good relative pitch, you can locate and identify any note based on a single reference pitch. Once you have memorized the shapes of the intervals on the fingerboard, you can quickly learn to play what you are hearing. Whenever you identify an interval, visualize yourself playing it on the fingerboard.

We've seen how the ear is already familiar with the sound of each interval through repeated previous exposure in Ex. 4.1. Even so, learning to recognize and identify the intervals can be a long and tedious process. Practice faithfully, and you will see—or should I say *hear*—the results. Ear-training never stops. Keep listening and always be on the lookout for new melodies. Sharpen your skills by garnering melodic ideas from recordings, live performances, or even the sounds of nature, then transfer them to your instrument. Your ultimate goal is to be able to play anything you hear.

It is best to begin with the sounds of the major and perfect intervals within one octave. Most ears are already familiar with the sound of the major scale via the *solfeggio* sight-singing system (*Do-Re-Mi-Fa-So-La-Ti-Do*) or, more likely, that damn "deer song" from *The Sound of Music*. Use any major scale fingering starting on any root for the following exercises. As you learn more scales, incorporate them into your ear-training in the same manner.

To practice ascending or descending major scales:

• Play and then sing any chosen root note.

• Sing up or down the scale while simultaneously playing it on the guitar.

• Sing the numerical scale degrees that correspond to the ascending and descending intervals—"1, 2, 3," and so on.

• Sing the scale again without playing it.

• Repeat the entire process, singing the names of the notes instead of the scale degrees—for example, "C, D, E," and so on.

Practice until you can sing an ascending or descending major scale starting on any root.

To practice ascending or descending major and perfect intervals individually:

• Play and then sing any chosen root note.

• Simultaneously play and sing by major scale degrees up or down to any chosen major or perfect interval.

• Sing and then play from the root directly to the chosen interval, eliminating all in-between notes.

• Repeat all of the above, singing the names of the notes instead of their numerical scale degrees.

Repeat the entire process for all major and perfect intervals.

To practice individual ascending or descending minor intervals and ♭5s:

• Play and then sing any chosen root.

• Simultaneously play and sing scale degrees up or down to the nearest major or perfect interval above any chosen minor or ♭5 interval.

• Sing and play the chosen minor or ♭5 interval by lowering the major or perfect interval located one half-step above it.

• Sing and then play from the root directly to the chosen interval, eliminating any in-between notes.

- Repeat all of the above, singing the names of the notes instead of their numerical scale degrees.

Repeat the entire process for all minor intervals and ♭5s.

Ask a friend who plays any instrument to record a half-hour of random melodic intervals, playing each pair of notes three times apiece. Try to identify each interval by ear from the recording, then check your results on the guitar. If you have access to—and are unfamiliar with—keyboard instruments, play any two consecutive notes and try to name the melodic interval.

For the ultimate self-test, radically retune your guitar, then play familiar interval shapes anywhere on the fingerboard and try to name them. In altered tunings, the shapes you play will produce different intervals than the ones you've memorized. This prevents you from identifying an interval by sight or feel, and forces you to do it purely by ear.

Eventually, you will be able to identify every note of the chromatic scale from a single reference pitch. Keep recalling any familiar melodies to help your retention of each interval. Every interval has a characteristic sound. Wire these and you'll be able to identify any type of interval, even without a reference pitch. Your objective is the immediate recognition and identification of the sound and distance of any interval.

CHAPTER FIVE

Harmony

Like people, individual notes tend to behave much differently in groups. Welcome to the alchemistic world of harmony, or—as I prefer to define it—the politics of music.

HARMONIC INTERVALS

A harmonic interval occurs when both notes of a melodic interval are sounded simultaneously. Harmonic intervals are the building blocks of chords. Melodic and harmonic intervals share the same fingerboard shapes (Chapter 4, Ex. 4.2), but—unless produced electronically or by two guitars—harmonic intervals can only be played on separate strings. (There are a few manual methods which allow you to produce a limited amount of harmonic intervals on a single string. These will be detailed in the next chapter.)

Any scale can be harmonized and any interval may be constructed from each scale degree. Harmonic intervals built from each note of a single scale can have a diatonic or parallel relationship to the scale. Diatonic harmony uses only scale tones, resulting in major, minor, perfect, or flatted intervals in accordance with the scale's step formula. Parallel harmony builds the same interval from each scale degree, regardless of the note's absence or presence in the scale.

The chart in **Ex. 5.1** (next page) illustrates all diatonic and parallel harmonic intervals within one octave in the key of C. Compare them to the melodic intervals back in Ex. 4.2.

Play these diatonic and parallel harmonic intervals in all keys, using any major scale fingering. Notice that when each harmonic interval is arpeggiated, or played melodically, the result is an interval sequence (see Chapter 4, Ex. 4.45). Remember to adjust the shape of an interval when the upper note falls on the *B* string, and, in some cases, the high *E* string. Use the shapes in Ex. 4.2 (Chapter 4) to form all extended diatonic and parallel intervals.

After exhausting the major scale, adapt all harmonic intervals to other scales and transpose them to all keys. All motifs, interval sequences, and their permutations are eligible for harmonization. Pick any scale system and get to work, keeping in mind that whatever applies to melody also applies to harmony.

Ex. 5.1

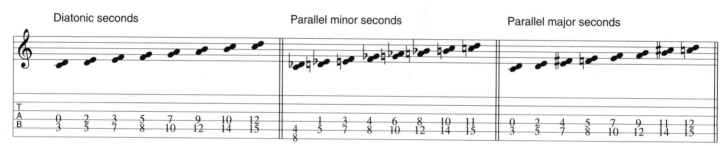

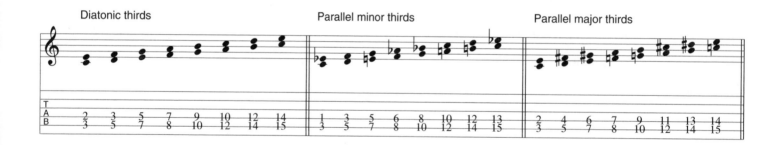

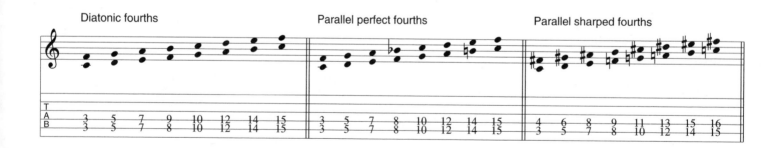

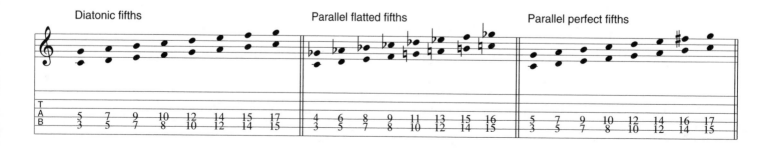

Ex. 5.1 (continued)

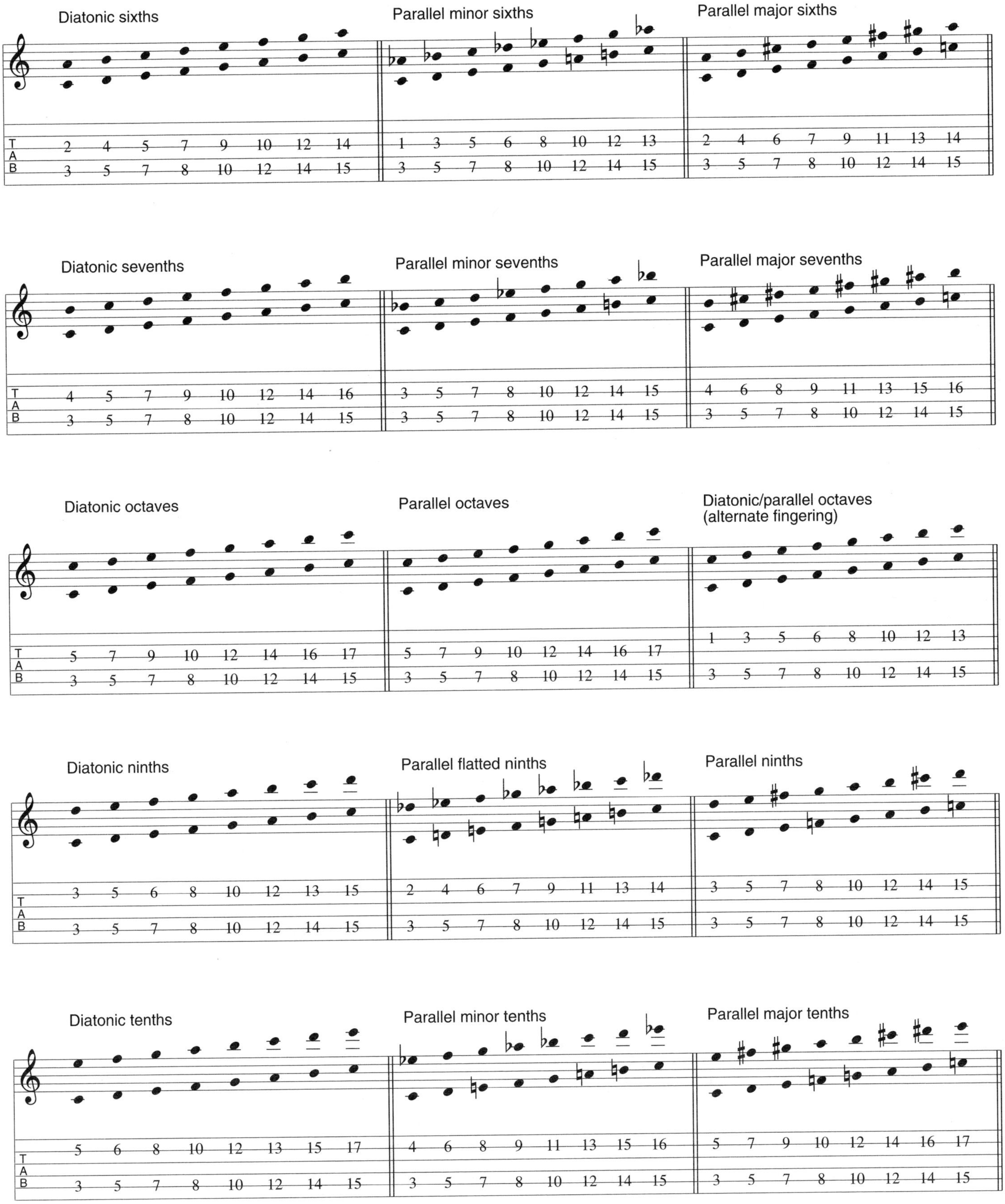

Diatonic sixths

Parallel minor sixths

Parallel major sixths

Diatonic sevenths

Parallel minor sevenths

Parallel major sevenths

Diatonic octaves

Parallel octaves

Diatonic/parallel octaves
(alternate fingering)

Diatonic ninths

Parallel flatted ninths

Parallel ninths

Diatonic tenths

Parallel minor tenths

Parallel major tenths

CHORD CONSTRUCTION

Chords consist of two or more harmonic intervals played simultaneously. There are three basic chord sounds: major, minor, and dominant. Every chord fits into one of these categories. Though harmonic intervals can suggest chords, the triad—or three-note chord—is the smallest official chordal unit.

On a structural level, chords are assembled by adding various degrees of the chromatic scale to various triads in accordance with specific formulas. This creates additional interval measurements from both the root and other chord tones—intervals within intervals within intervals, so to speak.

The following chart (**Ex. 5.2**) lists the name, formula in scale degrees, and written symbol for all common unaltered chords in all three chord categories.

Ex. 5.2

Name of chord	Formula in scale steps	Chord symbols
MAJOR CHORD TYPES		
Major triad	Root, 3, 5	C
Major sixth*	Root, 3, 5, 6	C6
Major seventh	Root, 3, 5, 7	Cmaj7, CM7, C∆7
Major ninth	Root, 3, 5, 7, 9 (2)	Cmaj9, CM9, C∆9
Major six/nine	Root, 3, 5, 6, 9 (2)	C6/9
Major thirteenth	Root, 3, 5, 7, 9 (2), 13 (6)	Cmaj13, CM13, CM∆13
Major add 4	Root, 3, 4, 5	Cadd4
Major add 9	Root, 3, 5, 9 (2)	Cadd9
Suspended 2**	Root, 2, 5	Csus2
Suspended 4**	Root, 4, 5	Csus4
MINOR CHORD TYPES		
Minor triad	Root, ♭3, 5	Cm, Cmi, C-
Minor sixth	Root, ♭3, 5, 6	Cm6, Cmi6, C-6
Minor seventh	Root, ♭3, 5, ♭7	Cm7, Cmi7, C-7
Minor ninth	Root, ♭3, 5, ♭7, 9 (2)	Cm9, Cmi9, C-9
Minor eleventh	Root, ♭3, 5, ♭7, 9 (2), 11 (4)	Cm11, Cmi11, C-11
Minor/major seventh	Root, ♭3, 5, 7	Cm/maj7, Cmi/maj7, C-/∆7
DOMINANT CHORD TYPES		
Dominant seventh	Root, 3, 5, ♭7	C7
Dominant ninth	Root, 3, 5, ♭7, 9 (2)	C9
Dominant eleventh	Root, 3, 5, ♭7, 9 (2), 11 (4)	C11
Dominant thirteenth	Root, 3, 5, ♭7, 9 (2), 13 (6)	C13
Dominant seventh suspended fourth	Root, 4, 5, ♭7	C7sus4, C7sus
Dominant ninth suspended fourth	Root, 4, 5, ♭7, 9	C9sus4, C9sus
Dominant thirteenth suspended fourth	Root, 4, 5, ♭7, 9, 13	C13sus4, C13sus

* Major sixth chords can function as both major or dominant.
** Sus2 and Sus4 chords can function as major, minor, or dominant.

ALTERED CHORDS

There are four possible alterations to any chord: ♭5 (sometimes labeled #11), #5 (sometimes labeled ♭6 or ♭13), ♭9, and #9. **Ex. 5.3** lists all common altered chords in all three categories by name, construction, and written symbol.

To form chord voicings over the entire fingerboard, use these charts in conjunction with the five major scale fingering patterns.

Ex. 5.3

Name of chord	Formula in scale steps	Chord symbols
ALTERED MAJOR CHORDS		
Augmented triad	Root, 3, #5	Caug, C+
Major seventh flat 5 (#11)	Root, 3, ♭5 (#11), 7	Cmaj7♭5, CΔ7♭5, Cmaj7#11
Major seventh sharp 5	Root, 3, #5, 7	Cmaj7#5, Cmaj7+5, CΔ7+5
Major six/nine flat 5 (#11)	Root, 3, ♭5, 6, 9	C6/9♭5, C6/9#11
Suspended sharp 4	Root, #4, 5	Csus#4
Suspended flat 2	Root, ♭2, 5	Csus♭2
ALTERED MINOR CHORDS		
Diminished triad*	Root, ♭3, ♭5	Cdim, C°, (E♭°, G♭°, A°)
Minor seventh flat 5	Root, ♭3, ♭5, ♭7	Cm7♭5, Cmi7♭5, C-7♭5, Cø
Minor seventh sharp 5	Root, ♭3, #5, ♭7	Cm7♭5, Cmi7♭5, Cm7♭+5, Cmi7+5, C-7#5, C-7+5
ALTERED DOMINANT CHORDS		
Dominant seventh sharp 5	Root, 3, #5, (♭13), ♭7	C7#5, C7+5, Caug7, C+7, C7♭13
Dominant seventh flat 5	Root, 3, ♭5, ♭7	C7♭5
Dominant seventh flat 9	Root, 3, 5, ♭7, ♭9	C7♭9, C7-9
Diminished seventh* **	Root, ♭3, ♭5, ♭7 (6)	Cdim7, C°7 (E♭°7, G♭°7, A°7)
Dominant seventh sharp 9	Root, 3, 5, ♭7, #9	C7#9, C7+9
Dominant seventh sharp 5 flat 9	Root, 3, #5, ♭7, ♭9	C7#5♭9, C+7♭9
Dominant seventh sharp 5 sharp 9	Root, 3, #5, ♭7, #9	C7#5#9, C+7#9
Dominant ninth sharp 5	Root, 3, #5, ♭7, 9	C9#5, C+9
Dominant ninth flat 5	Root, 3, ♭5, ♭7, 9	C9♭5
Dominant thirteenth flat 9	Root, 3, 5, ♭7, ♭9, 13	C13♭9
Dominant seventh flat 5 flat 9	Root, 3, ♭5, ♭7, ♭9	C7♭5♭9

* Any note in a diminished triad or diminished seventh chord can function as the root: C°(7)=E♭°(7)=G♭°(7)=A°(7).

** A diminished seventh chord functions as a 7♭9 chord rooted 1/2 step lower than any of its component notes:
C°7, E♭°7, G♭°7, A°7=B7♭9, D7♭9, F7♭9, A♭7♭9 or C7♭9, E♭7♭9, G♭7♭9, A7♭9 =D♭°7, E°7, G°7, B♭°7.

MAJOR SCALE HARMONY

While construction formulas reveal how random chords are formed on a molecular level, major scale harmony clarifies how they relate to scales, keys, and other chords. In fact, related chords are nothing more than every other note of a given scale played vertically, or harmonically, rather than horizontally, or melodically.

MAJOR SCALE HARMONY IN THIRDS

Traditionally, tertian (built in diatonic thirds) harmony is the system used to derive chords from any major scale and its modes. To harmonize the major scale in thirds, stack the 3rd scale degree on top of the root, then continue up the scale through the octave, with each note of the scale joined by the note one diatonic third above it. This produces only two-note intervals, and these harmonized thirds cannot yet be called chords. However, any two-note diad can *suggest* chord sounds, especially when a root is provided by another instrument. Each harmonized-third diad is designated major or minor in accordance with its interval structure. Its position in the scale is defined by the same Roman numerals used to identify the steps, or degrees, of the major scale. **Ex. 5.4a** illustrates how it works in the key of C.

Ex. 5.4a

C major scale harmonized in diatonic thirds

Major Scale Harmony Rule #1: In any major key, diatonic thirds built on steps I, IV, and V are major. Diatonic thirds built on steps II, III, VI, and VII are minor.

Ex. 5.4b illustrates the remaining major scales harmonized in diatonic thirds.

Ex. 5.4b

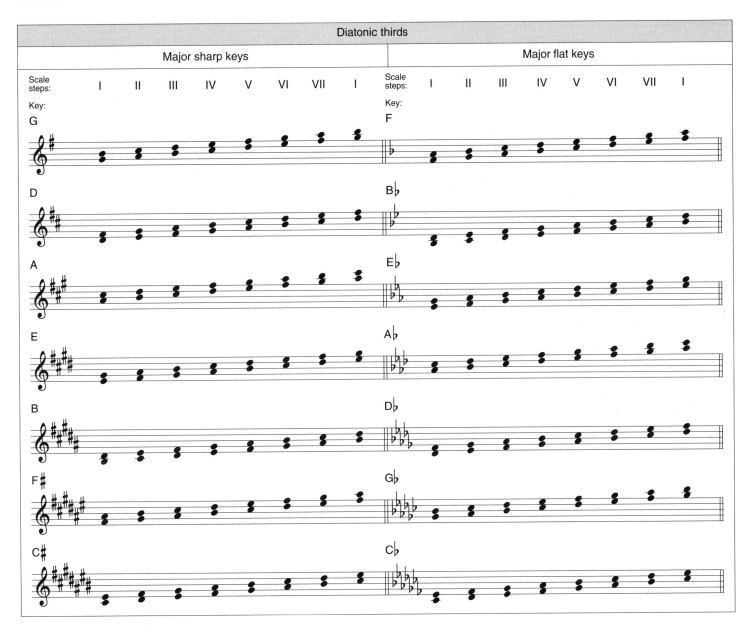

Write and play all major scales in thirds, using all previously shown tetrachord and scale fingerings.

MAJOR SCALE HARMONY IN TRIADS

Familiarity with harmony in thirds is a prerequisite to understanding triadic (three notes at a time) harmony. A triad contains three different notes: root, 3, and 5. There are three types of triads present in any diatonic major scale system: major, minor, and diminished.

To harmonize diatonic triads, stack the major scale on top of its thirds harmony starting with the 5 (a diatonic third above the 3) and continue through the octave (as shown in **Ex. 5.5a**). This forms a series of related triads which are named by their interval structures and located by their Roman numerical scale degrees. (Notice how each string tracks the major scale starting on a different degree.)

Ex. 5.5a

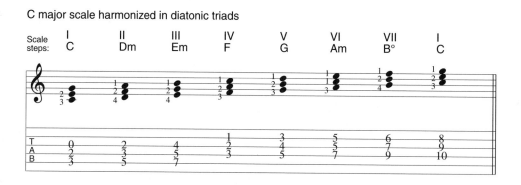

C major scale harmonized in diatonic triads

Major Scale Harmony Rule #2: In any major key, the I, IV, and V chords are major triads, the II, III, and VI chords are minor triads, and the VII chord is a diminished triad.

Ex. 5.5b illustrates the remaining major scales harmonized in diatonic triads. Write and play all triads in all major keys. Use the chord construction chart in conjunction with the five major scale fingering patterns to form triads all over the fingerboard. Your objective is to memorize any triad's position in any key. Drill yourself constantly—What is the II chord in the key of *D*? How about in the key of *E*, *A♭*, or *F♯*? What is the IV chord in *G*? How about in *B♭*, *A*, *D♭*, and so on?

Though only three appear in any major key, there are actually five types of triads: major, minor, augmented, diminished, and suspended. An augmented triad is a major triad with a ♯5, while a diminished triad is a minor triad with a ♭5, placing both triads

Ex. 5.5b

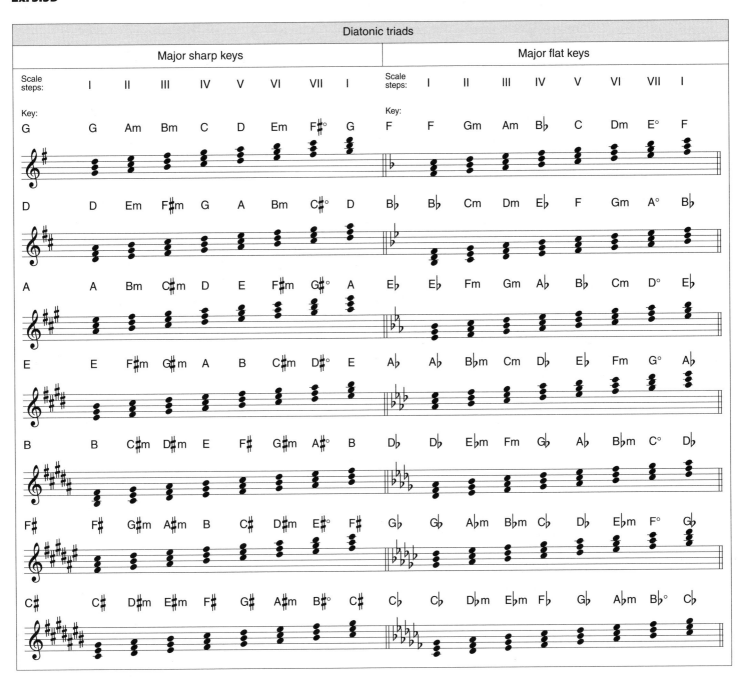

in the altered category. In contemporary music, these two chords often function as altered dominant-7th chords. For example, *Caug=C7#5*, and *Cdim=B7♭9*, *D7♭9*, and *F7♭9* (as well as just plain *A♭7*). In a suspended triad, the 3 is replaced by its upper or lower neighboring scale tone–2, 4, ♭2, or #4–for such chords as *Csus2* and *B♭sus#4*.

MAJOR SCALE HARMONY IN 7TH CHORDS

Familiarity with triadic harmony is a prerequisite to understanding 7th-chord harmony. By definition, a 7th chord contains four different notes—root, 3, 5, and 7. There are four types of 7th chords present in any harmonized diatonic major scale system—major-7th, minor-7th, dominant-7th, and minor-7th-♭5. To build diatonic 7th chords (**Ex. 5.6a**), stack a 7 (a diatonic third above the 5) on top of each diatonic triad within a key.

Ex. 5.6a

C major scale harmonized in diatonic seventh chords

Major Scale Harmony Rule #3: In any major key, the I and IV chords are major-7th; the II, III, and VI chords are minor-7th; the V chord is dominant-7th; and the VII chord is minor-7th-♭5.

Ex. 5.6b illustrates the remaining major scales harmonized in diatonic 7th chords. Revoice them into more manageable fingerings as necessary.

Drill yourself in the same manner as triads. Memorize the Imaj7, IIm7, IIIm7, IVmaj7, V7, VIm7, and VIIm7♭5 chords in every key. Write them, play them, and practice them mentally, away from the guitar. Practice all harmonized major scales through each intervallic cycle and incorporate chordal adaptations of rhythmic and melodic motifs, sequences, and permutations. Once again, whatever applies to melody also applies to harmony.

Ex. 5.6b

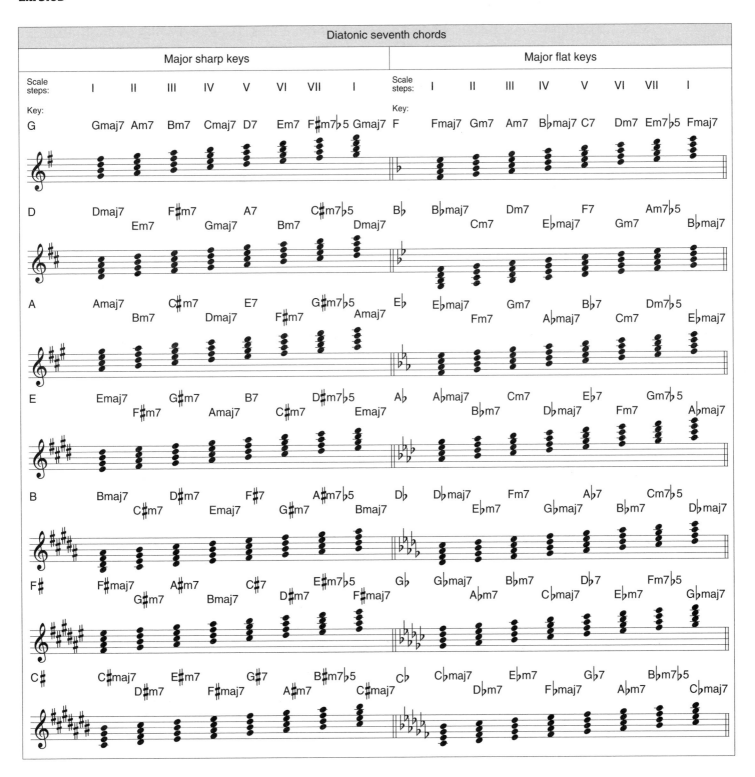

EXTENDED HARMONY

Harmony can be extended beyond 7ths to include 9ths, 11ths, and 13ths, as illustrated in **Ex. 5.7a**. Of course, on a 6-string guitar, it is impossible to play every note of these seven-note monsters—but who would want to?

Ex. 5.7a

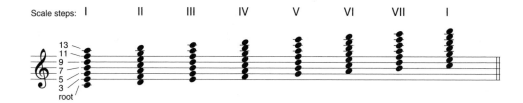

Ex. 5.7b looks at some rootless partial voicings (implied roots in parentheses) that concentrate on extensions above the 7 (excluding the 11). The four-note voicings in **Ex. 5.7c** utilize the 3, 5, and 9, and drop the 13 down into the 6 slot—a common practice in chord construction. Notice how the identical fingerings in each example shift to function differently over each implied root.

Ex. 5.7b

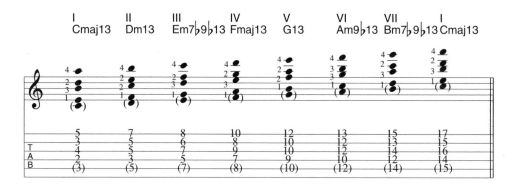

Ex. 5.7c

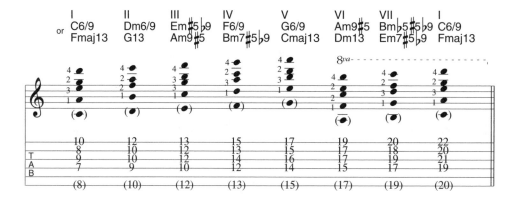

Any scale may be extended harmonically beyond 7ths. Use intervallic cycles, sequences, and permutations to explore extensions in all keys.

MINOR SCALE HARMONY

By harmonizing any major scale, you also harmonize its relative modes. As we've seen, the *A* natural minor scale (Aeolian mode) consists of the same notes as its relative *C* major scale, but relocates the tonic to *C*'s 6th scale degree, *A*. The resulting diatonic harmonies are identical to those found in the major scale.

MINOR SCALE HARMONY IN THIRDS

To harmonize the natural minor scale in thirds (**Ex. 5.8**), stack the 3 (a ♭3, actually) of the scale on top of the root and continue through the octave.

Ex. 5.8

A minor scale harmonized in diatonic thirds

Minor Scale Harmony Rule #1: In any natural minor key, diatonic thirds built on steps I, II, IV, and V are minor. Diatonic thirds built on steps ♭III, ♭VI, and ♭VII are major.

Write out—and then play—all 15 minor scales harmonized in diatonic thirds. Make your own chart similar to Ex. 5.4b. Explore all minor scale fingerings by converting the five connecting major scale patterns to a movable, minor-key *CAGED* template.

MINOR SCALE HARMONY IN TRIADS

To harmonize the minor scale in diatonic triads (**Ex. 5.9a**), stack the scale on top of its thirds harmony starting with the 5 (a diatonic third above the ♭3) and continue up through the octave.

Ex. 5.9a

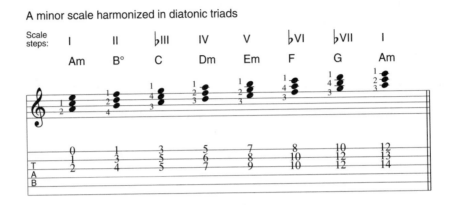

A minor scale harmonized in diatonic triads

Minor Scale Harmony Rule #2: In any natural minor key, the I, IV, and V chords are minor triads, the ♭III, ♭VI, and ♭VII chords are major triads, and the II chord is a diminished triad.

The chart in **Ex. 5.9b** names the diatonic triads in all remaining natural minor keys. Using the provided chord symbols, write them out in standard notation and play them in all keys.

Ex. 5.9b

	Minor sharp keys — triads								Minor flat keys — triads						
Scale steps:	I	II	♭III	IV	V	♭VI	♭VII	I	Scale steps:	I	II	♭III	IV	V	♭VI	♭VII	I
Em	Em	F#°	G	Am	Bm	C	D	Em	Dm	Dm	E°	F	Gm	Am	B♭	C	Dm
Bm	Bm	C#°	D	Em	F#m	G	A	Bm	Gm	Gm	A°	B♭	Cm	Dm	E♭	F	Gm
F#m	F#m	G#°	A	Bm	C#m	D	E	F#m	Cm	Cm	D°	E♭	Fm	Gm	A♭	B♭	Cm
C#m	C#m	D#°	E	F#m	G#m	A	B	C#m	Fm	Fm	G°	A♭	B♭m	Cm	D♭	E♭	Fm
G#m	G#m	A#°	B	C#m	D#m	E	F#	G#m	B♭m	B♭m	C°	D♭	E♭m	Fm	G♭	A♭	B♭m
D#m	D#m	E#°	F#	G#m	A#m	B	C#	D#m	E♭m	E♭m	F°	G♭	A♭m	B♭m	C♭	D♭	E♭m
A#m	A#m	B#°	C#	D#m	E#m	F#	G#	A#m	A♭m	A♭m	B♭°	C♭	D♭m	E♭m	F♭	G♭	A♭m

MINOR SCALE HARMONY IN 7TH CHORDS

To harmonize the natural minor scale in diatonic 7th chords (**Ex. 5.10a**), stack the scale on top of its diatonic triads starting with the 7 (a diatonic third above the 5) and continue through the octave.

Ex. 5.10a A minor scale harmonized in diatonic seventh chords

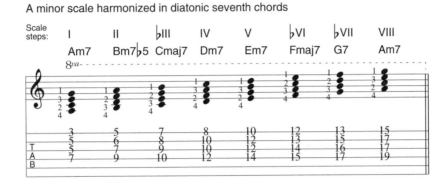

Minor Scale Harmony Rule #3: In any natural minor key, the I, IV, and V chords are minor-7th, the ♭III and ♭VI chords are major-7th, the ♭VII chord is dominant-7th, and the II chord is minor-7th-♭5.

The chart in **Ex. 5.10b** names the diatonic 7th chords in all remaining natural minor keys. Using the provided chord symbols, write them out in standard notation and play them in all keys through each intervallic cycle. Revoice them into more manageable fingerings as needed. To leave no stone unturned, write, play, sequence, and permute all harmonized diatonic and parallel modes in all keys.

Ex. 5.10b

	Minor sharp keys — seventh chords								Minor flat keys — seventh chords							
Scale steps:	I	II	♭III	IV	V	♭VI	♭VII	I	Scale steps:	I	II	♭III	IV	V	♭VI	♭VII	I
Em	Em7	F#m7♭5	Gmaj7	Am7	Bm7	Cmaj7	D7	Em7	Dm	Dm7	Em7♭5	Fmaj7	Gm7	Am7	B♭maj7	C7	Dm7
Bm	Bm7	C#m7♭5	Dmaj7	Em7	F#m7	Gmaj7	A7	Bm7	Gm	Gm7	Am7♭5	B♭maj7	Cm7	Dm7	E♭maj7	F7	Gm7
F#m	F#m7	G#m7♭5	Amaj7	Bm7	C#m7	Dmaj7	E7	F#m7	Cm	Cm7	Dm7♭5	E♭maj7	Fm7	Gm7	A♭maj7	B♭7	Cm7
C#m	C#m7	D#m7♭5	Emaj7	F#m7	G#m7	Amaj7	B7	C#m7	Fm	Fm7	Gm7♭5	A♭maj7	B♭m7	Cm7	D♭maj7	E♭7	Fm7
G#m	G#m7	A#m7♭5	Bmaj7	C#m7	D#m7	Emaj7	F#7	G#m7	B♭m	B♭m7	Cm7♭5	D♭maj7	E♭m7	Fm7	G♭maj7	A♭7	B♭m7
D#m	D#m7	E#m7♭5	F#maj7	G#m7	A#m7	Bmaj7	C#7	D#m7	E♭m	E♭m7	Fm7♭5	G♭maj7	A♭m7	B♭m7	C♭maj7	D♭7	E♭m7
A#m	A#m7	B#m7♭5	C#maj7	D#m7	E#m7	F#maj7	G#7	A#m7	A♭m	A♭m7	B♭m7♭5	C♭maj7	D♭m7	E♭m7	F♭maj7	G♭7	A♭m7

HARMONIC MINOR AND
MELODIC MINOR SCALE HARMONY

The structural difference between harmonic and melodic minor and parallel natural minor scales causes significant harmonic alterations. Most notably, the natural 7 present in both scales changes the V chord harmony from a minor triad or minor-7th chord to a major triad or dominant-7th chord. Again, the process of harmonization is tertian, or built in thirds. Harmonic and melodic minor key signatures are borrowed from the parallel natural minor key, and accidentals are added as needed.

HARMONIC MINOR SCALE HARMONY IN THIRDS

To harmonize the harmonic minor scale in thirds (**Ex. 5.11**), stack the scale on top of itself starting with the ♭3 and continue up through the octave. The results are identical to the harmonized *A* natural minor scale, but with all *G*s sharped.

 Ex. 5.11

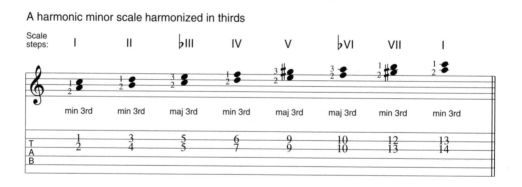

A harmonic minor scale harmonized in thirds

Harmonic Minor Scale Harmony Rule #1: In any key, steps I, II, IV, and VII are minor thirds, while steps ♭III, V, and ♭VI are major thirds.

HARMONIC MINOR SCALE HARMONY IN TRIADS

To harmonize the harmonic minor scale in triads (**Ex. 5.12a**), stack the scale on top of itself starting with the 5 (a diatonic third above the ♭3) and continue through the octave. Again, the results are identical to the harmonized *A* natural minor scale, but with all *G*s sharped.

Ex. 5.12a   A harmonic minor scale harmonized in triads

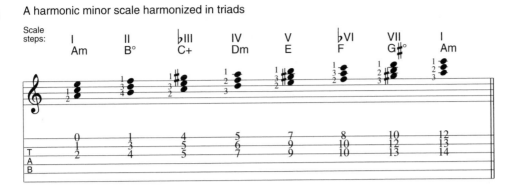

Harmonic Minor Scale Harmony Rule #2: In any key, the I and IV chords are minor triads, the V and ♭VI chords are major triads, the II and VII chords are diminished triads, and the ♭III chord is an augmented triad.

The chart in **Ex. 5.12b** lists the harmonized triads in the remaining harmonic minor scales. Using the provided chord symbols, write them out in standard notation, and play them in all keys.

Ex. 5.12b

Harmonic minor sharp keys — triads								Harmonic minor flat keys — triads							
Scale steps: I	II	♭III	IV	V	♭VI	VII	I	Scale steps:	I	II	♭III	IV	V	♭VI	VII	I
Em	F#°	G+	Am	B	C	D#°	Em	Dm	Dm	E°	F+	Gm	A	B♭	C#°	Dm
Bm	C#°	D+	Em	F#	G	A#°	Bm	Gm	Gm	A°	B♭+	Cm	D	E♭	F#°	Gm
F#m	G#°	A+	Bm	C#	D	E#°	F#m	Cm	Cm	D°	E♭+	Fm	G	A♭	B°	Cm
C#m	D#°	E+	F#m	G#	A	B#°	C#m	Fm	Fm	G°	A♭+	B♭m	C	D♭	E°	Fm
G#m	A#°	B+	C#m	D#	E	Fx°	G#m	B♭m	B♭m	C°	D♭+	E♭m	F	G♭	A°	B♭m
D#m	E#°	F#+	G#m	A#	B	Cx°	D#m	E♭m	E♭m	F°	G♭+	A♭m	B♭	C♭	D°	E♭m
A#m	B#°	C#+	D#m	E#	F#	Gx°	A#m	A♭m	A♭m	B♭°	C♭+	D♭m	E♭	F♭	G°	A♭m

HARMONIC MINOR SCALE HARMONY IN 7TH CHORDS

To harmonize the harmonic minor scale in 7th chords (**Ex. 5.13a**), stack the scale on top of itself starting with the 7 (a third above the 5) and continue through the octave. Once again, the results are identical to the harmonized *A* natural minor scale with all *G*s sharped. Note that this produces seven different types of chords.

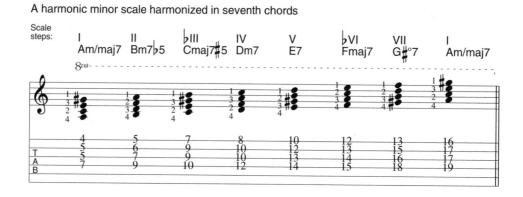

A harmonic minor scale harmonized in seventh chords

Harmonic Minor Scale Harmony Rule #3: In any key, the I chord is minor/major-7th, the II chord is minor-7th-♭5, the ♭III chord is major-7th-#5, the IV chord is minor-7th, the V chord is dominant-7th, the ♭VI chord is major-7th, and the VII chord is diminished-7th.

The chart in **Ex. 5.13b** lists the harmonized 7th chords in all remaining harmonic minor scales. Again, use the provided chord symbols to write them out in standard notation, revoice them into more manageable fingerings as needed, and play them in all keys.

Scale steps:	Harmonic minor sharp keys — seventh chords								Scale steps:	Harmonic minor flat keys — seventh chords							
	I	II	♭III	IV	V	♭VI	VII	I		I	II	♭III	IV	V	♭VI	VII	I
Em	Em/maj7	F#m7	Gmaj7#5	Am7	B7	Cmaj7	D#°7	Em/maj7	Dm	Dm/maj7	Em7♭5	Fmaj7#5	Gm7	A7	B♭maj7	C#°7	Dm/maj7
Bm	Bm/maj7	C#m7	Dmaj7#5	Em7	F#7	Gmaj7	A#°7	Bm/maj7	Gm	Gm/maj7	Am7♭5	B♭maj7#5	Cm7	D7	E♭maj7	F#°7	Gm/maj7
F#m	F#m/maj7	G#m7	Amaj7#5	Bm7	C#7	Dmaj7	E#°7	F#m/maj7	Cm	Cm/maj7	Dm7♭5	E♭maj7#5	Fm7	G7	A♭maj7	B°7	Cm/maj7
C#m	C#m/maj7	D#m7	Emaj7#5	F#m7	G#7	Amaj7	B#°7	C#m/maj7	Fm	Fm/maj7	Gm7♭5	A♭maj7#5	B♭m7	C7	D♭maj7	E°7	Fm/maj7
G#m	G#m/maj7	A#m7	Bmaj7#5	C#m7	D#7	Emaj7	Fx°7	G#m/maj7	B♭m	B♭m/maj7	Cm7♭5	D♭maj7#5	E♭m7	F7	G♭maj7	A°7	B♭m/maj7
D#m	D#m/maj7	E#m7	F#maj7#5	G#m7	A#7	Bmaj7	Cx°7	D#m/maj7	E♭m	E♭m/maj7	Fm7♭5	G♭maj7#5	A♭m7	B♭7	C♭maj7	D°7	E♭m/maj7
A#m	A#m/maj7	B#m7	C#maj7#5	D#m7	E#7	F#maj7	Gx°7	A#m/maj7	A♭m	A♭m/maj7	B♭m7♭5	C♭maj7#5	D♭m7	E♭7	F♭maj7	G°7	A♭m/maj7

Write, play, sequence, and permute all harmonic minor scales and their modes in all keys through each intervallic cycle. Don't forget to explore their extended harmonies.

MELODIC MINOR SCALE HARMONY IN THIRDS

To harmonize the melodic minor scale in thirds (**Ex. 5.14**), stack the scale on top of itself starting with the ♭3 and continue through the octave. The results are identical to the harmonized *A* natural minor scale, but with all *F*s and *G*s sharped.

Ex. 5.14   A melodic minor scale harmonized in thirds

Melodic Minor Scale Harmony Rule #1: In any key, steps I, II, VI, and VII are minor thirds and steps ♭III, IV, and V are major thirds.

MELODIC MINOR SCALE HARMONY IN TRIADS

To harmonize the melodic minor scale in triads (**Ex. 5.15a**), stack the scale on top of itself starting with the 5 (a third above the ♭3) and continue through the octave. Again, the results are identical to the harmonized *A* natural minor scale, with all *F*s and *G*s sharped.

Ex. 5.15a   A melodic minor scale harmonized in triads

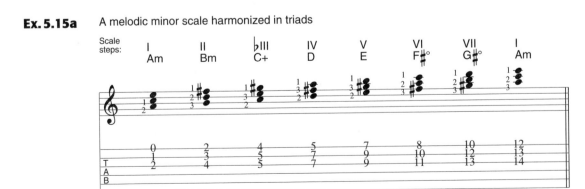

Melodic Minor Scale Harmony Rule #2: In any key, the I and II chords are minor triads, the IV and V chords are major triads, the VI and VII chords are diminished triads, and the ♭III chord is an augmented triad.

The chart in **Ex. 5.15b** lists the harmonized triads in the remaining melodic minor scales. Using the provided chord symbols, write them out in standard notation and play them in all keys.

Ex. 5.15b

Melodic minor sharp keys — triads									Melodic minor flat keys — triads								
Scale steps:	I	II	♭III	IV	V	VI	VII	I	Scale steps:	I	II	♭III	IV	V	VI	VII	I
Em	Em	F#m	G+	A	B	C#°	D#°	Em	Dm	Dm	Em	F+	G	A	B°	C°	Dm
Bm	Bm	C#m	D+	E	F#	G#°	A#°	Bm	Gm	Gm	Am	B♭+	C	D	E°	F°	Gm
F#m	F#m	G#m	A+	B	C#	D#°	E#°	F#m	Cm	Cm	Dm	E♭+	F	G	A°	B♭°	Cm
C#m	C#m	D#m	E+	F#	G#	A#°	B#°	C#m	Fm	Fm	Gm	A♭+	B♭	C	D°	E♭°	Fm
G#m	G#m	A#m	B+	C#	D#	E#°	Fx°	G#m	B♭m	B♭m	Cm	D♭+	E♭	F	G°	A♭°	B♭m
D#m	D#m	E#m	F#+	G#	A#	B#°	Cx°	D#m	E♭m	E♭m	Fm	G♭+	A♭	B♭	C°	D♭°	E♭m
A#m	A#m	B#m	C#+	D#	E#	Fx°	Gx°	A#m	A♭m	A♭m	B♭m	C♭+	D♭	E♭	F°	G♭°	A♭m

MELODIC MINOR SCALE HARMONY IN 7TH CHORDS

To harmonize the melodic minor scale in 7th chords (**Ex. 5.16a**), stack the scale on top of itself starting with the 7 (a third above the 5) and continue through the octave. Once again, the results are identical to the harmonized *A* natural minor scale, with all *F*s and *G*s sharped.

Ex. 5.16a

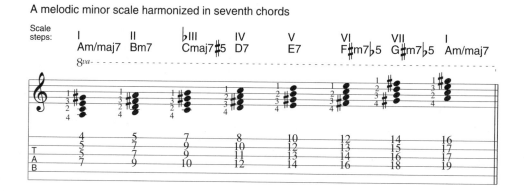

A melodic minor scale harmonized in seventh chords

Melodic Minor Scale Harmony Rule #3: In any key, the IV and V chords are dominant-7th, the VI and VII chords are minor-7th-♭5, the I chord is minor/major-7th, the II chord is minor-7th, and the ♭III chord is major-7th-♯5.

The chart in **Ex. 5.16b** lists the harmonized 7th chords in all remaining melodic minor scales. Again, use the provided chord symbols to write them out in standard notation, revoice them into more manageable fingerings as needed, and play them in all keys.

Ex. 5.16b

Scale steps:	Melodic minor sharp keys — seventh chords								Scale steps:	Melodic minor flat keys - seventh chords							
	I	II	♭III	IV	V	VI	VII	I		I	II	♭III	IV	V	VI	VII	I
Em	Em/maj7	F♯m7	Gmaj7♯5	A7	B7	C♯m7♭5	D♯m7♭5	Em/maj7	Dm	Dm/maj7	Em7	Fmaj7♯5	G7	A7	Bm7♭5	C♯m7♭5	Dm/maj7
Bm	Bm/maj7	C♯m7	Dmaj7♯5	E7	F♯7	G♯m7♭5	A♯m7♭5	Bm/maj7	Gm	Gm/maj7	Am7	B♭maj7♯5	C7	D7	Em7♭5	F♯m7♭5	Gm/maj7
F♯m	F♯m/maj7	G♯m7	Amaj7♯5	B7	C♯7	D♯m7♭5	E♯m7♭5	F♯m/maj7	Cm	Cm/maj7	Dm7	E♭maj7♯5	F7	G7	Am7♭5	Bm7♭5	Cm/maj7
C♯m	C♯m/maj7	D♯m7	Emaj7♯5	F♯7	G♯7	A♯m7♭5	B♯m7♭5	C♯m/maj7	Fm	Fm/maj7	Gm7	A♭maj7♯5	B♭7	C7	Dm7♭5	Em7♭5	Fm/maj7
G♯m	G♯m/maj7	A♯m7	Bmaj7♯5	C♯7	D♯7	E♯m7♭5	F×m7♭5	G♯m/maj7	B♭m	B♭m/maj7	Cm7	D♭maj7♯5	E♭7	F♭7	Gm7♭5	Am7♭5	B♭m/maj7
D♯m	D♯m/maj7	E♯m7	F♯maj7♯5	G♯7	A♯7	B♯m7♭5	C×m7♭5	D♯m/maj7	E♭m	E♭m/maj7	Fm7	G♭maj7♯5	A♭7	B♭7	Cm7♭5	Dm7♭5	E♭m/maj7
A♯m	A♯m/maj7	B♯m7	C♯maj7♯5	D♯7	E♯7	F♯m7♭5	G×m7♭5	A♯m/maj7	A♭m	A♭m/maj7	B♭m7	C♭maj7♯5	D♭7	E♭7	Fm7♭5	Gm7♭5	A♭m/maj7

Write, play, sequence, and permute each harmonized melodic minor scale and its modes in all keys, through all intervallic cycles.

PENTATONIC SCALE HARMONY

Due to its construction, a five-note pentatonic scale cannot be harmonized strictly in thirds. Harmonizing the pentatonic major scale using every other note reveals the combination of thirds and fourths in **Ex. 5.17a** (next page). Since the scale has no 4 or 7, there is virtually no harmonic tension present. **Ex. 5.17b** illustrates relative pentatonic minor harmony. Explore both major and minor pentatonic harmony, plus the three remaining pentatonic modes in all keys, using motifs, sequences, and permutations.

Ex. 5.17a

C pentatonic major harmony

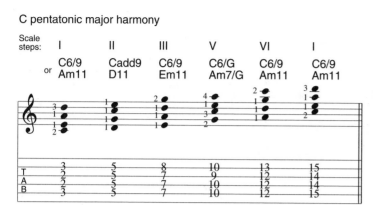

Ex. 5.17b

A pentatonic minor harmony

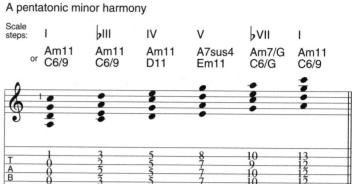

DIMINISHED SCALE HARMONY

Apply thirds harmony to any diminished scale and you'll get nothing but diminished triads and diminished-7th chords. In both harmonized diminished scales, every other chord is an inversion of itself. This means that there are only two different diminished chords in any harmonized diminished scale. And because the two types of diminished scales have one chord in common, there are actually only three different diminished triads and diminished-7th chords! These are always located three frets apart. **Examples 5.18a** and **5.18b** shows the whole-half and half-whole diminished scales harmonized in 7th chords. Revoice them into friendlier, more manageable fingerings.

As you may recall, any diminished-7th chord can also function as four different dominant-7th-♭9 chords, with roots one half-step lower than each of the notes in the

Ex. 5.18a

C whole-half diminished harmony

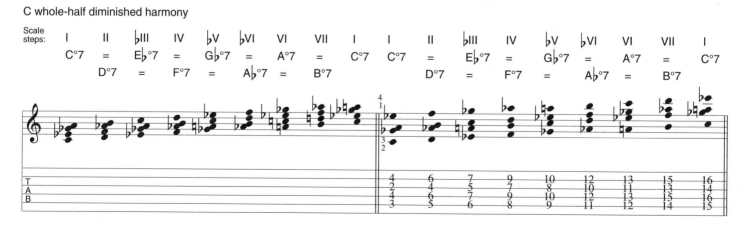

Ex. 5.18b

C half-whole diminished harmony

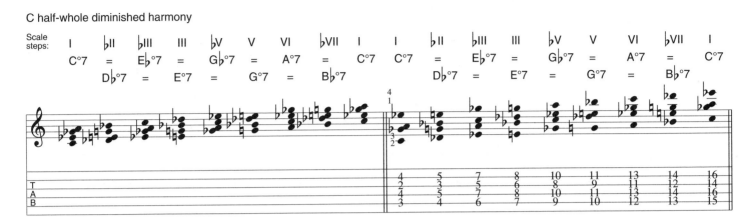

diminished–7th chord. Explore these implications and you will never be at a loss when it's time to create altered tension.

WHOLE-TONE SCALE HARMONY

Apply thirds harmony to any whole-tone scale (**Ex. 5.19**) and you'll get nothing but augmented triads. That's right—no 7th chords! As with diminished triads and 7th chords, every other chord is an inversion of itself. Since combining two whole-tone scales one half-step apart produces a chromatic scale, there are actually only two whole-tone scales. Together, these produce a total of four different augmented chords.

Adapt all harmonized diminished and whole-tone scales to intervallic cycles, motifs, sequences, and permutations. Still hungry for more new sounds? Harmonize the exotic scales in Chapter 4, Ex. 4.40.

Ex. 5.19

C whole-tone harmony

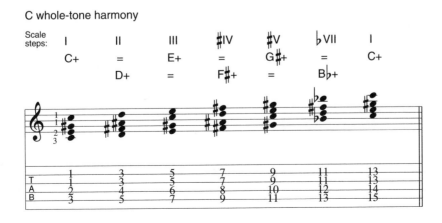

CHORDAL EXTENSIONS AND EMBELLISHMENTS

Any triad or 7th chord may be embellished, or colored, using natural extensions (9, 11, and 13) or alterations (♭5, ♯5, ♭9, and ♯9) without compromising its basic major, minor, or dominant quality and function. Though theoretically incorrect, 9, 11, and 13 are commonly added to chords as 2, 4, and 6, instead of an octave-plus above the root, as their formula dictates. Playing extensions an octave lower does impact the sound of a chord, but the decision to include these notes is often dictated by physics. In other words, grab them wherever you can!

Ever been faced with a "rhythm guitar" chart consisting of endless bars of static major, minor, or dominant-7th chords? Sparse chord charts, lame sheet music, or lousy show-band arrangements can all be brought to life using chord embellishments. **Examples 5.20a–5.20c** illustrate ways to add motion to otherwise stagnant harmonic situations by alternating *Cmaj6* and *Cmaj7* chords with a *C* triad, *Am7* and *Am6* with *Am*, and *G7sus4*, *G6*, and *G9sus4* with *G7*. Replacing a chord's 3 with its 2 or 4 creates a momentary period of harmonic unrest or tension, which is called a suspension. Returning to the 3 results in harmonic resolution.

Ex. 5.20a

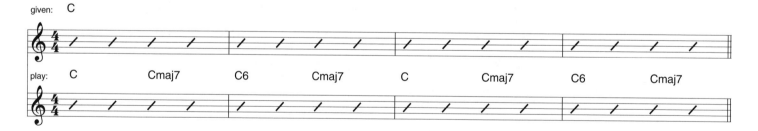

Ex. 5.20b

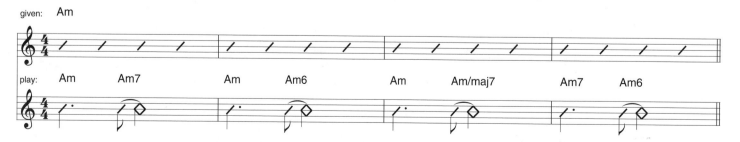

Ex. 5.20c

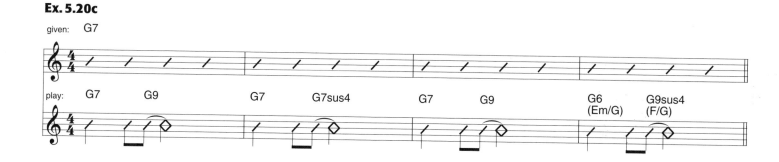

Alterations can cause unwanted tension, or harmonic unrest—especially in major and minor chords—and should be used with caution. Allow the melody of the moment to dictate chordal embellishments and generate rhythmic ideas. Apply extensions and alterations at your discretion, while always striving to stay in the context of whatever style of music you are playing.

To summarize:

- For major embellishments, use any major chord type in Ex. 5.2. Consider the melody carefully and use alterations sparingly.
- For minor embellishments, use any minor chord type in Ex. 5.2. Consider the melody carefully and use alterations sparingly.
- For dominant-7th embellishments, use major-6th chords or any dominant chord type in Ex. 5.2. Dominant chords accept altered extensions more readily than major or minor types, but consideration for the melody is still important. Any dominant chord type may also be reduced to a major triad.

BUILDING CHORDS ON THE FINGERBOARD

It is not necessary—and often impossible—to play a chord as it is spelled literally. The physical layout of the guitar frequently necessitates rearranging, duplicating, or deleting notes from a chord formula. The order of notes in a chord, spelled from low to high, is called a "voicing." Theoretically, any chord will yield as many inversions as it has notes. **Ex. 5.21a** (next page) shows the three inversions of a *C* major triad—root position (R–3–5), first inversion (3–5–R), and second inversion (5–R–3).

Ex. 5.21a

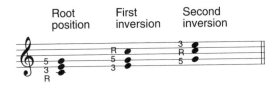

Ex. 5.21b reveals that our basic "open *C*" chord contains all three major triad inversions combined.

Ex. 5.21b

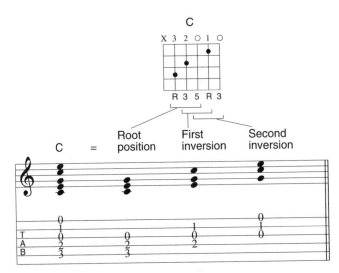

Due to the two-octave range available in any stationary position, guitar voicings typically double or even triple notes in a chord. This holds true for all five open-position triad fingerings—*C, A, G, E,* and *D*. They all use five or six strings, but may also be fragmented into several three- and four-note partial voicings on various string groups (**Ex. 5.21c**).

Ex. 5.21c

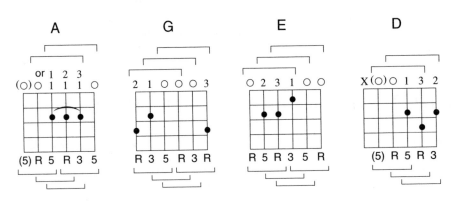

These five open-position triad shapes are the foundation on which all 7th, extended, and altered chords are constructed. Simply add or alter notes in accordance with any chord formula. Think of each string as a separate "voice," apply the formulas, and you'll discover thousands of chord voicings using various three-, four-, five-, and six-string groupings. Use the transposable *CAGED* template to locate any scale degree you wish to add in any key. Know your intervals, and you'll never be lost.

THE RELATIVE WEIGHT OF CHORD TONES

Some chord tones carry more harmonic weight than others. They are listed here in their order of importance.

- The 3 defines a chord's basic quality as major or minor.
- The 7, in conjunction with the 3, further defines a chord as major-7th, minor-7th, or dominant-7th.
- The root strengthens the overall sound of a chord and is usually provided by the bass in an ensemble. Though it names the chord, it is often omitted from guitar voicings in favor of embellishments, extensions, and alterations.
- The 5, in conjunction with the root, also strengthens the overall sound of a chord, but harmonically it is the most inactive and therefore the most expendable note.

Use the above information to edit chord formulas when you build voicings on the fingerboard. For instance, you can't play an embellished, extended, or altered chord without its embellishments, extensions, or alterations, so something else may have to go.

In heavy rock music where guitars tend to use a heavily distorted sound, harmony tends to be more basic and the importance of chord tones often reverses. Many rock voicings contain only roots and 5s. Essentially, this converts the chord to a "power chord," which takes to distortion like a buzz saw to cedar.

Chordal 3s and 7s sound great in clean-toned chords, but when things get really fuzzed-out they often cause undesirable overtones. (Tech tip: This holds truer for stomp-box and preamp distortion than power-amp saturation, where thirds can sound quite creamy.) However, perfect fifths invert to equally cutting perfect fourths, and a lot of harmonic ground can be covered using these two intervals when a bass player is providing the root. For instance, in any key, play a perfect fourth interval consisting of the 3 and 7 against a bassist's root for a metal-approved major-7th chord. Identify the different intervals contained within any chord and analyze how they function against the root. Sometimes, less is more.

ARPEGGIOS

Arpeggios are simply the notes of any chord played one at a time. Unlike chords, arpeggios are not limited to one note per string. This allows the inclusion of every note in a chord formula. Playing these in consecutive ascending or descending order outlines or implies harmony using only single notes. Arpeggios may be formed along the length of a single string, across one or more adjacent strings, or by combining both actions. **Ex. 5.22a** shows an arpeggiated root-position *G* major triad and its inversions on a single string.

Ex. 5.22a

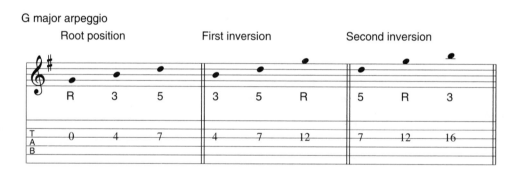

Three- and four-note arpeggios played on adjacent strings create easy-to-memorize fingerboard shapes and patterns. **Examples 5.22b** and **5.22c** transpose the shapes on beat "one" of each measure to extend the *G* major and *Gmaj7* arpeggios for three octaves. Draw them on a fingerboard grid to aid visualization and improve retention.

Ex. 5.22b

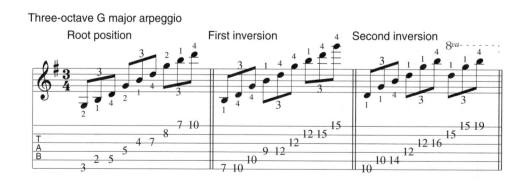

Ex. 5.22c

Three-octave G major seventh arpeggio

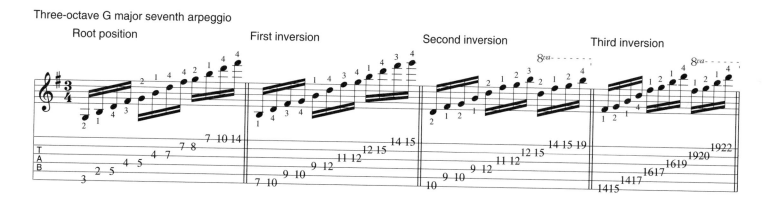

Arpeggios played "in position" are extracted from the five major scale fingering patterns and relate to the five open-position major triad fingerings—*C, A, G, E,* and *D*. **Ex. 5.23a** (next page) illustrates the connection. Use the five shapes to form any type of arpeggio by adding, deleting, or altering notes in accordance with the chord formula. Building arpeggios from these patterns is the same as building chords, except every note of the formula is utilized—unlike chord voicings, no notes are left out.

Ex. 5.23b features in-position ascending and descending diatonic 7th-chord arpeggios using major scale Pattern 4 in the key of *C*. This is identical to a root-3-5-7 motif sequenced in diatonic seconds. Arpeggiate any of the upcoming voice-leading examples for similar results. For additional brain twisting, give first, second, and third-inversion arpeggios the same treatment.

Your goal is to be able to play an arpeggio for every chord you know. To learn them in all keys, play them through all intervallic cycles. Create melodic arpeggio motifs and permute them.

Ex. 5.23a

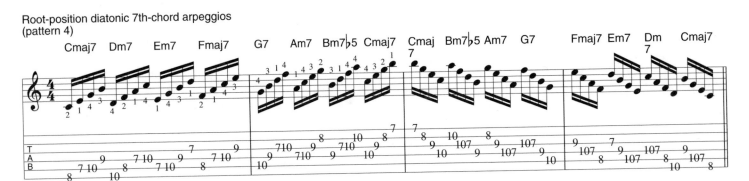

	C major triad arpeggios	Cmaj7 arpeggios	C minor triad arpeggios	Cm7 arpeggios	C7 arpeggios
Pattern 1 ("C" shape)					
Pattern 2 ("A" shape)					
Pattern 3 ("G" shape)					
Pattern 4 ("E" shape)					
Pattern 5 ("D" shape)					

Ex. 5.23b

Root-position diatonic 7th-chord arpeggios
(pattern 4)

TRANSFERRING CHORD VOICINGS TO ADJACENT STRINGS

Any chord voicing transferred to a different group of strings will retain its intervallic formula, as long as notes on the *B* and *E* strings are adjusted as necessary. In **Examples 5.24a–5.24f**, six types of root-position, first-inversion, and second-inversion triads—major, minor, augmented, diminished, sus2, and sus4—are transferred across four different string groups.

Ex. 5.24a

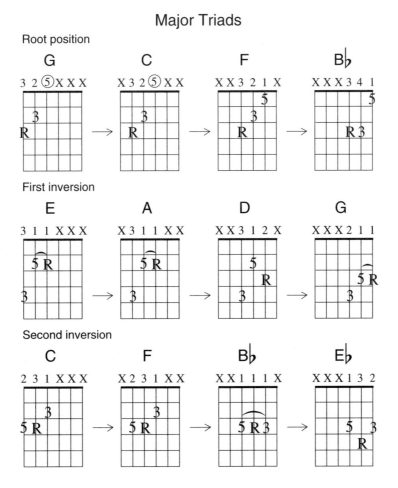

Ex. 5.24b

Minor Triads

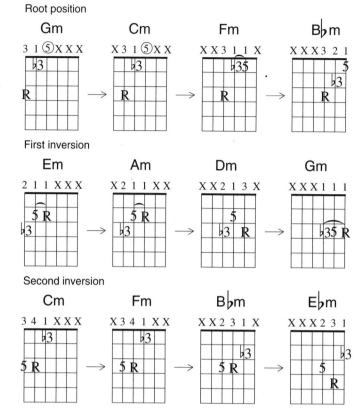

Ex. 5.24c

Augmented Triads

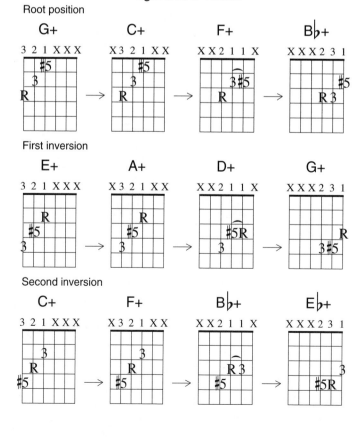

Ex. 5.24d

Diminished Triads

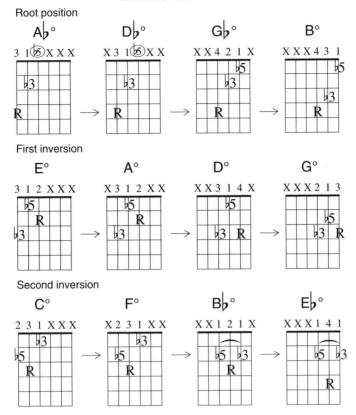

Ex. 5.24e

Sus 2 Triads

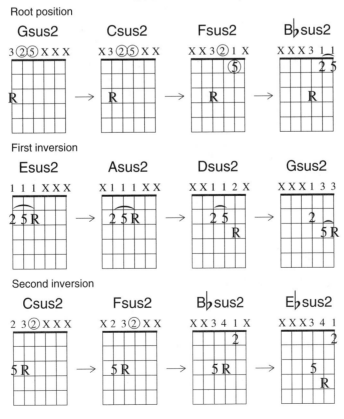

Ex. 5.24f

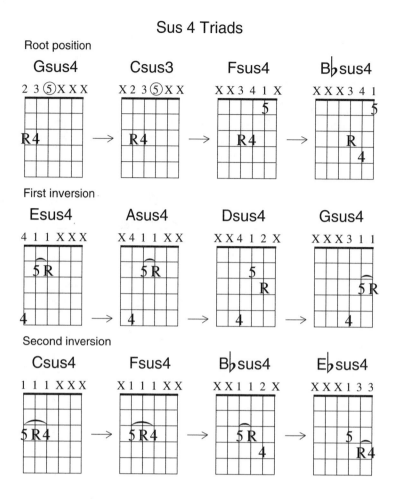

Sus 4 Triads

BUILDING CHORD VOICINGS ON THE FINGERBOARD
USING THE FIVE MAJOR SCALE FINGERING PATTERNS

You don't need a chord dictionary to find hundreds of voicings anywhere on the fingerboard. Locate and memorize the position of each scale degree in each major scale fingering pattern, apply the chord formulas, and you'll have hundreds of chords at your fingertips.

Align the *CAGED* template to a chosen key center. Choose a major scale pattern and highlight its resident major triad shape. Convert it to minor, if necessary. Sharp and flat scale degrees are located between major and perfect intervals. Apply the remaining scale degrees from any given chord formula and document the voicing. If a desired note is awkward in one pattern, it may be borrowed from a neighboring pattern. Edit voicings by deleting notes of lesser importance (see "The Relative Weight of Chord Tones" in this chapter). Not every chord has to be big to sound big. Remember that even two notes can suggest a chord sound. For example, any dominant-7th chord can be reduced to two different ♭5 diads, each consisting of the dominant chord's 3 and ♭7. Try it!

Examples 5.25a and **5.25b** illustrate the process using major scale Patterns 1 and 2 in the key of E.

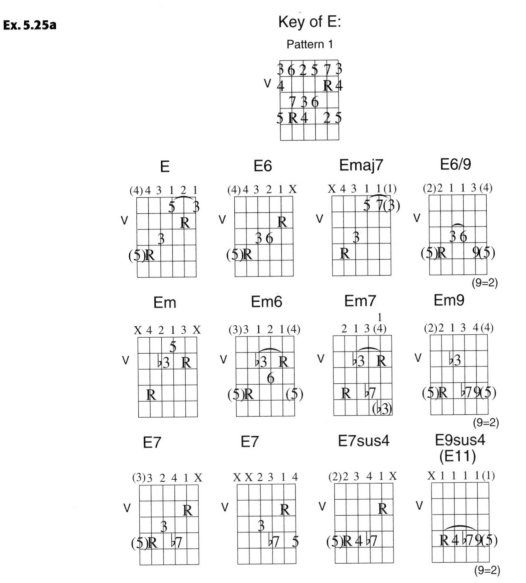

Ex. 5.25a

Ex. 5.25b

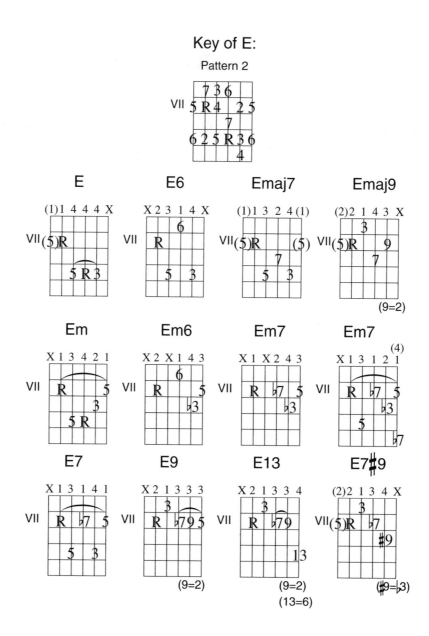

Follow suit with the remaining three major scale patterns. Find voicings you like, document and memorize them, then put them to use as soon as possible. Memorize chords visually, by their shape on the fingerboard, and structurally, by their notes and intervals. Play them in all positions through all intervallic cycles. Your objective is to have the facility to play at least one voicing of any chord in any key within any five-fret span.

SLASH CHORDS

Slash chords are a contemporary method for writing chord sounds using triad-over-bass-note symbols. The upper letter indicates the triad while the bottom names the bass note. These are separated by a diagonal slash. Horizontal slashes between letters indicates a poly-chord, meaning one triad stacked on top of another.

Playing a triad over a bass note other than its root can have a drastic effect on its sound and function. Since there are 12 notes, there are 12 possible triad-to-root relationships. To translate a slash chord to a more familiar language, analyze the notes in the triad against its bass note. The bass note can also function as chord tones other than the root. The chart in **Ex. 5.26a** translates the 12 major triad slash chords to their enharmonic standard chord symbols.

Ex. 5.26a

Slash chords				
Slash chord symbol	Triad/Root relationship	Relationship of notes in triad to C bass	Enharmonic chord name(s)	Chord quality
C/C	I/I	Root, 3, 5	C	Major
D♭/C	♭II/I	♭9 (♭2), 4, #5	C11#5♭9, D♭maj7 (7 in bass), B♭m9 (9 in bass)	Dominant (alt.), Major or Minor
D/C	II/I	9 (2), ♭5 (#II), 6	C6/9♭5, C6/9#11, or D7 (♭7 in bass)	Major (alt.) or Dominant
E♭/C	♭III/I	♭3, 5, ♭7	Cm7	Minor
E/C	III/I	3, #5, 7	Cmaj7#5 or E7#5 (#5 in bass)	Major (alt.) or Dominant (alt.)
F/C	IV/I	4, 6, Root	C13sus4 or F (5 in bass)	Dominant
F#(G♭)/C	#IV(♭V)/I	♭5, ♭7, ♭9	C7♭5♭9	Dominant (alt.)
G/C	V/I	5, 7, 9	Cmaj9 (no 3)	Major
A♭/C	♭VI/I	#5, Root, ♭3	Cm#5 or A♭ (3 in bass)	Minor (alt.) or Major
A/C	VI/I	6, ♭9, 3	C13♭9 (no 7)	Dominant (alt.)
B♭/C	♭VII/I	♭7, 9, 4(11)	C11	Dominant
B/C	VII/I	7, ♭3, ♭5	Cm/maj7♭5, B7♭9 or D13♭9 (♭7 in bass)	Minor (alt.) or Dominant (alt.)

Ex. 5.26b voices the 12 different major triads over a C (fifth string, 3rd fret) bass note.

Ex. 5.26b

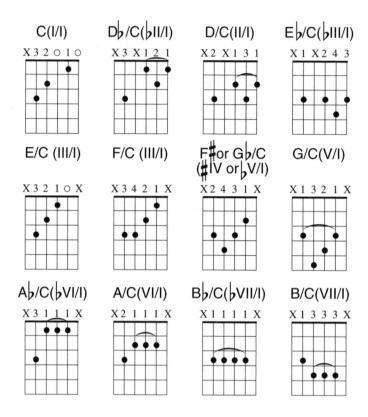

Conduct your own analysis of the 12 minor triad slash chords. Substitute slash chords for major, minor, and especially altered dominant sounds as often as possible. Apply the same principle to single-note melodic lines and watch a new universe unfold.

OPEN-STRING VOICINGS

There is no reason to limit chord voicings that utilize open strings to open position. Open strings vibrate along their full length and have a vibrant, shimmering quality. Incorporating one or two into any chord can facilitate voicings that are impossible otherwise. Move each of the five open-position major triads up the neck in half-steps, while leaving one or two strings open, then analyze and name each chord. Initially, the chords will be easier to name if you maintain the root as the lowest chord tone. The chart in **Ex. 5.27a** analyzes and names 12 different chords produced from the transposed E major triad shape using two open strings.

Ex. 5.27a

Open string voicings				
Root	E type fingering	Relation to root: Open B	Relation to root: Open E	Chord name and type
E	open position	5	Root	E
F	1st position	♭5(#11)	7	Fmaj7♭5(#11)
F#(G♭)	2nd position	4 (11)	♭7	F# (11)
G	3rd position	3	6	G6
A♭(G#)	4th position	♭3 (#9)	#5	A♭#5#9
A	5th position	2 (9)	5	Aadd9
B♭	6th position	♭2 (♭9)	♭5	B♭(♭5 ♭9)
B	7th position	Root	4 (11)	Badd4, B11
C	8th position	7	3	Cmaj7
D♭(C#)	9th position	♭7	♭3	D♭7#9 (C#7#9)
D	10th position	6	2	D6/9
E♭	11th position	#5	♭2 (♭9)	E♭ #5♭9
E	12th position	5	Root	E

Repeat this with as many major and minor triads as possible. You'll notice that not all of these chords are pleasing to the ear. In your search for open-string voicings, memorize those which sound good to you, but don't discard the dissonant ones too quickly. They can be extremely valuable as altered dominant-7th substitutions.

The process works with any type of chord. Play each voicing in **Ex. 5.27b** in all 12 positions while maintaining its open strings. Analyze and name the resulting chords.

Ex. 5.27b

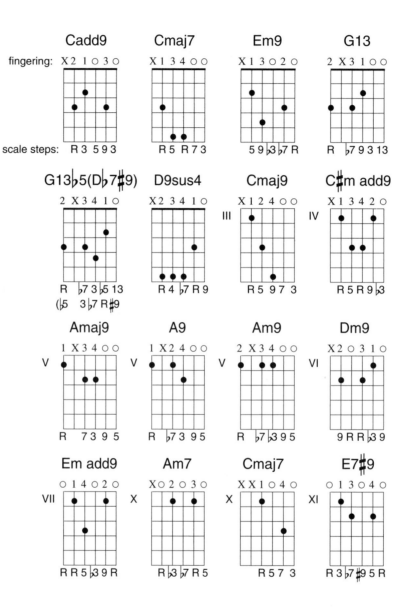

CHORD SUBSTITUTIONS

A chord substitute replaces one thing with another capable of the same function. The following harmonic substitution principles apply to chords and scales that bear them.

Diatonic Substitution Rule #1: In any major key, substitute the IIIm chord for the I chord. The IIIm chord is also called the secondary relative minor of I.

Ex. 5.28a illustrates how combining diatonic I and IIIm triads produces a Imaj7 chord while the sum of the Imaj7 and IIIm7 chords is a Imaj9 chord.

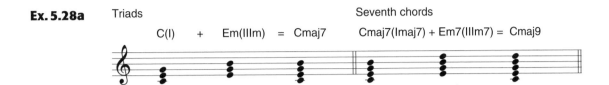

Ex. 5.28a

Diatonic Substitution Rule #2: In any major key, substitute the IV chord for the IIm chord.

Ex. 5.28b illustrates how combining diatonic IIm and IV triads produces a IIm7 chord while the sum of the IIm7 and IVmaj7 chords is a IIm9 chord.

Ex. 5.28b

♭5 **Substitutions:** You may substitute any two chords a ♭5 apart.

The *G7♭5* and *D♭7♭5* chords in **Ex. 5.28c** contain identical notes and are inversions of each other. This explains the substitution principle, but ♭5 subs do not have to consist of the same notes. Additionally, the quality of a subbed chord may or may not stay the same. Use ♭5 subs to add harmonic tension when chords are in motion—rather than static—and steer clear of using them on the tonic.

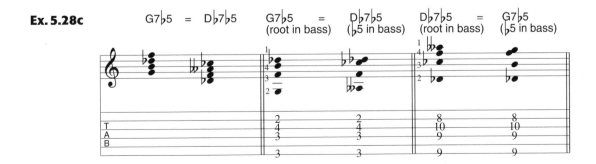

Ex. 5.28c

Ex. 5.28d shows several alternatives to a common IIm7–V7–I chord progression, incorporating ♭5 subs.

Ex. 5.28d

Given:	Dm7	G7	Cmaj7
Play:	Dm7	D♭7	Cmaj7
	Dm7	D♭maj7	Cmaj7
	A♭m7	D♭7	Cmaj7
	A♭maj7	D♭maj7	Cmaj7
	A♭7	G7	Cmaj7

HARMONIC MOTION

Harmonic motion describes the movement of one voice in a chord or interval to that of another. There are four basic flavors of harmonic motion: similar, parallel, oblique, and contrary.

- Similar motion occurs when voices move in the same direction—up or down—using mixed intervals, as in diatonic harmony.
- Parallel motion features voices moving in the same direction using identical intervals.
- Oblique motion is characterized by a moving voice against a stationary voice.
- Contrary motion uses voices moving in opposite directions.

Examples 5.29a–5.29d illustrate each type of harmonic motion using simple harmonic intervals from the key of *A* minor. Play them melodically as well as harmonically.

Ex. 5.29a–b

Similar motion

Parallel motion

Ex. 5.29c–d   Oblique motion   Contrary motion

Examples 5.30a–5.30d apply each flavor to a blues turnaround in the key of *G*. Try playing each melodic interval harmonically.

Ex. 5.30a–b   Similar motion   Parallel motion

Ex. 5.30c–d   Oblique motion (top and bottom voices only)
Combined oblique and parallel motion (all
voices)   Contrary motion

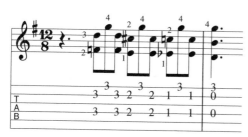   

DIATONIC VOICE-LEADING

We've seen how melodic motifs and chords can be moved stepwise through any diatonic system to which they belong. Similar harmonic motion is the foundation of diatonic voice-leading. Each note of a chord moves to its neighboring diatonic scale degree. This is the chordal adaptation of a sequenced scale or melodic motif. Arpeggiate each chord in any of the following examples and *poof*—it's a sequence. Use diatonic voice-leading to extrapolate an entire relative "chord scale" from any single voicing.

Examples 5.31-5.31d apply diatonic voice-leading to four different major triads. As you play them, notice how you are actually tracking the major scale on three different strings at the same time.

Ex. 5.31a

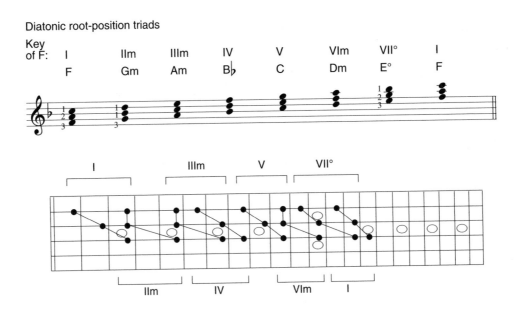

Ex. 5.31b

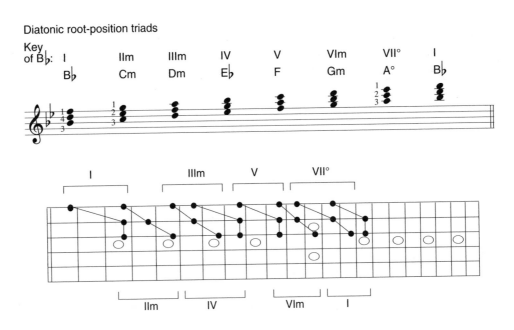

Ex. 5.31c   Diatonic second-inversion triads

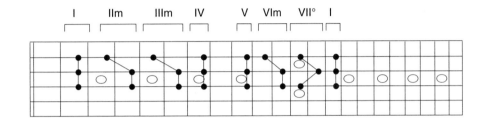

Ex. 5.31d   Diatonic second-inversion triads

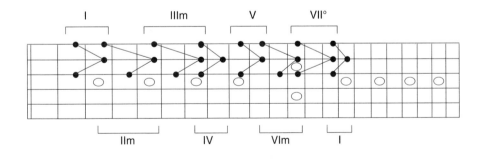

This also works with embellished triads. **Examples 5.32a** and **5.32b** use second-inversion *Dsus2* (5-root-4) and *Dsus4* (5-root-2) voicings. Try unusual structures, such as root-2-6, root-3-6, root-3-4, and 2-5-6.

Ex. 5.32a

Diatonic second-inversion sus4 triads

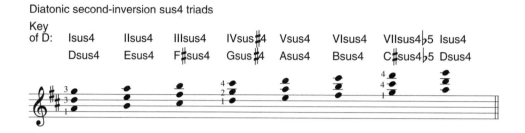

Ex. 5.32b

Diatonic second-inversion sus2 triads

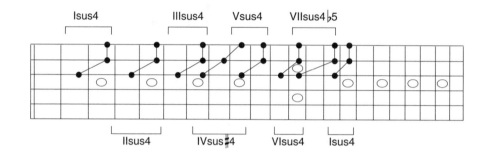

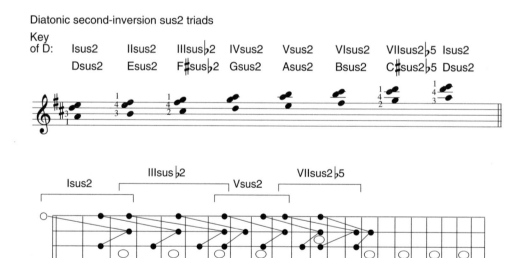

Ex. 5.33 follows an embellished chord sequence (*G-Gsus4-Gsus2-G*) through its family of related diatonic voicings. Beef up each measure rhythmically, and you've got seven cool modal vamps (See Examples 5.35a–5.35c).

Ex. 5.33

Diatonic sus4 & sus2 embellishments (key of G)

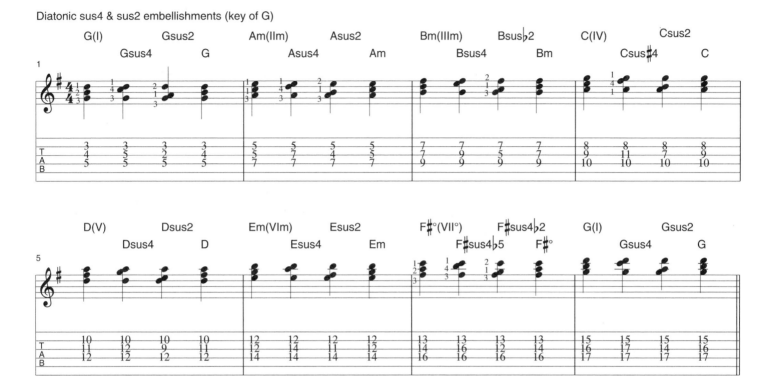

The grids in **Examples 5.34a–5.34d** illustrate diatonic voice-leading applied to garden-variety major-7th voicings in four different keys. Other common major-7th voicings include root-5-7-3, 3-root-5-7, 3-7-root-5, and 5-root-3-7. Apply diatonic voice-leading, write them out, then play them through all intervallic cycles.

Ex. 5.34a   Diatonic seventh chords (R, 3, 5, 7)

Key of G:

Imaj7	IIm7	IIIm7	IVmaj7	V7	VIm7	VIIm7♭5	Imaj7
Gmaj7	Am7	Bm7	Cmaj7	D7	Em7	F♯m7♭5	Gmaj7

Ex. 5.34b

Diatonic seventh chords (R, 3, 5, 7)

Key of C:	Imaj7	IIm7	IIIm7	IVmaj7	V7	VIm7	VIIm7♭5	Imaj7
	Cmaj7	Dm7	Em7	Fmaj7	G7	Am7	Bm7♭5	Cmaj7

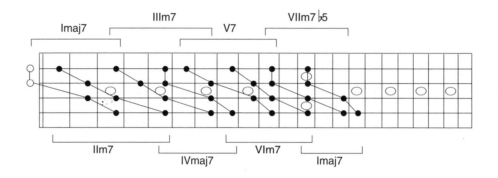

Ex. 5.34c

Diatonic seventh chords (R, 5, 7, 3)

Key of B♭:	Imaj7	IIm7	IIIm7	IVmaj7	V7	VIm7	VIIm7♭5	Imaj7
	B♭maj7	Cm7	Dm7	E♭maj7	F7	Gm7	Am7♭5	B♭maj7

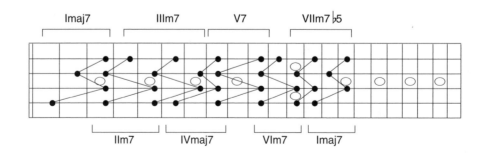

Ex. 5.34d   Diatonic seventh chords (R, 7, 3, 5)

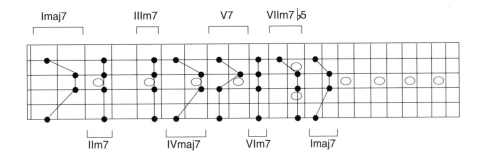

STATIC MODAL HARMONY

Harmony can be either functional or static, that is, in motion or not. Static harmony centers around one chord which acts as a modal tonic. A modal vamp, or short, repetitive progression consisting of the modal tonic plus one or two diatonic neighboring chords, can introduce motion to otherwise static harmony.

To create static harmony for a given mode, play rhythmically on the modal tonic chord—*D* Dorian=*Dm* or *Dm7*, *E* Phrygian=*Em* or *Em7*, *F* Lydian=*F* or *Fmaj7*, and so on. To create a modal vamp, alternate the modal tonic with its upper or lower diatonic neighboring triad, or seventh chord. Any chord in a modal vamp may be embellished (see Ex. 5.33).

Ex. 5.35a (next page) uses this formula to extract a pair of *D* Dorian vamps from the harmonized *C* major scale.

Try playing the root of the modal tonic for both chords, as in **Ex. 5.35b**. This maintains a common pedal tone in the bass and reinforces the characteristic flavor of the mode.

Ex. 5.35a

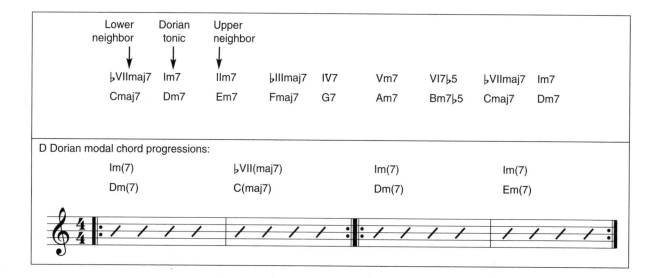

Ex. 5.35b

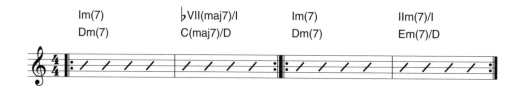

Another way to construct modal vamps is to alternate relative major-key IV and V triads over any related modal tonic. **Ex. 5.36** (facing page) lists the seven possible modal vamps using the IV and V triads in the key of C. Notice how one chord creates harmonic tension while the other provides resolution.

Transpose these vamps to all keys, experiment with different triad voicings, and play them through all intervallic cycles. Jazz them up with your favorite rhythmic motifs and embellish them using extensions. Record the vamps, then practice modal melodic motifs, permutations, and sequences over them. This will tune your ear to the characteristics of the seven modal tonalities, or modalities. Listen for them in all music.

Ex. 5.36

Modal slash-chord vamps		
C Ionian (major) $\frac{4}{4}$	F/C : / / / /	G/C :
D Dorian $\frac{4}{4}$	F/D : / / / /	G/D :
E Phrygian $\frac{4}{4}$	F/E : / / / /	G/E :
F Lydian $\frac{4}{4}$	F : / / / /	G/F :
G Mixolydian $\frac{4}{4}$	F/G : / / / /	G :
A Aeolian (natural minor) $\frac{4}{4}$	F/A : / / / /	G/A :
B Locrian $\frac{4}{4}$	F/B : / / / /	F/B :

CHORD PROGRESSIONS

When two or more different chords are strung together and played consecutively over a specified number of bars, the harmony becomes functional, as opposed to static. This is often called a "chord progression." A chord progression is any group of related or unrelated chords that—in most cases—move, or progress, towards a predetermined point of arrival. Ideally, chords should connect smoothly and be in agreement with the melodies from which they are derived. Chord progressions can be as simple or complex as desired.

STRONG ROOT PROGRESSIONS

The foundation of any harmonic progression is its root motion. A strong root progression is a progression of bass notes which, when harmonized, creates a strong harmonic pull from one chord to the next and causes harmonic movement towards a point of arrival. Harmonizing a strong root progression forms a strong chord progression. The chart in **Ex. 5.37a** (next page) decodes the three strongest root progressions—up a perfect fourth, down a perfect fifth, and down a minor second—in any key. Movement to a point of arrival is from left to right.

Ex. 5.37a

G♭ (F♯)	F	E	E♭	D	D♭	C	B	B♭	A	A♭	G	G♭ (F♯)
C	B	B♭	A	A♭	G	G♭ (F♯)	F	E	E♭	D	D♭	C

Table title: Strong root progressions

To use the chart, choose any note as the point of arrival and approach it diagonally or horizontally from left to right as in **Ex. 5.37b**. The chosen approach note becomes a new point of arrival which may be approached in the same manner. Repeat this process until the desired amount of harmonic motion has been achieved.

Ex. 5.37b

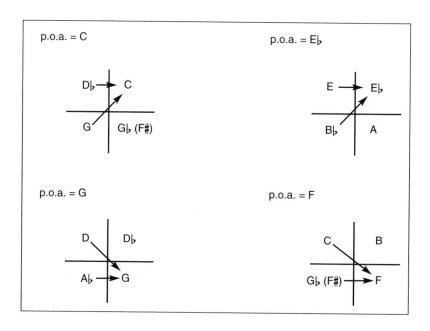

DIATONIC CHORD PROGRESSIONS

Like scales and scale harmony, diatonic chord progressions are built from a single key and use only related chords. Chord types assigned to diatonic root progressions are predetermined in accordance with the scale harmony. Diatonic root/chord progressions can be notated using Roman numerals assigned to any key. A root progression notated numerically is called a "figured bass" line.

Any melody built from a single diatonic scale system may be harmonized using only the I, IV, and V chords. Combined, these three chords contain every note of the major scale.

In a diatonic system, some chords create motion by requiring resolution while others are content to stand still. It is important to understand the function and tendency of each chord in relation to its tonic.

- The I chord, or *tonic*, names the key and is the most common resolution or point of arrival.

- The IIm chord, or *super-tonic*, creates motion away from the tonic. Since IIm is the V of V, there is a strong pull toward the V chord.

- The IIIm chord, or *mediant*, also known as the secondary relative minor, is a diatonic substitution for the I chord, and therefore creates little harmonic pull away from the tonic.

- The IV chord, or *sub-dominant*, is built on an active scale tone and exerts a strong pull toward and away from the tonic. The IV chord commonly resolves to the tonic or its relative minor, the VIm chord.

- The V chord, or *dominant*, contains both active major scale tones—4 and 7—and exerts the strongest pull to the tonic. The V chord commonly resolves to the tonic.
- The VIm chord, also known as the *sub-mediant* or *super-dominant*, provides an "in-house" key change to the relative minor. It also functions as the V of IIIm.

- The VIIdim chord, or *sub-tonic*, also called the leading tone, is built on the scale's other active note and commonly resolves to the tonic.

Cadence describes the final harmonic movement to a point of arrival. In diatonic progressions, the tonic, or I chord, is commonly the point of arrival and is most often preceded by its V chord. This forms the strongest root motion—up a fourth or down a fifth—which is called a V-I cadence. If a chord other than V precedes I, and it is non-diatonic, chances are it is one of five other substitutions. **Ex. 5.38** (next page) diagrams the six ways to approach a C tonic.

Ex. 5.38

Six ways to a tonic			
	II	V	I
1	Dm7	G7	
2	A♭m7	D♭7	
3	Bm7♭5	E7	
4	Fm7♭5	B♭7	Cmaj7 (Am7 = C6) (Em7 = Cmaj9)
5	F♯m7	B7	
6	Cm7♭5	F7	

- #1 is a diatonic IIm7–V7–I progression in the key of C.
- #2 shows the ♭5 subs for #1.
- #3 is a IIm7♭5–V7–Im progression targeting the relative minor, *Am7*.
- #4 shows the ♭5 subs for #3.
- #5 is a IIm7♭5–V7–Im progression targeting the secondary relative minor, *Em7*.
- #6 shows the ♭5 subs for #5.

Each V chord substitution may precede the major tonic, its relative minor, or its secondary relative minor. That's six different approaches to three different points of arrival. The IIm chords can also be paired with the V subs in any combination. Almost any conceivable chord progression lurks within these six subs.

Any 7th chords appearing on the chart can be reduced to triads. Remember that these six substitutions are applicable to melodic lines, scales, arpeggios, and chords. This chart may be the most valuable item in this book. Think of it as your secret decoder ring. Return to it whenever you encounter a perplexing progression, and all will be revealed.

Back to diatonic progressions. In the key of C, a harmonized V–I progression becomes G (V) or G7 (V7) moving to C (I) or Cmaj7 (Imaj7). Because V–I is such a strong root progression, any chord may be preceded by one built from its V. The V of G is D.

In the key of *C, D* is harmonized diatonically as the IIm7 chord. This forms the ever popular IIm7-V7-I progression, or *Dm7-G7-Cmaj7*. Contemporary IIm7-V7-I progressions favor 7th chord harmonies and extensions over triads.

Replacing the IIm7 chord with the subdominant (see "Chord Substitutions," Ex. 5.28b) converts the progression to IV-V-I, or *F-G-C*. Progressions built from any combination of I, IV, and V are frequently harmonized as triads or dominant-7th chords and their extensions, rather than diatonic 7th chords (see "Blues Progressions," Examples 5.42a–5.42c).

There are six permutations of each progression. Notice how each permutation shifts the point of arrival. Play them in all keys using triads and diatonic 7th chords.

I–IV–V	IIm–V–I
I–V–IV	IIm–I–V
IV–I–V	I–IIm–V
IV–V–I	I–V–IIm
V–I–IV	V–I–IIm
V–IV–I	V–IIm–I

Any melody built from a single diatonic scale system may be harmonized using only the I, IV, and V chords. Collectively, these three chords contain every note of the major scale. Many rock, blues, folk, country, and popular songs consist of standardized 8-, 12-, and 16-bar progressions using only I, IV, and V chords. Memorize the figured bass progressions in **Examples 5.39a–5.39d** in all keys. Let the style of music dictate the use of triads or 7th chords.

Ex. 5.39a

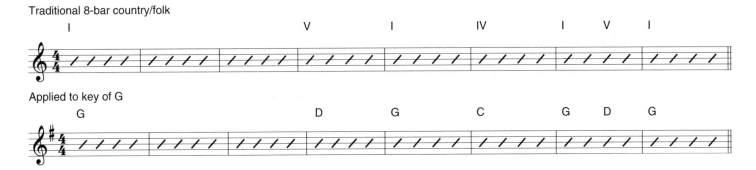

Traditional 8-bar country/folk

Applied to key of G

Ex. 5.39b

8-bar rock and roll

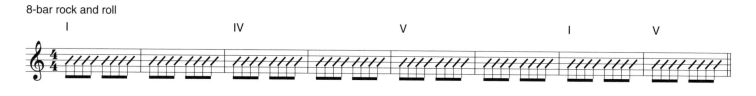

Ex. 5.39c

12-bar rock/blues

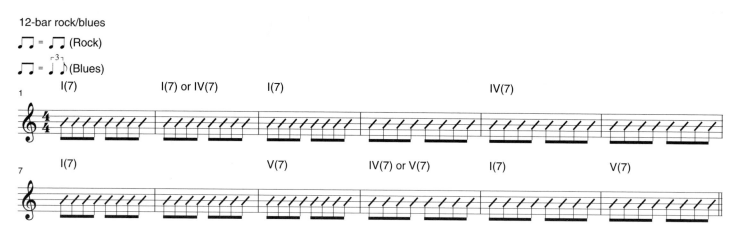

Ex. 5.39d

16-bar country/gospel

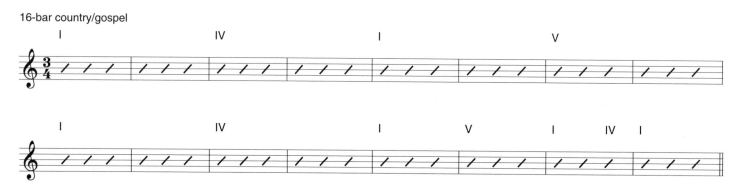

In blues, the progression in Ex. 5.39c is commonly played using all dominant-7th chords and their extensions, and is not truly diatonic. The progression does remain diatonic when harmonized in triads.

To build longer diatonic progressions, precede each chord with its V. The diatonic V of *D* is *Am* or *Am7*—the VI chord in *C*—and the V of *A* is *Em* or *Em7*—the III chord in *C*. This lengthens the progression to IIIm7-VIm7-IIm7-V7-I, or *Em7-Am7-Dm7-G7-Cmaj7*. The V-of-V process is called "backcycling" because the root motion follows the cycle of fifths in reverse order. Forward root-motion inverts to the cycle of fourths.

Substituting the I chord for the III chord forms the very common I–VIm–IIm–V progression, or *C–Am–Dm–G*. Since VI subs for II, this easily becomes I–VIm–IV–V, or *C–Am–F–G*.

There are 24 permutations of any four-chord progression.

For IIIm–VIm–IIm–V:

IIIm–VIm–IIm–V	VIm–IIm–V–IIIm	IIm–V–IIIm–VIm	V–IIIm–VIm–IIm
IIIm–VIm–V–IIm	VIm–IIm–IIIm–V	IIm–V–VIm–IIIm	V–IIIm–IIm–VIm
IIIm–IIm–V–VIm	VIm–V–IIIm–IIm	IIm–IIIm–VIm–V	V–VIm–IIm–IIIm
IIIm–IIm–VIm–V	VIm–V–IIm–IIIm	IIm–IIIm–V–VIm	V–VIm–IIIm–IIm
IIIm–V–VIm–IIm	VIm–IIIm–IIm–V	IIm–VIm–V–IIIm	V–IIm–IIIm–VIm
IIIm–V–IIm–VIm	VIm–IIIm–V–IIm	IIm–VIm–IIIm–V	V–IIm–VIm–IIIm

For I–VIm–IV–V:

I–VIm–IV–V	VIm–IV–V–I	IV–V–I–VIm	V–I–VIm–IV
I–VIm–V–IV	VIm–IV–I–V	IV–V–VIm–I	V–I–IV–VIm
I–IV–V–VIm	VIm–V–I–IV	IV–I–VIm–V	V–VIm–IV–I
I–IV–VIm–V	VIm–V–IV–I	IV–I–V–VIm	V–VIm–I–IV
I–V–VIm–IV	VIm–I–IV–V	IV–VIm–V–I	V–IV–I–VIm
I–V–IV–VIm	VIm–I–V–IV	IV–VIm–I–V	V–IV–VIm–I

For I–VIm–IIm–V permutations, replace all IV chords with IIm chords. Play all permutations in all keys using as many voicings as possible, then adapt them to modes and relative minor keys.

Once established, chord progressions may be embellished using extensions and alterations. Alterations are most effective on functioning dominant-7th chords, so apply them to any V chord. Remember: A diminished-7th chord played a half-step higher than a dominant-7th chord produces a dominant-7th-♭9 chord—*G♯dim7= G7♭9*.

Diatonic progressions may also move scalewise—I-IIm-IIIm-IV, IV-IIIm-IIm-I, and so on—or in sequence—I-IIIm-IIm-IV, IV-IIm-IIIm-I, and so on. Familiarize yourself with all possible diatonic chord progressions in all major, minor, and modal keys, and memorize those you like best. The bottom line: There is no right or wrong. Whatever *sounds* right *is* right.

MODULATION

Not all chord progressions are purely diatonic. Chords often travel through several modulations, or key changes, before reaching a final destination. This is accomplished via cyclic or parallel root motion, or by borrowing harmonized root progressions from other keys.

Moving, or modulating, any chord voicing through any intervallic cycle produces a nondiatonic, parallel harmonic progression which eventually returns to its point of departure. **Examples 5.40a** and **5.40b** show major-7th chords cycled in fourths and minor-9th chords cycled in minor thirds.

Ex. 5.40a

Major seventh chords w/ascending fourths

Ex. 5.40b

Minor ninth chords w/ascending minor thirds

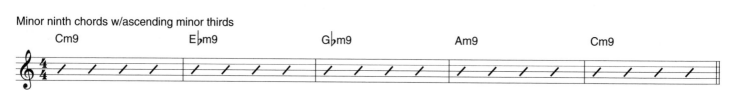

This also works with entire chord progressions. All or part of any previously illustrated progression may be modulated through any intervallic cycle. **Examples 5.40c** and **5.40d** feature a diatonic IV-IIIm-IIm-I progression modulated through the cycle of fourths, and a jazzy IIm-V7-I progression that runs the cycle of major thirds. Both begin

in the key of *G*.

Ex. 5.40c

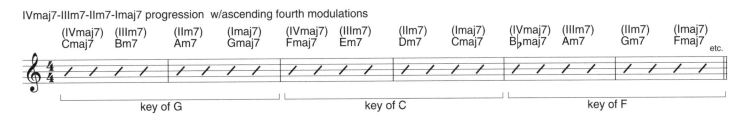

Ex. 5.40d

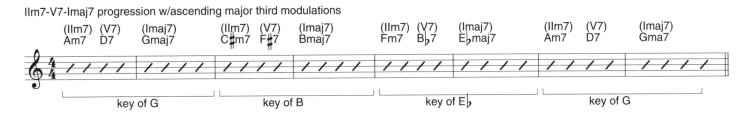

Intervallic motion and chord types are variable within any cycle. **Ex. 5.40e** illustrates

alternating major-7th and minor-7th chords built on alternating ascending major and

minor second intervals. **Ex. 5.40f** begins with a series of major-7th and minor-7th

chords descending in minor seconds. The last three chords form a IIm7♭5-V7-Im pro-

gression in *D* minor, with *B♭maj7* as the ♭5 substitute for *Em7♭5*.

Ex. 5.40e

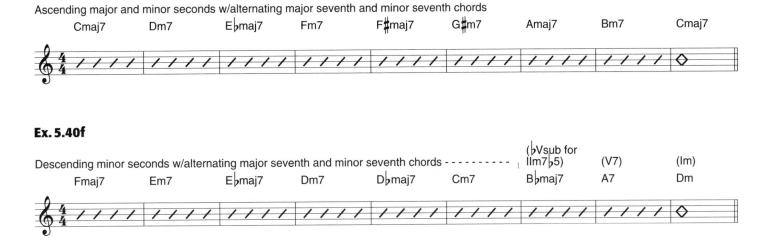

Ex. 5.40f

Another common way to modulate is through the use of secondary dominant chords. This is identical to V-of-V backcycling, but uses dominant-7th chords exclusively to precede the point-of-arrival chord. Each major key has only one resident dominant-7th chord, so adding more results in temporary modulations to other keys. **Ex. 5.41** converts a diatonic IIIm–VIm–IIm–V–I progression to secondary dominant chords.

Ex. 5.41

IIIm7	VIm7	IIm7	V7	Imaj7	converted to secondary dominants:	III7	VI7	II7	V7	Imaj7
		Dm7	G7	Cmaj7				D7	G7	Cmaj7
	Am7	Dm7	G7	Cmaj7			A7	D7	G7	Cmaj7
Em7	Am7	Dm7	G7	Cmaj7		E7	A7	D7	G7	Cmaj7

The dominant cycle in the last progression forms the bridge to the well-worn jazz standard, "I've Got Rhythm." Using ♭5-subs, this becomes *B♭7–E♭7–A♭7–D♭7–C*.

BLUES PROGRESSIONS

There are two primary schools of blues—the rural and urban blues that spawned acoustic and electric disciples from Mississippi and Chicago to Texas and Britain, and the jazz blues of the '50s and '60s hard-bop masters. Though each hosts its own vocabulary of stylistic techniques and note choices, both share a common 12-bar form. Analyzing a blues progression in either style reveals that most differences are simply a matter of harmonic density.

The I, IV, and V chords form the foundation of any 12-bar blues. All three are commonly harmonized as dominant-7th chords and extended with 9s and 13s. Theoretically, this places them in three separate major keys (there is only one dominant-7th chord—the V—in any harmonized major scale), but blues music doesn't always conform to traditional rules of harmony.

Examples 5.42a and **5.42b** show the two most common basic 12-bar blues progressions in the key of C. This type of harmonically unadorned progression is typical of the rural and urban schools. Transpose the progression to all other keys and embellish each chord to taste, using 9s and 13s. Play the progression using a variety of rhythms and grooves.

Transpose the four common I-chord ideas in **Ex. 5.42c** to cover the IV and V chords by shifting them to the appropriate position. For example, move the figures in bars 1

Ex. 5.42a

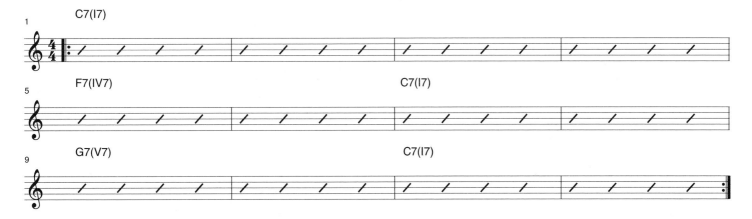

Ex. 5.42b

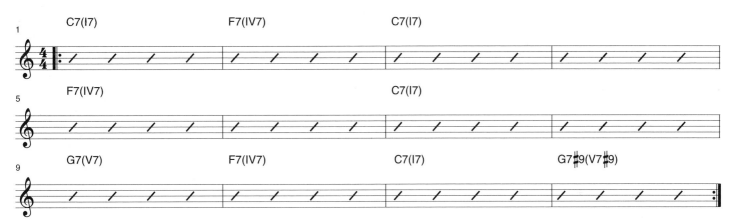

and 2 to the first position for the IV chord (*F*), and third position for the V (*G*). Or, you could transfer them to the fourth and fifth strings, remain in eighth position for the IV, and shift up a whole-step to tenth position for the V. Bars 3 and 4 swing harder due to

Ex. 5.42c

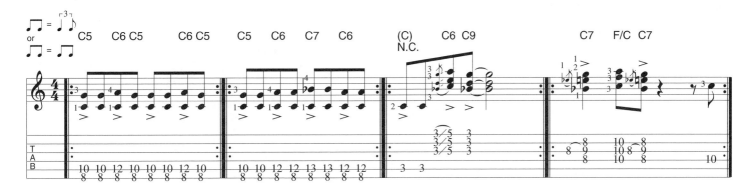

the emphasis on the *and* of beat 2. Try sliding back into the *C9* in bar 3 without picking it. Once you get the hang of bar 4's comfy groove, it practically plays itself.

In blues styles, chords are often omitted in favor of single-note lines (often doubled by the bassist), such as the I-chord figures in **Ex. 5.42d**. Transpose each riff to the IV and V chords as well.

Ex. 5.42d

In jazz-based blues styles, progressions are made more complex by increasing their harmonic activity. Using the V-of-V technique to backcycle from bars 5, 10, and 12 creates busier root motion, which is harmonized here as a series of IIm-V7 progressions descending in whole-steps. Analyze the root motion in **Ex. 5.42e** using the strong root progressions chart in Ex. 5.37a.

Ex. 5.42e

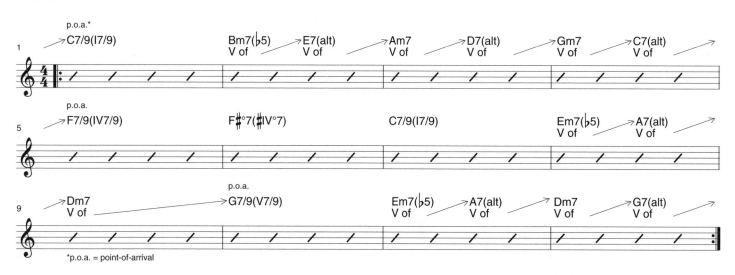

Use this concept to add movement to stagnant chord progressions. Remember: Anything that applies to chords also applies to single-note melodic lines.

CHORD-MELODY STYLE

Chord-melody is a pianistic approach to guitar playing that allows guitarists to play melodies and chords at the same time and break free of the "rhythm or lead" mentality. Though melodies may be assigned to the middle or bottom voice of a chord, the basic premise of chord-melody is to voice chords with the melody notes on top. To become fluent in the style, you must possess the ability to play any chord with any chord tone as the highest note. (Non-chord tones will always be within close reach of the nearest chord tone.)

In 4/4, play one or two chords per bar, voiced below the melody notes on beats "one" and "three"—or adjust them to fit rhythmic motifs as necessary. (In 3/4, one chord per bar is usually sufficient.) Play all other melody notes—including chord tones and non-chord tones—as single notes over the sustained chords. For contrast, try punctuating staccato chords beneath a sustained melody.

Ex. 5.43 shows one possible chord-melody treatment of a given single-note melody and chord symbols. (Notice how the chordal rhythms in bars 2 and 4 have been adjusted to fit the rhythm of the melody.) The original *G7* and *A7* chords have been extended to *G13* and *A13*, and the altered *A7♯5* chordal "kick" in bar 4—not part of the original melody—increases the harmonic pull back to *Dm*.

Ex. 5.43

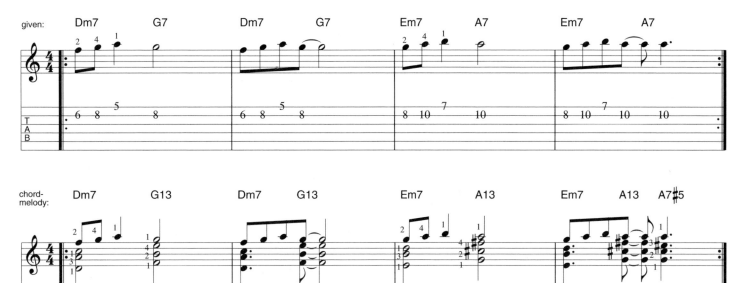

Follow these guidelines to arrange your own chord-melodies. Any melody, regardless of its simplicity or complexity, may be arranged in chord-melody style, but it works best with strong, active melodies, as found in traditional songs, jazz standards, and pop tunes—especially ballads. Strive to keep the song's original melody intact. In chord-melody style, you are limited only by the extent of your chordal vocabulary and harmonic awareness.

REHARMONIZATION

Reharmonization can cause a drastic change in the way a listener perceives a melody. Essentially, this is accomplished by changing and reharmonizing a melody's original root progression. This alters the harmonic climate in which the melody resides and which is largely responsible for the way it is perceived emotionally.

A melody with only a few basic chord changes can be reharmonized to various degrees of complexity, while complex progressions may be simplified to create sparse modal environments. You can reharmonize an entire song or just chosen sections.

To reharmonize any part of any melody, refer to the strong root progressions chart in Ex. 5.37a and follow these six steps:

First, select a melody and examine its original harmony. **Ex. 5.44a** reprises the first four bars of "Mary Had a Little Lamb."

Ex. 5.44a

Then, choose a point of arrival as the last melody note to be reharmonized. The point of arrival can be the original chord or a reharmonization. In **Ex. 5.44b**, the point of arrival—*E*, on the third beat of bar 2—uses the original *C* root.

Ex. 5.44b

Next, decide how many chords each measure will contain—two, for example. Then, working backwards from the point of arrival, use the strong root progressions chart to determine the three possible approaches. Choose an approach to *C*, then to the note approaching *C*, then to the note approaching that note, and so on. Continue backwards until you reach the beginning of the reharmonization. In **Ex. 5.44c**, *G* is used to approach *C*, *D* approaches *G*, and *E♭* approaches *D*.

Next, analyze each melody note in relation to its new root and name the resulting intervals. The skeletal structures in **Ex 5.44d** suggest harmonic possibilities for each chord.

Ex. 5.44c

Choose new root progression (work backwards from p.o.a.)

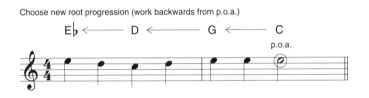

Ex. 5.44d

Analyze melody against new root progression

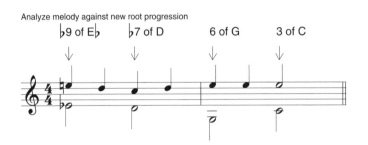

Finally, after defining chord qualities, add desired embellishments, extensions, and alterations. Certain chord tones should be avoided on certain chord types. Avoid ♭9, ♯9, and ♭7 on major chords, ♭9 and 3 on minor chords, and ♮7 on dominant chords. **Ex. 5.44e** shows the fleshed-out progression. Play the reharmonization over prerecorded chords, or play it chord-melody style.

Ex. 5.44e

Fill in chords suggested by root/melody intervals

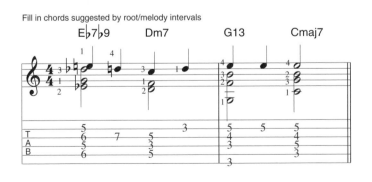

Ex. 5.44f

Same melody w/different root progression

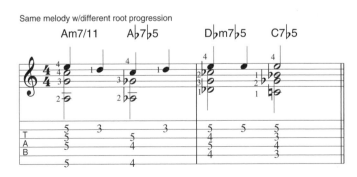

If these results are undesirable, experiment with different root progressions and chord types with these few considerations in mind. When choosing a point of arrival, determine whether it is functional (creating harmonic pull) or static (at rest). The idea is to create a feeling of arrival or finality when the point of arrival is at a resolution point in the progression. Major and minor chord types best suit this purpose. Dominant-7th chords usually function as the V of another chord and encourage harmonic movement (not rest), so they are best suited to the tension points in a progression. However, since we are dealing with the first two bars of a four-bar progression, a dominant arrival works well at the end of bar 2. The reharmonization in **Ex. 5.44f** targets *C7♭5*.

Examples 5.45a–5.45d show four more possibilities using two different points of arrival—*A♭* (*G♯*) and *A*.

Ex. 5.45a

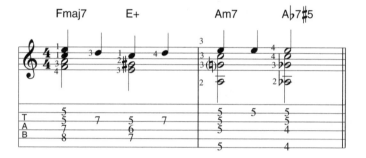

Ex. 5.45b

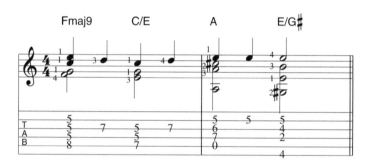

Ex. 5.45c

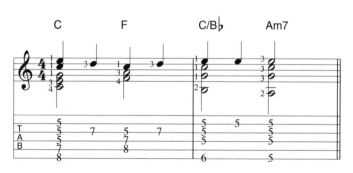

Ex. 5.45d

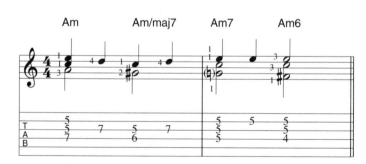

For static modal reharmonizations, pedal any note of the *C* major scale below the melody, or import relative modal vamps from Examples 5.35 and 5.36. This only works with diatonic melodies. When melodic key changes occur, modal drones or vamps must also be transposed.

QUARTAL HARMONY

Not all harmony is tertian. Any consecutive intervals stacked on top of a scale tone will produce unique harmony, though some prove more useful than others. For instance, while harmony stacked in seconds can sound harsh, "quartal" harmonies—chords built in fourths—impart an airy ambiguity that invites several harmonic interpretations.

As with tertian harmony, quartal harmony can be either diatonic or parallel. **Ex. 5.46a** shows three-part quartal harmony in diatonic fourths derived from the *C* major scale. Each chord has been named in relation to three different roots. **Ex. 5.46b** illustrates quartal chords built in parallel fourths.

Ex. 5.46a

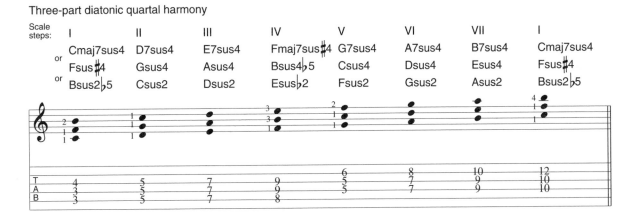

Ex. 5.46b

Examples **5.47a** and **5.47b** feature the previous diatonic and parallel quartal harmonies extended to four parts.

Ex. 5.47a   Four-part diatonic quartal harmony

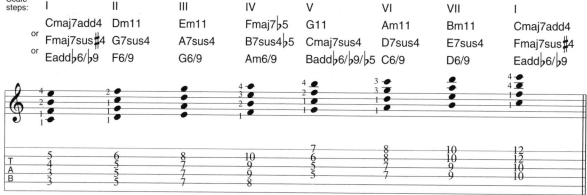

Ex. 5.47b   Four-part parallel quartal harmony

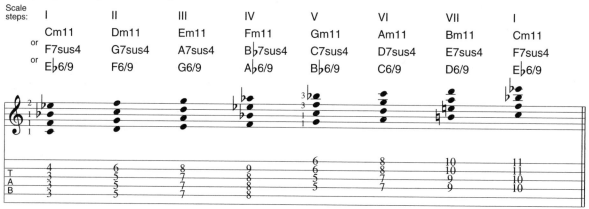

Due to the guitar's standard, fourth-based tuning scheme, five- and six-voice quartal chords fall comfortably on the fingerboard. **Examples 5.48a** and **5.48b** map five-part diatonic and parallel quartal harmonies in the key of *C*. For six-note chords, add a low *G* (sixth string, 3rd fret) to each I chord and continue ascending diatonically, thinking of the notes on your sixth string (*G*, *A*, *B*, *C*, and so on) as the roots.

Ex. 5.48a

Five-part diatonic quartal harmony

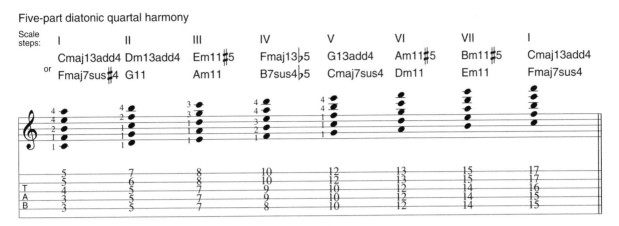

Ex. 5.48b

Five-part parallel quartal harmony

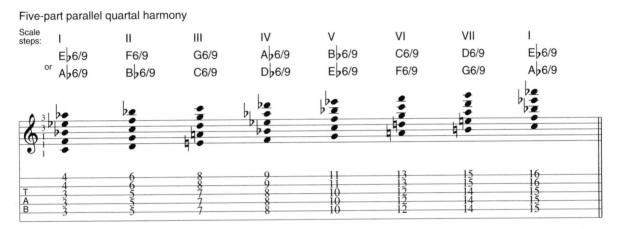

The floating, suspended sound of quartal chords makes them ideal for modern modal vamping. Choose the appropriate modal tonic, and use its family of diatonically related quartal chords to improvise rhythmic modal vamps or chord solos. To temporarily travel outside the key, switch to parallel quartal chords. For actual key changes, transpose the modal tonic accordingly. Increase your harmonic awareness by exploring scales harmonized in diatonic and parallel seconds, fifths, sixths, and sevenths.

HARMONIC EAR-TRAINING

HARMONIC INTERVALS

The first goal in harmonic ear-training is the immediate recognition of all harmonic intervals relative to a given pitch. The procedure is the same as with melodic intervals, except both notes are sounded simultaneously (see Chapter 4, "Melodic Ear-Training").

TRIADS

Once the harmonic intervals become ingrained in your ears, move on to triads. Begin by singing and playing arpeggiated major and minor triads in all three inversions as shown in **Examples 5.49a** and **5.49b**. Strum each triad slowly, sing its ascending and descending arpeggio, then play the chord again. Repeat this, moving up the neck chromatically or through any intervallic cycle.

Ex. 5.49a

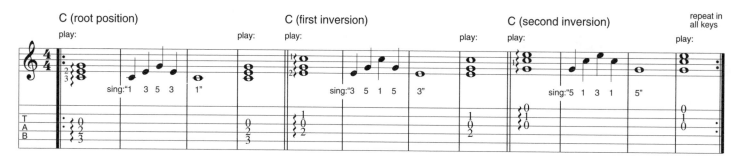

Ex. 5.49b

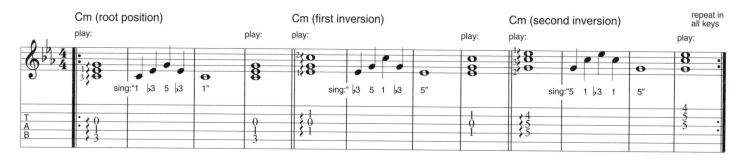

Practicing these triad inversions diatonically will tune your ear to the mix of major, minor, and diminished triads present in any harmonized major scale system (**Examples 5.50a–5.50c**). Remember—a diminished triad is just a minor triad with a flatted 5.

Ex. 5.50a

Root-position diatonic triads

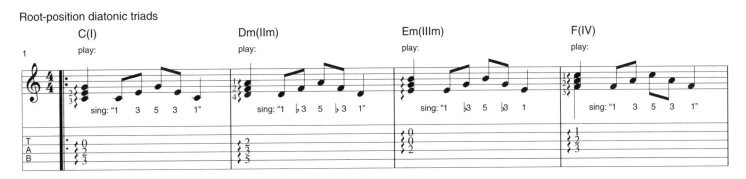

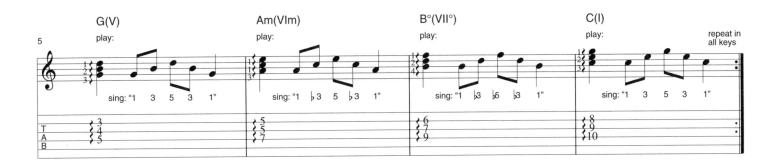

Ex. 5.50b

First-inversion diatonic triads

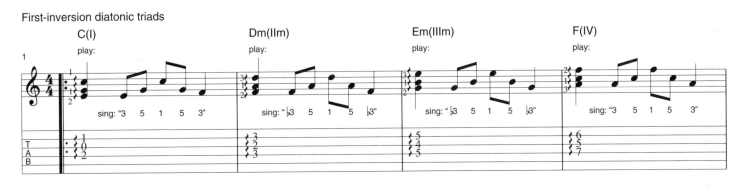

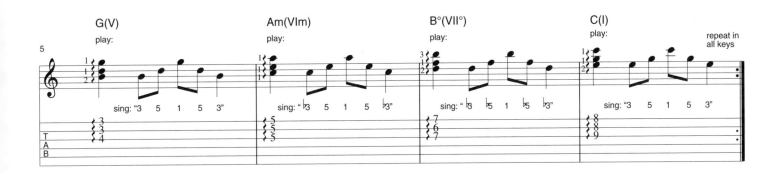

Ex. 5.50c

Second-inversion diatonic triads

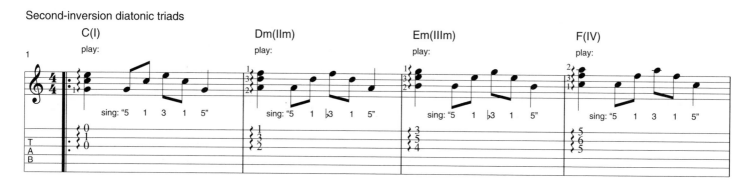

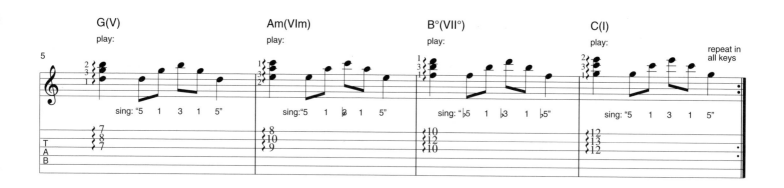

Practice these examples in all keys, using as many different fingerings as possible. Triad fingerings on the guitar are often based on four-, five-, and six-note voicings in which notes are doubled—or tripled—in separate octaves. The open *C, A, G, E,* and *D* chord shapes, for example, all contain notes which are repeated in multiple octaves. Each triad voicing has its own unique color. Listen to them carefully and each will eventually become ingrained in your tonal memory. Once you've wired the major and minor triads, it's easy to add suspensions or alter them to augmented and diminished.

Once again, enlist a pal to record a load of random triads, playing each three times, using any instrument. Try to identify the quality of each triad by ear before checking your guess on the guitar. First, locate the root—usually the bass note—then determine whether the third of the triad is major or minor. Gradually, you will develop an increased ability to recognize and recall chord sounds at will. Learn to trust your first impression of a chord's quality. Identify this first, then listen for its inversion or voicing.

You can also make your own tests by recording too many triads to memorize—

again, three times apiece—and listening them in random order or at various playback speeds. Use this opportunity to create your own personal chord dictionary by writing, recording, and practicing new voicings as you learn them. This way, you'll gradually learn to hear chord voicings while having the working knowledge to put them to use.

SEVENTH CHORDS

After you become adept at identifying triads, it's time to move on to seventh chords. Identify these in the same manner as triads. Locate the root, name the triad, then determine whether the chord contains a 7 or ♭7. There are four types of seventh chords found in a harmonized major scale: major-7th, minor-7th, dominant-7th, and minor-7th-♭5. (Sing and arpeggiate each in all inversions as you did with triads. Refer to the chord construction chart in Ex. 5.2 for the spelling of each chord type.)

Example 5.51 repeats the previous arpeggiated triadic drill using root-position 7th chords in the key of C. Be sure to transpose them to all keys.

Ex. 5.51

Root-position diatonic seventh chords

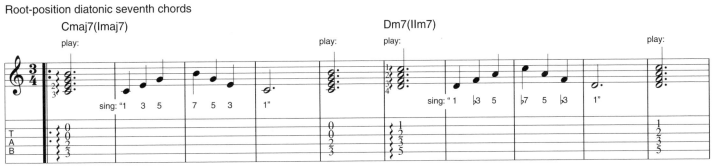

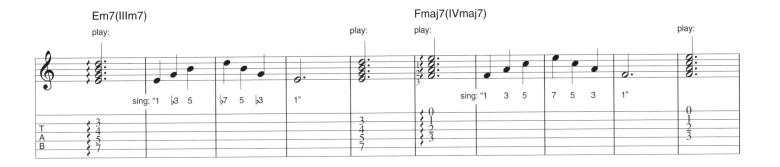

Ex. 5.51 (continued)

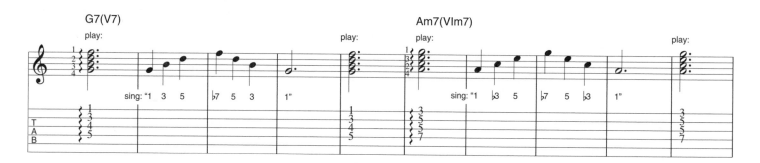

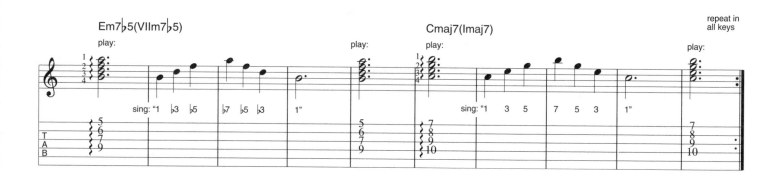

All 7th chords have four notes and, hence, four inversions—some of which are harmonic equivalents of other chords. **Ex. 5.52** illustrates four types of enharmonically related chords.

Ex. 5.52

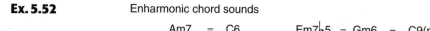

Enharmonic chord sounds

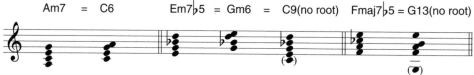

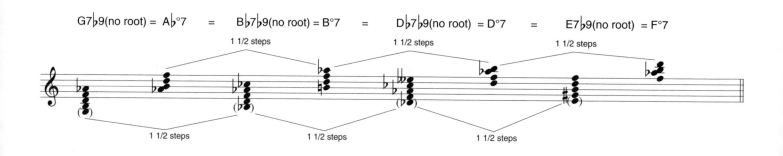

Practice singing and arpeggiating as many 7th-chord inversions as possible. Follow the same steps as triad inversions to practice parallel and diatonic inversions. This is an enormous undertaking, so it is advisable to initially deal with only one or two chord types per practice session.

Work closely with the chord construction chart in Ex. 5.2 to build and document common 7th-chord voicings. Have someone record a slew of these—three times each—and test yourself as you did with triads. To self-test, record new 7th-chord voicings as you learn them, then play them back and at random for identification. Make sure to record at least 50 voicings so you won't remember the order in which they were played. Vary playback speed to disguise them further.

EXTENSIONS

To hear extended chords—9th, 11th, and 13th chords, of major, minor, or dominant quality—first identify the quality of the triad followed by the 7th chord. Next, listen for the inclusion of a 9, 11, or 13. Voiced in a 7th chord, these may be heard as 2, 4, or 6, respectively.

ALTERATIONS

Chords containing one or more altered tone (♭5, ♯5, ♭9, or ♯9) create harsh, dissonant harmonies which usually demand resolution. Except for dominant-7th-♯9 chords, such as *G7♯9*, altered dominant chords are rarely found on their own. Look for them when chords are on the move—as opposed to static. Again, determine the quality of the triad, the 7th chord and any extensions, and finally, the alterations. The ♭9 and ♯9 may be heard as the ♭2 and ♭3, respectively. These will be the most difficult chord sounds to identify, but have patience and persist.

Harmonic ear-training never ends. Be aware of chordal sounds coming from the radio, elevator music, or even car horns. Listen carefully and your ears will grow daily.

CHAPTER SIX

Technique

Webster's dictionary defines technique as "the manner in which technical details are treated or basic physical movements are used." Notice there's no reference to "good," "bad," "right," or "wrong." Whether sloppy or refined, technique is a matter of personal choice.

For musicians, technique refers to the mental and physical command of music. Instrumental prowess may or may not be a musician's objective. There are great composers who don't perform and virtuoso instrumentalists and singers who don't compose. Regardless of your chosen niche or goal, acquiring the ability to manipulate music—mentally and/or physically—requires honing and balancing two totally different sets of chops.

The basic physical technique of playing the guitar requires total synchronization between both hands. We're not talking about brain surgery here, but that doesn't mean it's easy. The initial learning curve is steep—it can take from six to 18 months before your hands even begin to do what you ask of them. If you are just beginning to play, be patient and practice diligently. Learning and technique go hand in hand (forgive the pun)—the more you learn about music, the more technique you accumulate.

But acquiring technique is more than a physical ritual. The mechanics of the learning process can be divided into two areas of study: mental and motor. Each requires a different approach. On the mental side, ideas and concepts—such as scale and chord formulas, melodic and rhythmic fragments, and fingerboard shapes—can be understood, internalized, and recalled fairly quickly by reducing the information they convey to a series of short mental "snapshots." (People with so-called "photographic memories" excel at this process.) Performing the new idea—the *motor* side of the learning process—

is an entirely different matter. This involves training your nervous system to respond in new ways and requires considerable physical repetition before the action feels comfortable. Depending on its degree of difficulty, a new idea will become a reflex after about 50-100 repetitions. (Remember learning to write the alphabet?)

Until both hands and the mind converge, technique will remain spotty at best. An idea cannot be performed without hesitation or mistakes unless it is absolutely clear to the performer mentally. Practice new ideas at a tempo where you can play them flawlessly—otherwise you are just rehearsing your mistakes.

Musical memorization entails singing notes and rhythms in your head or aloud. If you can't hum, sing, or grunt some approximation of an idea, you'll certainly find it difficult to play. (Of course, you can't hum or sing chords, but you can learn to "hear" them internally.) Vocalizing new ideas shifts your focus to the sound of the notes—rather than how to physically play them—and allows you to synchronize mental and motor skills. The key to memorization and instant recall is working with small bits of information at very slow tempos and visualizing physical shapes on the fingerboard.

HOW TO PRACTICE

Practicing technique for its own sake definitely builds speed and endurance, but without strategy this goes nowhere. Avoid practicing aimlessly. Instead, use the following tips to maximize the time and energy you devote to practicing:

- Set up a weekly schedule and stick to it. Practicing efficiently for one year can produce amazing results. Devote as much time to practicing as possible. If you can't practice for extended periods, try to get in at least one 20-minute session daily.

- Arrange your practice time so there are no interruptions from phone calls or visitors. Designate a distraction-free practice zone in your home.

- Recognize and differentiate the two parts of the learning process. Mental learning requires intensely focused concentration, while repetitious motor learning is strictly physical and can be practiced while watching television.

- Define weaknesses in your playing and assign short time frames—three to five minutes—to each area. Always break new ideas down into small, digestible servings and devote all concentration to the moment. Valuable practice time is too often wasted with aimless noodling and lack of focus. Setting a reasonable goal within a short time frame yields attainable results.

- Don't practice any exercise for more than 10 minutes without a short break. If you burn out on an exercise, move on to other exercises—even if you haven't achieved your projected goal yet.

- Focus on learning new ideas. Practice them very slowly at first. Remember that if you make a mistake more than once, you are reinforcing that mistake. Slow down and do it right. Speed is a byproduct of concentration, clarity, and experience.

- Work with a metronome or drum machine to improve picking technique gradually and steadily. Choose and document a comfortable tempo—[♩]=60 bpm, for instance—and play non-stop eighth-notes for 10 minutes. No hammering-on, pulling-off, sliding, or bending—just straight alternate picking. Rest for a few minutes and repeat the same routine (not the same notes) three to five times daily, six days per week. Each day, advance the metronome two points. The gradual increase in tempo is barely perceptible from day to day, but in one week you will have advanced 10 points! Follow this procedure faithfully for two months and you'll amaze yourself with your growth.

- Don't incorporate ornaments such as hammer-ons, pull-offs, and slides into a line until you can pick each note accurately.

- Strive to maintain a smooth flow when you connect fragments of a long line. Some areas will require more repetition than others. Locate, isolate, and drill your trouble spots.

- Practice mental visualization of fingerboard shapes and equate them with their corresponding sounds. Try to see and hear yourself playing, then check your accuracy. Once you can mentally "play" an idea away from the guitar, it's yours to keep.

• Permute ideas to reveal their full potential.

• Increase your efficiency by learning to practice several things simultaneously. For example, play the intervallic scale sequence of your choice through the cycle of fourths in 5/4 while picking eighth-note triplets on each note.

• Practice with and without an amplifier. Switch between electric and acoustic guitars, and always strive for a good sound.

• Listen to all great musicians, regardless of their instrument or stylistic genre. Learn their lines, chords (when applicable), and concepts.

• Learn songs. Increase your repertoire weekly.

• Play with other musicians as often as possible.

• Here's an important one: *Know when to quit for the day*. If your heart isn't in the guitar, do something else for a while. During periods of intense practice, a certain magic occurs after a good night's rest, and the previous day's work seems a little easier to comprehend and perform. Take at least one day off per week to rejuvenate.

• Finally, learn to apply any musical concept to any other area of study. Formulate your own exercises and strive to make them as musical as possible. Remember that by limiting yourself to small amounts of information, you learn more efficiently and retain more of what you learn. All study has a cumulative effect. If you seek knowledge and practice faithfully, it will accumulate.

FRET-HAND TECHNIQUES

The following fret-hand techniques can be used to ornament most musical ideas. They offer guitarists a host of options for individual expression.

VIBRATO

Vibrato is a vocal technique adapted to musical instruments. True vibrato—or pitch modulation—refers to raising and lowering one or more pitch repeatedly at a desired depth (amount of pitch bend) and frequency (rate of speed). On the guitar, vibrato is generated with the fret hand or by using a mechanical vibrato bar (also called a tremolo bar—see Examples 6.48-6.50). A well-developed vibrato increases sustain, makes notes "sing" expressively, and ranges from subtle to over-exaggerated.

Fret-hand vibrato is generated using wrist, finger, or elbow motion to stretch a string slightly sharp and is not applicable to open strings. Stabilize your hand by backing up notes with one or more additional fingers on the same string. Think like a vocalist. ("Sweet" is the key word here.) Let a note sit before adding a tasty touch of vibrato and be careful not to overuse it to the point of being obnoxious—unless, of course, that's your intention.

Let's examine three flavors of fret-hand vibrato.

Push/pull or pull/push vibrato: Move the string slightly off its center axis in one direction and then an equal distance in the opposite direction. Repeat this subtle bending action in a smooth, steady motion. Start by pushing (towards the ceiling) or pulling (towards the floor)—the choice is yours (except for the low E string, which can't be pushed because it will creep off the fretboard). For wrist vibrato, rock your hand in a motion similar to twisting a doorknob or screwing in a light bulb. The fingers stay locked and all motion comes from the wrist. It's also possible to lock the arm and wrist and generate vibrato from the elbow. This produces a wonderfully wide, exaggerated vibrato.

For individual finger vibrato, each finger operates independently—as if you're trying to scratch your palm through the fingerboard. The strings are pulled towards the floor and released (except for both E strings, which may creep off the fretboard if pushed or pulled in the wrong direction). Finger vibrato works particularly well on the lower three strings.

Classical vibrato: Using a slight back-and-forth motion along the length of any fretted string gently sways its pitch sharp and flat for a true vibrato. Use this technique to cause a variable rise and fall in pitch—up to a half-step.

Circular vibrato: Push/pull or pull/push the string in a circular motion by combining the previous methods.

To strengthen manual vibrato of any of the above types, practice vibrating in rhythm. Play each measure in **Ex. 6.1a** four times with each finger. When you're done, transpose them over the entire fingerboard.

Ex. 6.1a

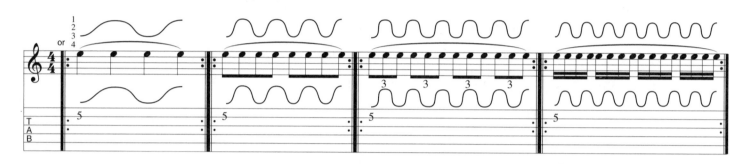

Vibrato is commonly notated with a general symbol (**Ex. 6.1b**), and the frequency and depth are left to the player's interpretation.

Ex. 6.1b

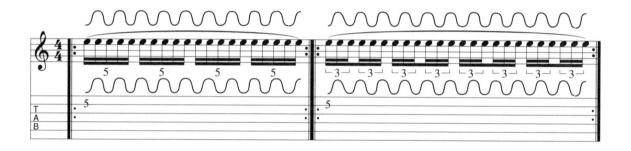

You can also generate vibrato using a number of unconventional methods. You can get physical and shake the entire guitar—particularly effective with chords—or bend the strings behind the nut (or the bridge, if your guitar has some string length behind the bridge). You can even bend the neck itself. Be adventurous, but don't put your axe in the hospital!

Like any technique, vibrato must be practiced,s so get to work and incorporate it into your music immediately. Don't be discouraged if it seems tough at first. Keep practicing, and listen to the great players for inspiration.

HAMMER-ONS, PULL-OFFS, SLIDES, AND BENDS

Playing the guitar involves much more than just picking the notes. There are many other techniques we can use to articulate notes—including hammer-ons, pull-offs, slides, and bends.

HAMMER-ONS

Following any picked note, one or more higher-pitched notes can be sounded by hammering down onto the same string with a different finger. You can also hammer without picking at all—for one-handed playing—but this tends to cause undesirable overtones from behind the hammered note. If that's your thing, invest in a string-dampening device. Hammer-ons are indicated by a tie between two or more different notes of ascending pitch in both standard and tablature (or "tab") notation.

Examples 6.2a–6.2d illustrate a variety of *A* pentatonic minor and *G* Mixolydian hammer-on applications.

Ex. 6.2a　　　　　　　　**Ex. 6.2b**　　　　　　　　**Ex. 6.2c**

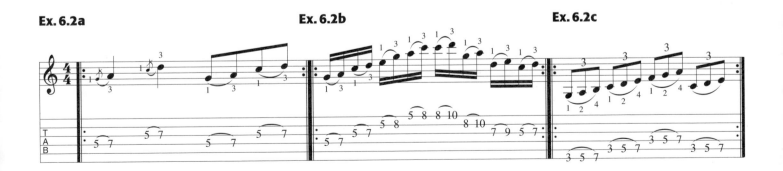

Ex. 6.2d

* Repeat in reverse

* Do not reverse order
of hammered notes.

Ex. 6.2e applies hammer-ons to a descending *C* major scale sequence played entirely on the second string. The index finger remains in contact with the string throughout. **Ex. 6.2f** shows the same sequence played one-handed. The index finger breaks contact with the string every other note to rehammer.

Ex. 6.2e

Repeat in reverse

Ex. 6.2f

Repeat in reverse

* Hammer w/out picking.

PULL-OFFS

Following any picked note—except for open strings—one or more prepared lower pitches can be sounded by pulling the same finger off the string quickly and at a slight angle. The fretting finger actually picks the string. The pull-off motion can be up or down, but down (towards the floor) is most common. Finger the picked and pulled-off notes simultaneously so the note you are pulling off to is prepped in advance.

Pull-offs are indicated by a tie between two or more different notes of descending pitch in both standard and tab notation. **Examples 6.3a–6.3d** show several *A* pentatonic minor and *G* Mixolydian pull-off applications.

Ex. 6.3a   **Ex. 6.3b**   **Ex. 6.3c**

Ex. 6.3d

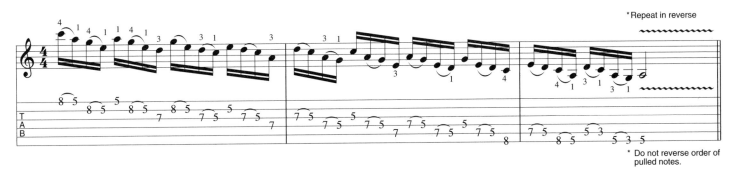

Ex. 6.3e applies pull-offs—this time starting on an upbeat—to a descending *C* major

scale sequence played entirely on the second string.

Ex. 6.3e

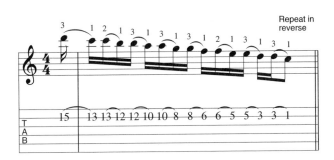

COMBINED HAMMER-ONS AND PULL-OFFS

Hammer-ons and pull-offs may be combined freely. Notice how each hammer-on in the
A pentatonic minor-based lines in **Examples 6.4a–6.4d** sets up a potential pull-off, and
vice versa.

Ex. 6.4a   **Ex. 6.4b**   **Ex. 6.4c**

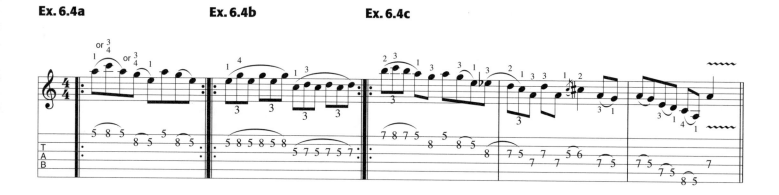

Ex. 6.4d

Ex. 6.4e combines techniques in a descending *C* major scale sequence played in
eighth-note triplets. Alternate the hammer-ons and pull-offs rapidly enough and they
become trills (**Ex. 6.4f**).

Ex. 6.4e   **Ex. 6.4f**

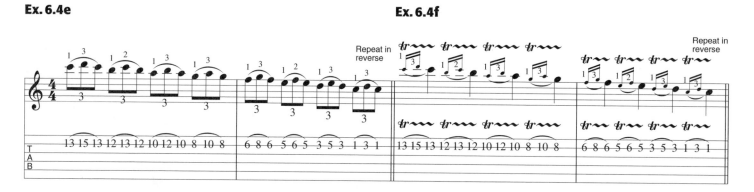

SLIDES

Following any pick attack, hammer-on, or pull-off, additional higher or lower pitches can be sounded by maintaining finger pressure on the string and sliding up or down the fingerboard to the next note.

Slides are indicated by a diagonal line—slanted in the direction of the slide—plus a tie between two or more notes of ascending or descending pitch in both standard and tab notation. **Examples 6.5a** and **6.5b** illustrate using an *A* pentatonic minor snippet and a *C* major scale played entirely on the second string.

Ex. 6.5a   **Ex. 6.5b**

When no tie is present, all notes are picked. Try alternating between 3rd and 1st fingers or omitting every other slide in **Ex. 6.6**.

Ex. 6.6

Ex. 6.7 combines hammer-ons, pull-offs, and slides. The entire second-string *C* major scale sequence is set into motion by a single pick attack.

 Ex. 6.7

1 7 7

Bends

Strings can be manually stretched across the fingerboard in either direction (towards the ceiling or towards the floor) to bend notes to a higher pitch. The three upper strings are usually pushed up while the bass strings are pulled down.

String bends originate at the wrist, using the same doorknob-twisting action as vibrato, but individual fingers also share the responsibility. Although you can bend strings with any finger, the bulk of the work seems to fall on the 3rd (ring) finger. The 1st (index) and 2nd (middle) fingers are often used to bend, but they are also used—individually or collectively—to back up whichever finger is doing the bending. To increase bending power, lock your 1st and 2nd fingers behind 3rd-finger bends—on the same string, of course—or your 1st finger behind 2nd-finger bends. It gets easier to bend strings as you move up the neck. (String tension increases closer to its points of suspension—in this case, the nut—making it more difficult to bend notes at the 1st and 2nd frets than it is in higher positions.)

Unlike hammer-ons, pull-offs, and slides, bends are not restricted to equally tempered pitches. Notes can be bent to specific intervals or to *any* pitch—not just the 12 notes in the chromatic scale. In standard tuning, a perfect fourth is about the reasonable bending limit. Half-step (minor second) and whole-step (major second) bends are most common, but minor third and major third (one-and-a-half steps and two whole-steps, respectively) and perfect-fourth (five half-steps) bends are also possible. Microtonal bends—approximately a quarter-step to three quarter-steps—can add bluesy or exotic expression to otherwise stagnant melodies.

Sustaining the pitch of a bent note requires practiced strength and control, and that takes time to master. Adding vibrato to a bend can be even trickier. The most common method is to bend to a desired pitch, release slightly, and bend back to pitch, repeating the action at a consistent rate. Practice vibrating bends rhythmically, in the same manner as unbent notes.

There are many notational systems in use which accurately portray pitch-bends on the guitar. The standard notation should reflect the actual bent pitch as well as the bend's point of origin. Symbols such as arrows are more appropriate for tab notation where they can graphically depict bending distances in half- or whole-steps. Though there is no standard notation system for guitar music, most publishers include a key to the symbols used in their books and transcription folios. The system in this book—the same as the one currently used in *Guitar Player*—is state-of-the-art, but who knows what tomorrow may bring?

The following examples illustrate nine common pitch-bending techniques. Our notation uses parenthetical note heads and tab numbers to indicate bent pitches and their hypothetical fret locations. In addition, a "B" symbol is aligned with the bent pitch between the standard and tab staves. The preceding grace note and first tab number designate the pitch where the bend originates.

HALF-STEP BENDS

Any note can be picked and bent up a half-step to a desired pitch in accordance with a specific rhythm. Half-step bends always originate one fret below a targeted pitch.

Ex. 6.8a compares half-step grace bends and rhythmic bends. Transpose them both over the entire fingerboard. In **Ex. 6.8b**, the idea is to play an unbent reference note and match it with a bend from a half-step lower. Try elongating the grace bends to eighth-notes or beyond.

Ex. 6.8a   **Ex. 6.8b**

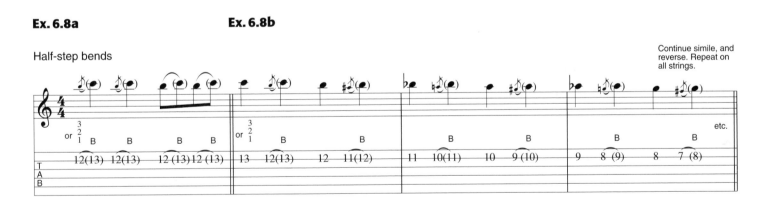

WHOLE-STEP BENDS

Any note can be picked and bent up a whole-step to a desired pitch in accordance with a specific rhythm. Whole-step bends always originate two frets below a targeted pitch.

Ex. 6.9a compares whole-step grace bends and rhythmic bends. Transpose them both over the entire fingerboard. In **Ex. 6.9b**, the idea is to play an unbent reference note and match it with a bend from a whole-step lower. Again, try elongating the grace bends to eighth-notes or beyond.

Ex. 6.9a

Whole-step bends

Ex. 6.9b

Except for the chromatic and whole-tone scales, all scales will contain some combination of half- and whole-steps. **Ex. 6.10a** is a sequenced *C* major scale combining half- and whole-step bends on the *B* string. **Ex. 6.10b** shows a similar sequence played in the seventh position using major scale Pattern 4.

Ex. 6.10a

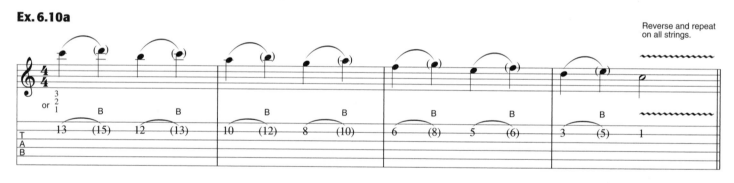

Ex. 6.10b

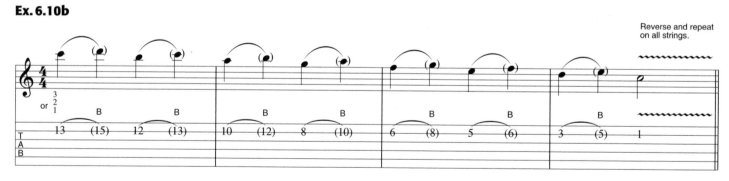

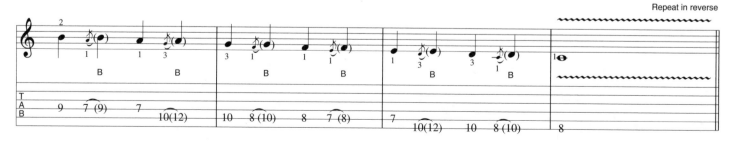

EXTENDED BENDS

Any note can be picked and bent up one-and-a-half, two whole, or two-and-a-half steps to a desired pitch in accordance with a specific rhythm. **Ex. 6.11** illustrates three extended grace and rhythmic bends. Extreme bends are best suited to the *B* string, *G* string, and lower—the lower the note, the lesser the tension. (Be prepared to snap a few high *E* strings.)

Ex. 6.11

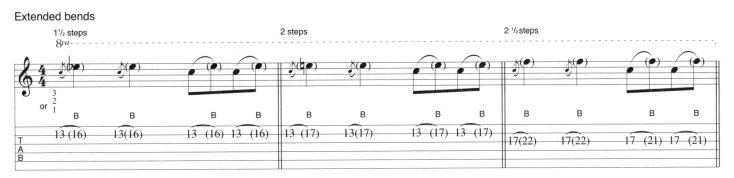

PRE-BENDS/GHOST BENDS

Any note can be bent to a desired pitch before it is picked so that only the bent pitch is heard. Pre-bends (or ghost bends) are notated the same as any other bend, except the original pitch—the grace note—is parenthesized and the "B" symbol between staves becomes "pre-B." When a pre-bend comes from an adjacent note, the grace note is eliminated.

Ex. 6.12a illustrates three different pre-bends while **Ex. 6.12b** (next page) applies half- and whole-step pre-bends to a descending *C* major scale sequence on the *B* string.

Ex. 6.12a

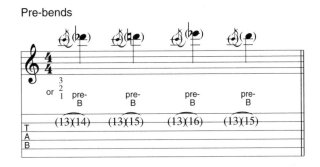

Ex. 6.12b

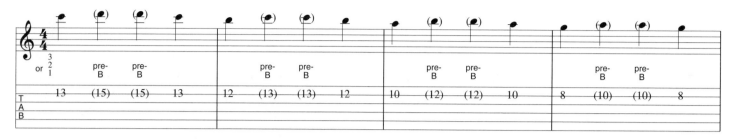

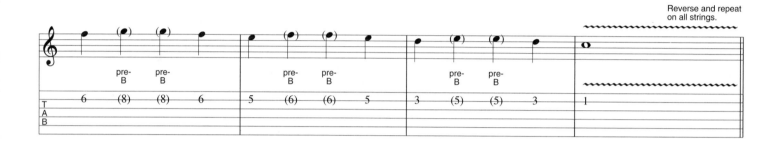

SUSTAINED BENDS

Any note can be bent any desired distance and held while the bent pitch is attacked repeatedly. The repeated attacks are notated in parentheses and a "hold - - -" indicator is added between staves, lasting the duration of the bend.

Ex. 6.13a shows grace and rhythmic sustained bends, and Ex. 6.13b applies both to a descending *C* major scale on the *B* string.

Ex. 6.13a   **Ex. 6.13b**

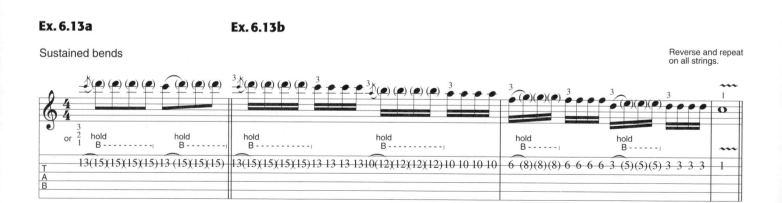

OBLIQUE BENDS

Any type of bend can be played simultaneously against one or more stationary notes. Though they appear as staggered tab numbers, pick the grace note and the stationary pitch(es) at the same time. Explore oblique pre-bends and sustained bends.

Oblique bends can be played anywhere, but are most common on the top three strings. **Examples 6.14a–c** illustrates oblique unison bends, oblique intervallic bends, and oblique bends played against double-stops—two notes on adjacent strings played at the same fret, often with the same finger.

Ex. 6.14a   **Ex. 6.14b**   **Ex. 6.14c**

Oblique unison bends   Oblique intervallic bends   Oblique bends w/ double stops

Be sure to experiment with oblique hammer-ons and pull-offs.

DOUBLE-STOP AND TRIPLE-STOP BENDS

Double-stop bends are most common on the *G* and *B* strings. **Ex. 6.15a** shows three different bends from the same two notes. In the first measure, both notes are bent a half-step. In the next bar, the bottom note is bent a whole-step while the top note only travels a whole-step. In the last bar, both notes are bent a whole-step. The torturous triple-stop bend in **Ex. 6.15b** is potentially pain-inducing—but well worth the effort.

Ex. 6.15a   **Ex. 6.15b**

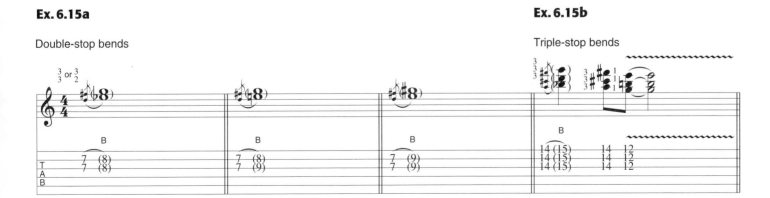

Double-stop bends   Triple-stop bends

MELODIC BENDS/RELEASED BENDS

What goes up must come down. So far, all of the pitch-bends we've examined have had inaudible releases. Audible releases vastly increase the melodic potential of pitch-bending. To release any bend, simply ease the string back into its starting position while maintaining enough pressure to sustain the note. It is up to you to determine whether or not the release of any bend will be audible. You can also release bends partially by pausing at any point during the string's arc. In music and tab, the released note must always be preceded by an audible or inaudible bend. Releases are notated using ties between noteheads and tab numbers, and an "R" symbol aligned with the released pitch between staves.

Ex. 6.16a showcases several possible techniques—including grace/pre-bent releases, rhythmic/melodic releases, and multiple bends/releases from a single pick attack.

Ex. 6.16a Bends w/ releases

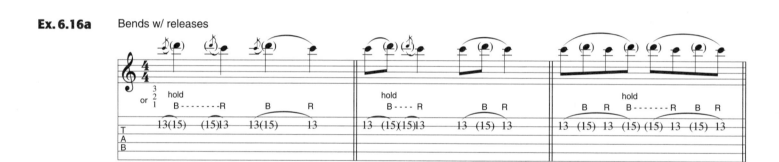

Ex. 6.16b applies melodic releases to the bends in a C major scale sequence played entirely on the B string. Maintain contact with the string throughout without creating an audible slide when shifting between notes. Once you can control this, it's easy to add audible slides at will. Ex. 6.16c shows the same sequence applied to eighth-note triplets.

Ex. 6.16b

Reverse and repeat on all strings.

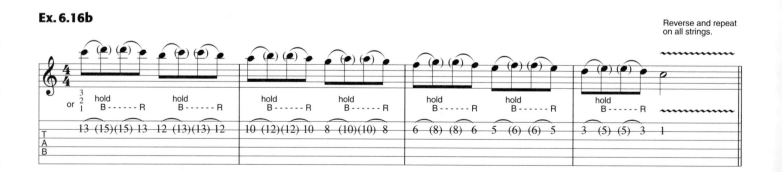

Ex. 6.16c

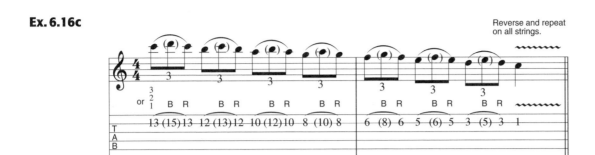

MICROTONAL BENDS

Unless you are intentionally trying to sound out-of-tune, microtonal, "in-between" bends of one quarter-step to three quarter-steps tend to sound best when added gradually or to the tail end of a note. **Ex. 6.17a** depicts how you might encounter a written quarter-step bend and the sweetest way to approach it. **Ex. 6.17b** applies a quarter-step bend to a pull-off following a bend/release combo. Use **Ex. 6.17c** as a model for oblique microtonal bends on different string groups.

Ex. 6.17a   **Ex. 6.17b**   **Ex. 6.17c**

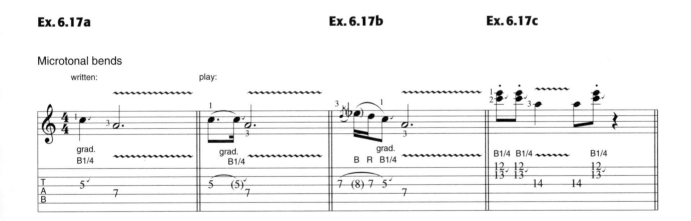

Well—that exhausts the most common fret-hand techniques. Let's now move on to the other hand.

PICK-HAND TECHNIQUES

The pick hand controls picking, muting, volume, and dynamics, plus special effects— such as artificial and pinched harmonics. We'll begin with flatpicking techniques.

ALTERNATE FLATPICKING

Any two consecutive notes can be picked using alternating down- and upstrokes. Try to align the down/up pick-hand motion with your foot-tapping. This isn't an inflexible rule, but it will help to develop and reinforce a strong sense of time. Play downbeats in **Ex. 6.18** using downstrokes (⊓) and the upbeats using upstrokes (V). A slight accent (>) on each downbeat will help you to keep your metric bearings. Practice, and this will become second nature.

Ex. 6.18

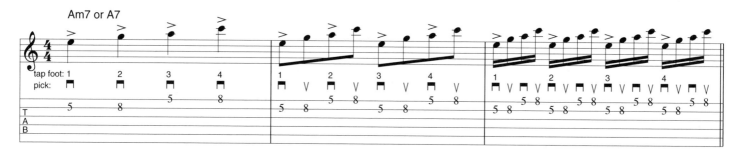

Keep this action—or at least the *feel* of it—constant even when resting between melody notes. Feel rests as if they were notes—just don't attack the strings. When the melody resumes, jump back in on the appropriate down- or upstroke without breaking the flow of time. (Remember, it's up to you to generate the time.) This is especially use-ful—and necessary—for playing single-note lines and chords at fast tempos. When the rests occur in **Examples 6.19a** and **6.19b**, do not make contact with the string, but maintain the feel of the down/up pick motion to lock in the time. (The "silent strokes" are parenthesized.)

Ex. 6.19a

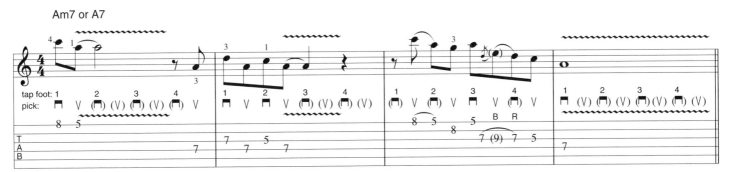

Ex. 6.19b

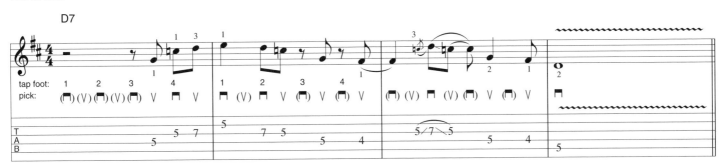

If it feels better to pick a phrase another way, do it. Alternate picking isn't the only way to fly. Any two consecutive notes can be played using the following combinations of pick strokes:

⊓ ⊓ (down/down), ⊓ V (down/up), V ⊓ (up/down), or V V (up/up).

Any three consecutive notes can be played using the following combinations:

⊓ ⊓ ⊓ (down/down/down), ⊓ ⊓ V (down/down/up), ⊓ V ⊓ (down/up/down),

⊓ V V (down/up/up), V V V (up/up/up), V V ⊓ (up/up/down), V ⊓ V (up/down/up),

V ⊓ ⊓ (up/down/down).

Applying alternate picking to repeated triplets shifts the downbeats to alternate down- and upstrokes:

⊓ V ⊓, V ⊓ V, ⊓ V ⊓, V ⊓ V, and so on; or V ⊓ V, ⊓ V ⊓, V ⊓ V, ⊓ V ⊓, and so on.

That's a lot of picking possibilities! What's the bottom line? Simply this: Your objective is to become fluent using any practical combination of down- and upstrokes.

SYNCHRONIZING BOTH HANDS

When you hammer-on, pull-off, slide, or bend notes, the rhythmic feeling of time shifts back and forth between your left and right hands—as the fret hand sounds a note, the pick hand is momentarily suspended. Again, concentrate on feeling strong pick-hand downbeats and the upbeats will naturally fall into place.

Ex. 6.20 consists of a dozen one-bar examples designed to help synchronize the left and right hands when hammering, pulling-off, sliding, or bending. Develop your own exercises based on these examples.

Ex. 6.20

Am7, A7, or D9

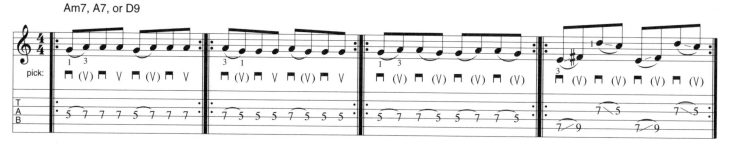

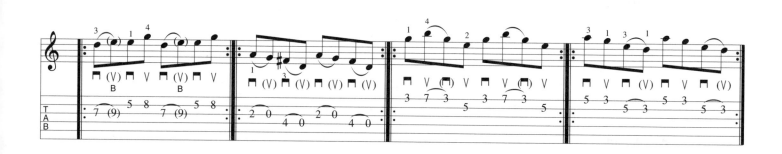

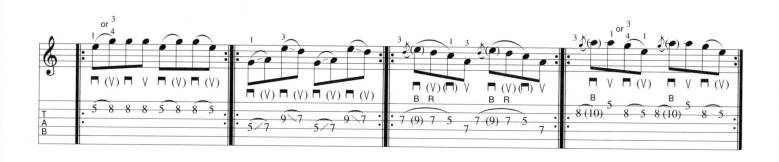

OTHER FLATPICKING TECHNIQUES

Guitar players often develop their own unique methods for picking extremely fast single-note lines. Terms such as "circular picking," "economy picking," "sweep picking," and "speed picking" have been used to describe some of these techniques.

ECONOMY PICKING

This technique—shown to me by the late, great jazz and studio guitarist Tommy Tedesco—involves playing passages with three notes per string. Each string is picked down/up/down (⊓ V ⊓) when ascending and up/down/up (V ⊓ V) when descending. This eliminates either an upstroke or a downstroke—depending whether you're ascending or descending. With practice, **Examples 6.21a** and **6.21b** can be smoothed to produce a lightning-fast cascade of triplets or sixteenth-notes that encompasses all six strings. For a real brain twister, permute the order of notes on each string. Use the same technique for any three-note grouping. (Try identical or symmetrical shapes, and so on.) Play them fast enough, hit your predetermined target—provided it's a good one—and almost any notes will do. (Tommy got a *lot* of mileage out of this technique.)

Ex. 6.21a

Ex. 6.21b

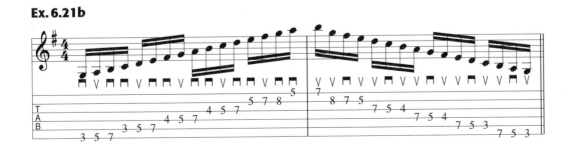

SWEEP PICKING

You can "sweep" the pick across two or more adjacent strings using consecutive down- or upstrokes to play lightning-fast, arpeggio-based lines that land on one note per string. Practice this technique using the various three- and four-note string groups in **Examples 6.22a** and **6.22b** before adding the chromatic and diatonic triad and 7th-chord arpeggios in **Examples 6.22c-6.22g**. Practice them in all keys and modalities, and remember—sweep picking can be combined with any other picking techniques.

Ex. 6.22a

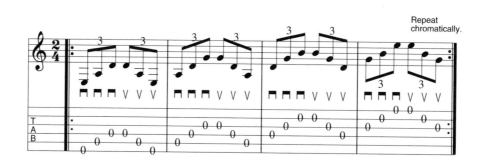

Ex. 6.22b

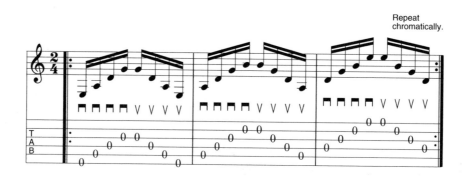

Ex. 6.22c   **Ex. 6.22d**

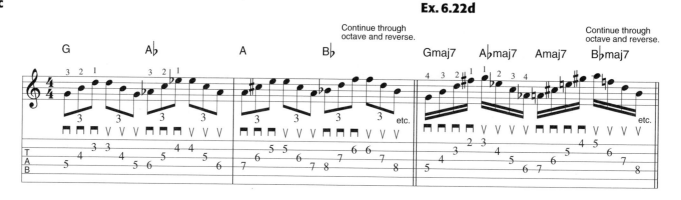

Ex. 6.22e

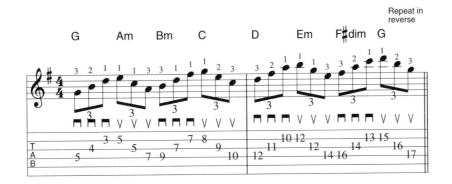

Ex. 6.22f

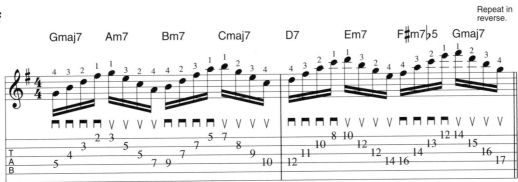

Ex. 6.22g

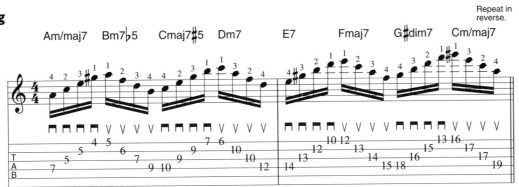

Any of these techniques can be combined and recombined. Always explore several pick- and fret-hand phrasing options when learning new lines. Internalize the ones that feel and sound best to you.

Ex. 6.23 shows the same line phrased and fingered four different ways.

Ex. 6.23

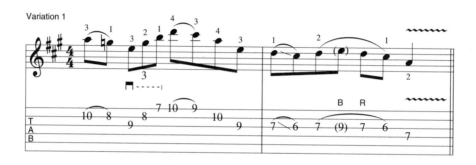

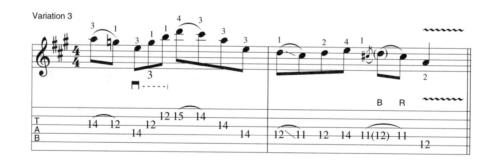

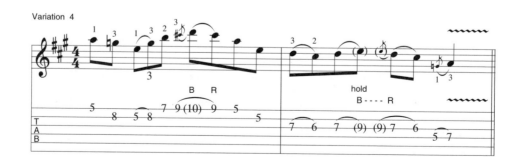

BASIC FINGERPICKING

To notate fingerstyle technique, the pick-hand fingers are labeled *"p"* for thumb, *"i"* for index, *"m"* for middle, and *"a"* for ring.

Ex. 6.24a adapts a useful and easy-to-grasp "Travis-style" fingerpicking pattern to three ascending major triads played over a *D* pedal bass. The thumb picks down while the index finger claws upward.

Ex. 6.24a

Each measure in **Ex. 6.24b** accents different beats to produce a variety of feels.

Ex. 6.24b

To apply this pattern to five- and six-note chord voicings, simply finger the entire chord and pick four strings, as shown in **Ex. 6.24c**. Incorporate your *m* and *a* fingers if you like. Link any two measures to create a two-bar pattern.

Ex. 6.24c

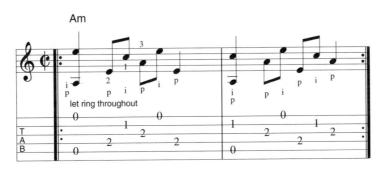

HYBRID PICKING

Flatpicking and fingerpicking can be combined into a hybrid form. You can hybrid-pick any of the previous fingerpicking examples by replacing the thumb with a picked downstroke and the index with the middle finger. This versatile technique has many single-note, intervallic, and chordal applications. **Examples 6.25a–6.25c** illustrate a pianistic approach to diatonic 7th chords. Hold each chord shape and hybrid-pick these harmonized arpeggios.

Ex. 6.25a   **Ex. 6.25b**

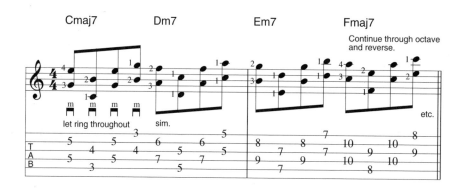

Ex. 6.25c

Ex. 6.25d features funky, hybrid "chicken picking" applied to descending diatonic sixths. Pull the notes indicated to snap outward with your middle finger, and allow them to recoil back against the fingerboard with an audible *pop*. **Ex. 6.25e** pedals a high *G* tonic over superimposed ascending *C* (IV) and descending *D* (V) arpeggios.

Ex. 6.25d

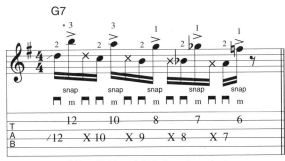

* Snap B-string w/middle finger throughout.

Ex. 6.25e

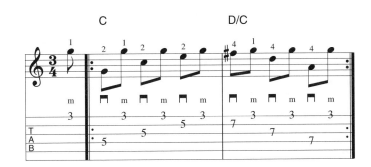

PALM MUTING

A muffled, percussive effect can be imposed on notes by allowing part of the palm of your pick hand to rest on the desired strings slightly above the bridge (towards the neck). **Ex. 6.26a** palm-mutes an ascending *A* harmonic minor scale sequence. **Ex. 6.26b** (next page) applies the technique to a single-note, "tic-toc" funk figure while **Ex. 6.26c** uses it in a modern rock context. The amount of palm pressure determines the intensity of the muting effect. With palm muting, pitches remain discernible regardless of the amount of pressure you apply. (Beware—if your guitar sports a floating tremolo tailpiece, excess pressure on the bridge will pull the strings sharp.)

Ex. 6.26a

Ex. 6.26b

Ex. 6.26c

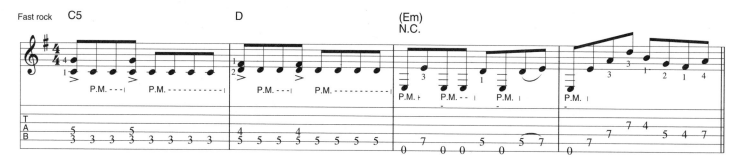

FRET-HAND MUTING

Another way to mute notes is to slightly release fret-hand pressure. This style of muting obscures the original pitch and is for percussive use only—unless you happen to hit a harmonic node (see "Harmonics"). **Ex. 6.27** illustrates two ways to notate fret-hand muting. The notation shows every note of an *E9* chord being played on every beat—muted or not. Don't take this too literally. On certain beats—especially fast sixteenth-note upbeats—the pick will brush only the upper strings. It's a natural byproduct of settling into a groove.

Ex. 6.27

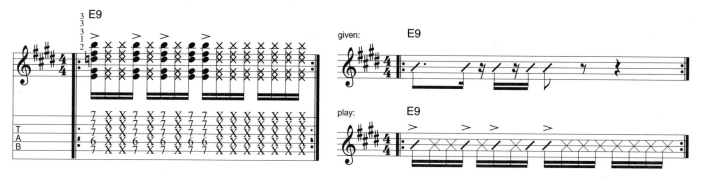

PICK-HAND HAMMER-ONS/FINGER TAPPING

Though the act is essentially the same, we'll refer to this technique as "tapping" to avoid confusion with fret-hand hammer-ons. To tap a note, hammer a pick-hand finger directly onto any string at its normally fretted position and hold it for the desired duration. Basic tapping technique can entail all taps or a combination of taps, hammer-ons, pull-offs, slides, and bends—using either hand. The latter can be demonstrated with any three notes on the same string.

TAPPED ARPEGGIOS

The following six examples (**6.28a–6.28f**, next page) utilize a C minor arpeggio (C-Eb-G) played on the G string. Its three notes yield six permutations (C-Eb-G, C-G-Eb, Eb-G-C, Eb-C-G, G-C-Eb, and G-Eb-C). Play each six-note group four times to complete a measure of 4/4, or adapt them to 2/4, 3/4, 5/4, and so on. Pick-hand pull-offs can be upward or downward. Whenever possible, keep the fret hand's 1st finger stationary and prepare the 4th finger while the pick hand is tapping.

In **Ex. 6.28a**, the first note is tapped and pulled off to the second note. The fret hand then pulls off to sound the third note.

In **Ex. 6.28b**, the first note is tapped and pulled off to the second note. The third note is hammered with the fret hand.

In **Ex. 6.28c**, the first two notes are sounded by hammering—without picking—and then pulling off with the fret hand. The third note is tapped and pulled off to repeat the triplet.

In **Ex 6.28d**, the first note is an unpicked, fret-hand hammer-on. The second note is tapped and then pulled off to sound the third. Another fret-hand hammer-on recycles the triplet.

In **Ex. 6.28e**, the first two notes are hammered with the fret hand. The third note is tapped and pulled off to recycle the triplet.

In **Ex. 6.28f**, the first note is hammered with the fret hand's 1st finger. The second note is tapped and then pulled off to sound the third. A fret-hand, fourth-finger pull-off recycles the triplet.

Ex. 6.28a

Ex. 6.28b

Ex. 6.28c

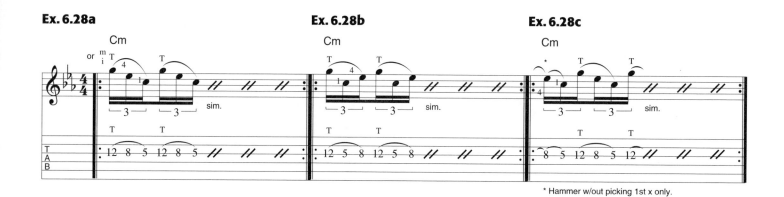

* Hammer w/out picking 1st x only.

Ex. 6.28d

Ex. 6.28e

Ex. 6.28f

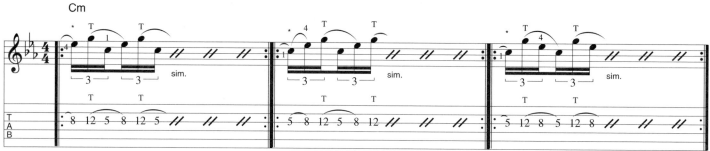

Adapt these ideas on all strings using different arpeggios. Explore rhythms beyond triplets by adding, deleting, or repeating notes. Experiment with two, four, five, and six-note groupings, open strings, pitch-bends, and so on. The sky's the limit!

Be sure to consider all inversions when adapting any chord progression to tapped arpeggios. Pair the voicings that flow smoothly from one chord to the next. All three of the following examples convey identical harmonic information—*Cm* (Im) to *G* (V)—but notice how **Ex. 6.29a** is much more awkward to perform than **Ex. 6.29b** or **Ex. 6.29c**. Transpose these examples—and your own spin-offs—to all strings and keys.

Ex. 6.29a

Ex. 6.29b

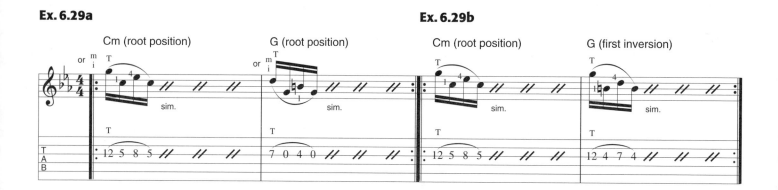

Ex. 6.29c

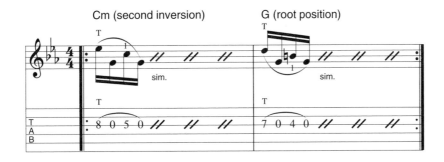

TAPPED SCALES

If you can tap chord tones, you can tap scale tones. Tapping scales along the length of a single string not only sounds great, it also improves your ability to visualize and retain scale formulas.

In the next three examples, the fret hand's 1st finger never breaks contact with the *B* string. The first two commence with "silent taps" as an alternative to the fret-hand hammer-ons in the previous examples. **Ex. 6.30a** features a *C* major scale sequence ascending the *B* string in sixteenth-note triplets. Each three-note motif is repeated twice. Use this "bought time" to think ahead.

Ex. 6.30a

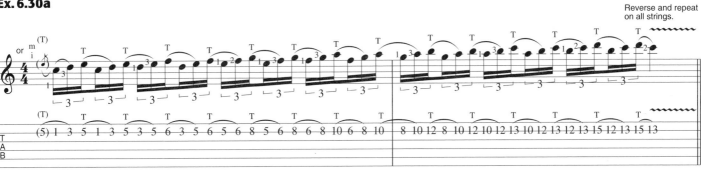

Ex. 6.30b adapts the same idea to a straight sixteenth-note motif and adds fret-hand finger slides, while **Ex. 6.30c** inverts the notes to accommodate tapped pick-hand slides.

Ex. 6.30b

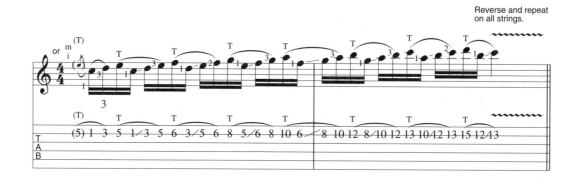

Ex. 6.30c

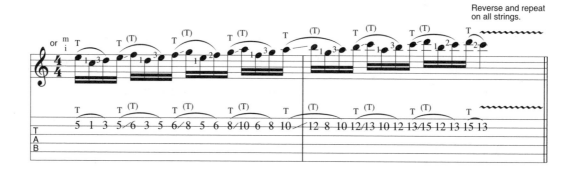

THE CHORDAL CAPO

You can hold any fret-hand chord shape while tapping out another shape higher up the fingerboard on the same strings. This "chordal capo" technique—a favorite of Jennifer Batten—is also applicable to parallel and diatonic voicings, polychords, or totally unrelated chords.

Ex. 6.31a frets a third-position *Gm* below a tapped, tenth-position inversion. **Ex. 6.31b** reorders the same notes into a string-skipping sequence. Both raise interesting melodic possibilities.

Ex. 6.31a

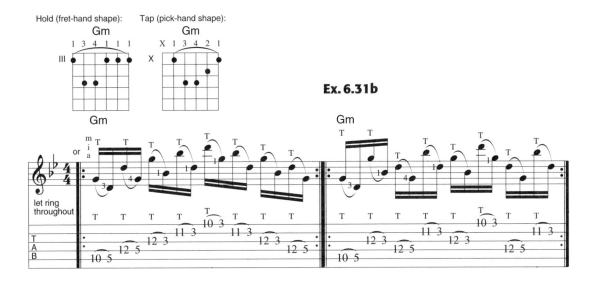

Ex. 6.31b

The sequenced third intervals in **Ex. 6.31c** use *Cmaj7* and *Dm7* chordal capos below tapped *Em7* and *Fmaj7* diatonic substitutions (see Chapter 5, Ex. 5.28). Remember: *Cmaj7+Em7=Cmaj9*, and *Dm7+Fmaj7=Dm9*. Continue the sequence up the harmonized *C* scale using diatonic 7th chords spaced a third apart.

Ex. 6.31c

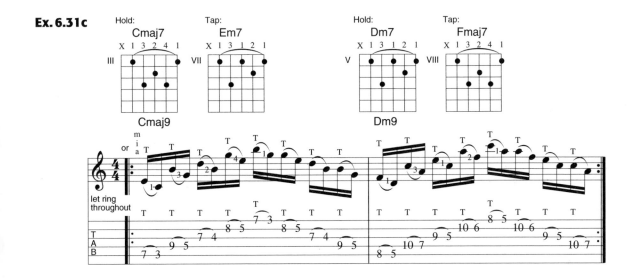

THE SCALE CAPO

Once again, whatever works for chords works for scales. Arrange any two scale patterns using the same number of notes per string with enough distance between them to keep your fingers from getting tangled. When each pattern contains two notes per string, begin with the upper tapped note pulled off to the upper fretted note, then follow suit with the lower tapped and fretted notes. Repeat this pattern on each string. Getting bored? Permute it!

Ex. 6.32a "capos" a fifth-position *A* pentatonic minor pattern with the fret hand and taps a higher inversion of the same scale based at the 10th fret. **Ex. 6.32b** features the same capo with a descending octave pattern tapped 12 frets higher while **Ex. 6.32c** taps a parallel twelfth-position *E* pentatonic minor pattern.

Ex. 6.32a

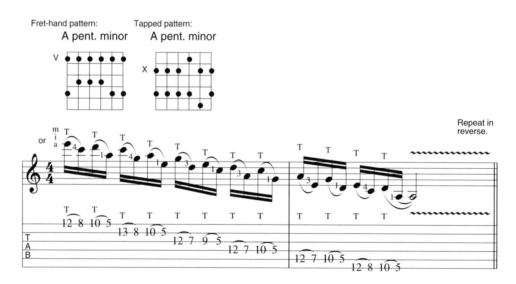

Ex. 6.32b

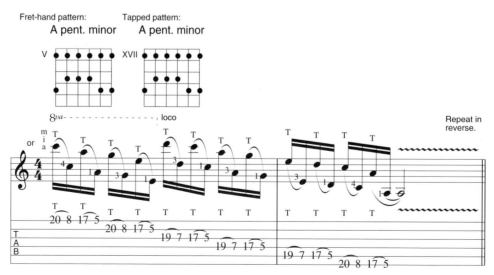

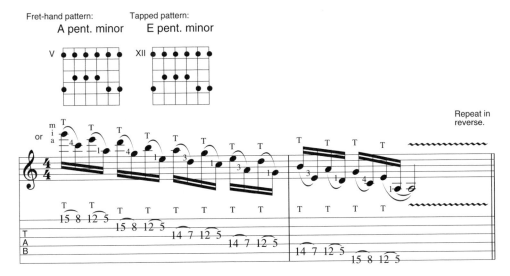

TWO-HANDED TAPPING

Tapped notes don't always have to be adorned with hammer-ons and pull-offs. Both hands have the ability to tap, but in lieu of a manual capo, it may become necessary to dampen the strings in order to prevent unwanted notes from "fretting out" behind the tapped notes. Buy the mechanical pro-model or tie a sock around the first fret (thanks again, Jennifer!)—the choice is yours. If you play loud enough, this won't even be an issue.

Ex. 6.33 (next page) breaks a *Cmaj7* voicing—root-5-7-3—into two string groups, assigns one to each hand, and follows suit up the harmonized *C* major scale. The fret hand handles the *A* and *G* strings, and the pick hand covers the *D* and *B* strings. The voicings are crammed but manageable, thanks to the Joe Satriani-style, castanet-influenced rhythm motif that lifts each pair of fingers out of the other's way in the nick of time. It's almost as much fun to watch as it is to play!

Ex. 6.33

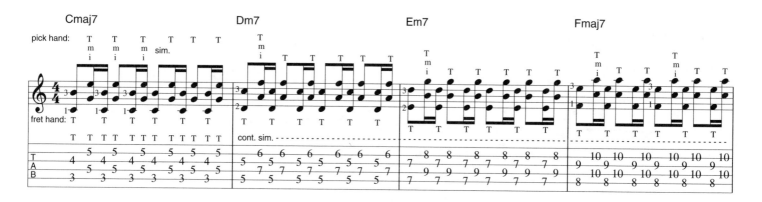

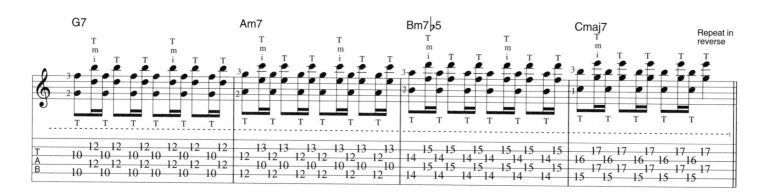

Another "manual capo" technique—also from Satriani's trick bag—uses the pick-hand's index finger to barre the strings *behind* the fret hand, and the fret hand to hammer on and pull off. Though it is limited to one fret at a time, the true value of this temporary finger capo lies in its extreme mobility.

HARMONICS

Harmonic nodes are non-vibrating, dead spots which manifest at equal divisions of a vibrating body. Setting a harmonic overtone into motion on the guitar divides the string's vibrational pattern into equal segments. Besides extending the range of the guitar, harmonics can add a lot of color to your palette. They sound pure when played with a soft attack—like a sine wave—and chimey when plucked harder. Distort them and they scream. Open strings produce "natural" harmonics while fretted notes yield "artificial" harmonics. Each are attainable in a number of ways.

When a string is plucked into motion, it vibrates between its two points of suspension—the nut and the bridge. Think of how a tub full of water would react if you tossed in a pebble. The waves spread in all directions until they hit a "shoreline" (the ends of the tub) and then travel back to the opposite shore until their energy dissipates. On the guitar, the string is the water, the nut and bridge are the shorelines, and the pick attack is the pebble. **Ex. 6.34** illustrates the vibrational path of a plucked open string.

Ex. 6.34

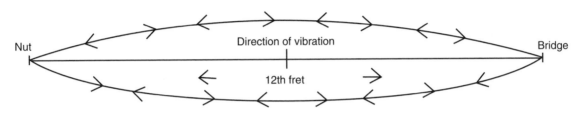

All notes—open and fretted—contain all harmonics in accordance with nature's overtone series: octave, octave+perfect fifth, two octaves, two octaves+major third, two octaves+perfect fifth, two octaves+minor seventh, two octaves+major ninth (or three octaves+major second), and so on. When we hear a fundamental pitch, it is actually the sum total of these harmonic overtones. By their physical nature, different instruments emphasize different harmonics. Guitarists should have no problem accessing the first ten.

NATURAL HARMONICS

Natural harmonics are notated using diamond-shaped noteheads and diamond-shaped brackets around tab numbers. Prepare natural harmonics by lightly placing a fret-hand finger directly over a desired node on an open string, avoiding contact with the fingerboard. Pluck the string and simultaneously remove your fret hand. The resulting node vibrates the string in equal parts.

Ex. 6.35 demonstrates the first 10 harmonic overtones generated by a low open-*E* fundamental. The overtone series generates mirror-image natural harmonics on either side of the 12th fret. As you'll see, it's hard to notate exact tab positions for the ones that fall between frets or off the fingerboard. Just fish around. As you locate each one, try to assign it a visual landmark.

Ex. 6.35

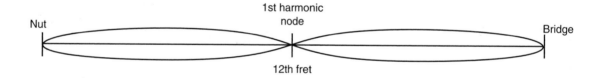

The first harmonic divides the string in half, directly above the 12th fret. The string vibrates in two equal parts and each node sounds one octave higher than the fundamental. **Ex. 6.36** shows the node and its vibrational path.

Ex. 6.36

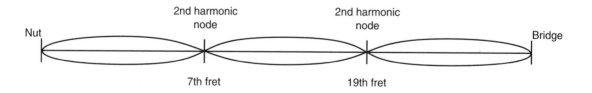

The second harmonic divides the string into thirds, directly above the 7th and 19th frets. The string vibrates in three equal parts and each node sounds one octave plus a fifth higher than the fundamental. **Ex. 6.37** shows both nodes and their vibrational path.

Ex. 6.37

The third harmonic quarters the string, directly above the 5th and 12th frets, and at the 24th fret (or the hypothetical 24th fret, if you don't have a 24-fret fingerboard). The string vibrates in four equal parts, and the nodes at the 5th and 12th frets sound two octaves higher than the fundamental, while the 12th-fret node sounds one octave higher. **Ex. 6.38** shows the three nodes and their vibrational path.

Ex. 6.38

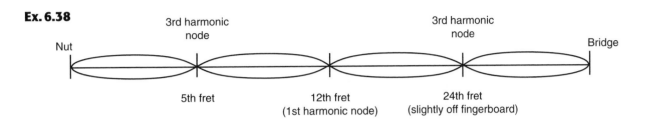

The fourth harmonic divides the string into fifths, directly above the 4th, 9th, and 16th frets, and off the fingerboard at the hypothetical 28th fret. The string vibrates in five equal parts and each node sounds two octaves plus a major third higher than the fundamental. **Ex. 6.39** shows the four nodes and their vibrational path.

Ex. 6.39

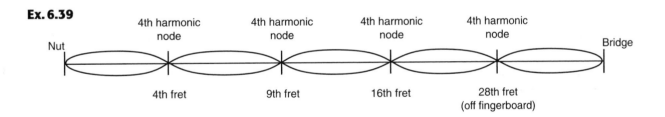

The fifth harmonic divides the string into sixths, between 3rd and 4th frets (closer to the 3rd fret), directly above the 7th and 12th frets, between 3rd and 4th frets (closer to the 3rd fret), directly above the 19th fret, at the real or hypothetical 24th fret. Each node sounds two octaves plus a perfect fifth higher than the fundamental, except for the 12th-fret node, which sounds an octave above the fundamental. **Ex. 6.40** shows the five nodes and their vibrational path.

Ex. 6.40

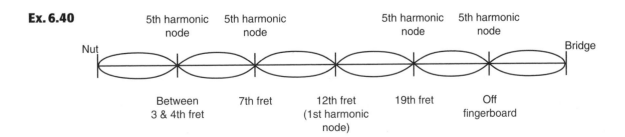

Get the idea? Now practice finding natural harmonics on each open string. If you haven't noticed yet, the overtone series contains all the notes of a major triad (root, 3, and 5), plus ♭7 and 9. You can make a lot of music with just those tones, especially if you've got a whammy bar.

There are harmonics that divide the strings into even smaller pieces: The sixth harmonic divides the string into seven equal parts and sounds two-octaves-plus-a-minor-seventh higher than the fundamental, the seventh harmonic divides the string into eight equal parts and sounds three octaves higher than the fundamental, and the eighth harmonic divides the string into nine equal parts and sounds three-octaves-plus-a-major-second (or two-octaves-plus-a-ninth) higher than the fundamental. These harmonics are harder to produce accurately, as the nodes sit closer and closer to each other when you divide the string more times. With perseverance, however, you'll be able to find them and—hopefully—incorporate them into your lines and chords.

Assuming you've already explored their inherent triad and dominant-7th and dominant-9th arpeggios, let's examine a few more ways to use natural harmonics. **Ex. 6.41** is an ascending *E* pentatonic minor scale—embellished with a 9—played entirely with natural harmonics.

Ex. 6.41

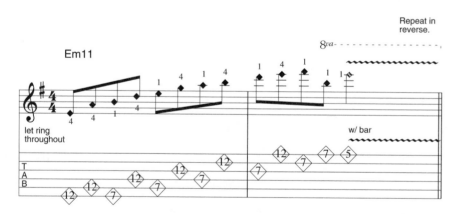

Combining natural harmonics with conventional notes also offers a lot of interesting musical possibilities. Play natural harmonics against static or moving bass notes to create shimmering chordal sounds. **Ex. 6.42a** will get you started. As an option, play the bass note before adding the harmonics. **Ex. 6.42b** forms 12 slash chords from a harmonic diad (*G-D*) played over ascending chromatic bass notes.

Ex. 6.42a

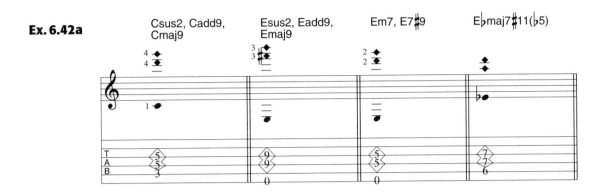

Ex. 6.42b

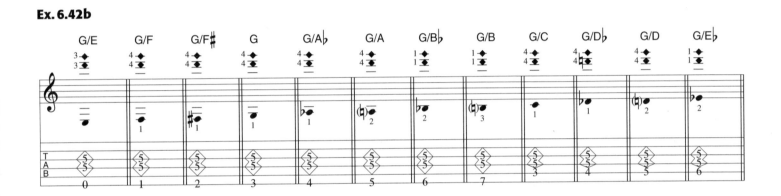

The chart in **Ex. 6.43** (next page) graphically locates the most available open-string harmonics in chromatic order. (Note: There is no natural *A♯/B♭* harmonic because this note doesn't appear in any open string's overtone series.)

Ex. 6.43

Chromatic open-string harmonics

Harmonics	⑥ (E) →	⑤ (A)	④ (D)	③ (G)	② (B)	① (E)
C	—	—	Just below 6th, 10th, 15th, and 22nd fret. Between 2nd and 3rd frets.	—	—	—
C#(Db)	—	4th, 9th, 16th, and 21st fret. Just above 6th fret. Between 1st and 2nd frets.	—	—	Just above 2nd, 10th, and 14th fret. Between 4th and 5th frets.	—
D	Just below 6th, 10th, 15th, and 22nd fret. Between 2nd and 3rd frets.	—	5th, 12th, and 24th fret. Just above 8th and 17th fret. Between 2nd and 3rd frets.	7th and 19th fret. Just above 3rd and 15th fret. Between 1st and 2nd frets.	—	Just below 6th, 10th, 15th, and 22nd fret. Between 2nd and 3rd frets.
D#(Eb)	—	—	—	—	4th, 9th, 16th, and 21st fret. Just above 6th fret. Between 1st and 2nd frets.	—
E	5th, 12th, and 24th fret. Just above 8th and 17th fret. Between 2nd and 3rd frets.	7th and 19th fret. Just above 3rd and 15th fret. Between 1st and 2nd frets.	Just above 2nd, 10th, and 14th fret. Between 4th and 5th frets.	—	—	5th, 12th and 24th fret. Just above 8th and 17th fret. Between 2nd and 3rd frets.
F	—	—	—	Just below 6th, 10th, 15th, and 22nd fret. Between 2nd and 3rd frets.	—	—
F# (Gb)	Just above 2nd, 10th, and 14th fret. Between 4th and 5th frets.	—	4th, 9th, 16th, and 21st fret. Just above 6th fret. Between 1st and 2nd frets.	—	7th and 19th fret. Just above 3rd and 15th fret. Between 1st and 2nd frets.	Just above 2nd, 10th, and 14th fret. Between 4th and 5th frets.
G	—	Just below 6th, 10th, 15th, and 22nd fret. Between 2nd and 3rd frets.	—	5th, 12th, and 24th fret. Just above 8th and 17th fret. Between 2nd and 3rd frets.	—	—
G# (Ab)	4th, 9th, 16th, and 21st fret. Just above 6th fret. Between 1st and 2nd frets.	—	—	—	—	4th, 9th, 16th, and 21st fret. Just above 6th fret. Between 1st and 2nd frets.
A	—	5th, 12th, and 24th fret. Just above 8th and 17th fret. Between 2nd and 3rd frets.	7th and 19th fret. Just above 3rd and 15th fret. Between 1st and 2nd frets.	Just above 2nd, 10th, and 14th fret. Between 4th and 5th frets.	Just below 6th, 10th, 15th, and 22nd fret. Between 2nd and 3rd frets.	—
A# (Bb)	—	—	—	—	—	—
B	7th and 19th fret. Just above 3rd and 15th fret. Between 1st and 2nd frets.	Just above 2nd, 10th, and 14th fret. Between 4th and 5th frets.	—	4th, 9th, 16th, and 21st fret. Just above 6th fret. Between 1st and 2nd frets.	5th, 12th, and 24th fret. Just above 8th and 17th fret. Between 2nd and 3rd frets.	7th and 19th fret. Just above 3rd and 15th fret. Between 1st and 2nd frets.

TAPPED AND SLAPPED HARMONICS

Harmonics can be produced by tapping or slapping one or more strings with a fret-hand finger at any desired node. **Ex. 6.44** illustrates with single and multiple notes. Tap sharply and remove the tapping finger quickly. Your aim is crucial on single notes. With chord slaps, you just have to be in the ballpark and approximate the basic angle of the shape with your index finger. Tapped harmonics are notated with appropriate left- and right-hand fingering and a "T" symbol above both staves. Slapped harmonics are notated with a "slap" indicator between staves and a half-tie to noteheads and tab numbers.

Ex. 6.44

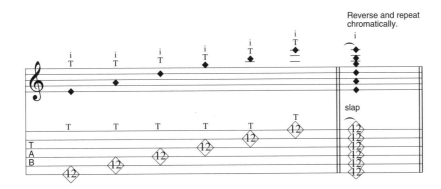

PINCHED/PICK HARMONICS

You don't actually "pinch" pinched harmonics. They are produced by allowing part of your thumb—usually the flesh near the base of the nail—to graze the string as soon as you pick it. The resulting harmonic comes from your thumb touching down on a random or selected node. Different harmonics will appear—in accordance with the overtone series—as you move your pick hand closer to the bridge or the neck. Choke up on the pick so only its tip is exposed.

Pinched harmonic notation shows both the fundamental note and its selected node; however, most of these are played off the neck over the pickups. You won't see the node in the tab either. You'll have to go fishing for most of the pinched harmonic overtone series generated from the lone *C* note in **Ex. 6.45** (next page)—which includes approximate tab positions for the nodes. Since these are generated from a fretted note, we're no longer talking about natural harmonics.

Ex. 6.45

ARTIFICIAL HARMONICS

Artificial harmonics are equal divisions of fretted (non-open) strings, and they follow the same principles as natural harmonics. The only difference lies in how they are produced. The fret hand is occupied elsewhere, so the pick hand must assume the responsibility of playing the nodes.

To play an artificial harmonic one octave above any fretted fundamental, touch the node 12 frets higher with the pick-hand index finger, and pick behind it—towards the bridge—with either the thumb or a pick. (If you use a pick, hold it between your thumb and middle fingers. If you use your thumb, duck the pick into your palm and hold it there with the middle and ring fingers.)

Artificial harmonics are notated the same as natural harmonics, with the addition of a parenthetical fundamental in both standard and tab notation. The same divisions that apply to open strings also apply to fretted notes: artificial harmonics seven frets above any fretted fundamental sound an octave plus a fifth higher, five frets above sounds two octaves higher, and so on. **Ex. 6.46a** demonstrates how to extract the first three artificial harmonics from a single note, while **Ex. 6.46b** pulls them from a B♭/C chord. **Ex. 6.46c** applies artificial harmonics to ascending diatonic 7th-chord arpeggios in the key of *G*. And, in case you haven't caught on yet, artificial harmonics can also be tapped, slapped, or pinched.

Ex. 6.46a

Ex. 6.46b

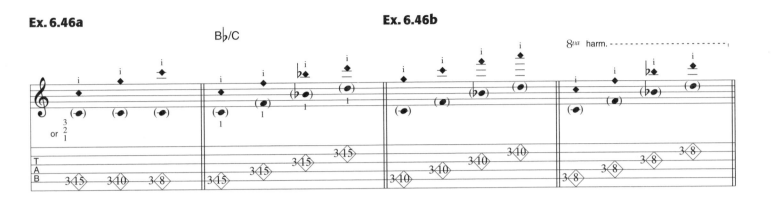

Ex. 6.46c

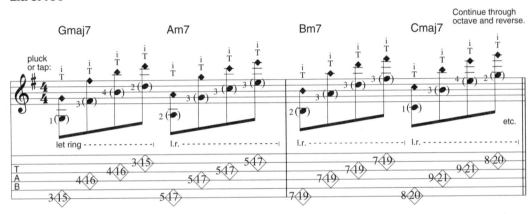

HARP HARMONICS

Harp harmonics—a favorite technique of the late, great fingerstylist Lenny Breau—blend natural or artificial harmonics with open strings or fretted notes to create cascades of chordal color. In **Ex. 6.47a** (next page), the fret hand holds a *Gm11* voicing (a straight barre across all six strings at the 3rd fret) while the pick hand sequences a series of two-string groups, with one fretted note and one artificial harmonic.

Follow these steps:

- Pick the *D* string using a middle-finger (*m*) upstroke. Then play the artificial harmonic at the 15th fret on the low *E* string. Use the thumb to pluck the string as your index finger touches the node.

- Continue alternating the same two-string pattern across the remaining adjacent string-groups: *G* string/3rd fret to *A* string/15th-fret harmonic, *B* string/3rd fret to *D* string/15th-fret harmonic, and high *E* string/3rd fret to *G* string/15th-fret harmonic.

- Reverse and descend the same pattern.

- Make it sound pretty.

- Move up a half-step (one fret higher) and repeat the previous steps.

Ex. 6.47a

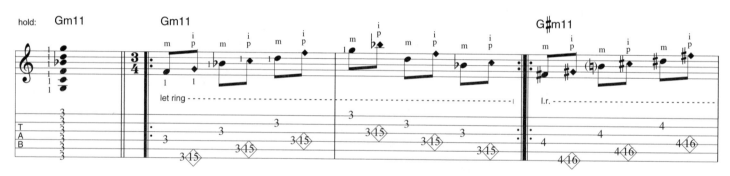

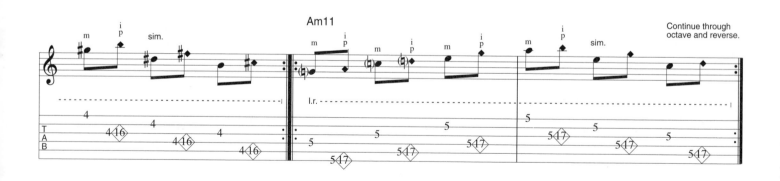

Ex. 6.47b offers five suggested chord voicings for harp harmonics. Be sure to follow the fretboard contour of each shape with your pick hand.

Ex. 6.47b

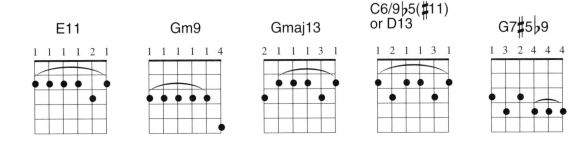

E11 Gm9 Gmaj13 C6/9♭5(♯11) or D13 G7♯5♭9

MECHANICAL VIBRATO

The vibrato bar—also known as the tremolo bar, whammy bar, wiggle stick, hand brake, and other cute names—has become a vital tool of expression for electric guitarists. Besides actual vibrato, the most obvious (and overused) bar technique is the "dive bomb" that dumps any note into flabby netherland. This sounds great with distorted harmonics and low open strings, but can wear thin quickly, so let's look at a few *musical* uses of the bar.

The bar's potential ranges from the ridiculous to the sublime. You can bend *into* notes as well as *from* them. Depress the bar slightly, pick any note, and release the bar to create a subtle *wang* or *yaw* effect that grows more pronounced the deeper you dip. **Ex. 6.48a** illustrates this technique and its notational symbols. Any drop in pitch can be notated using numerals written inside the "dip" symbol.

The bar can also be used to attack and sustain notes. **Ex. 6.48b** demonstrates how to "play the bar" to seven different rhythmic subdivisions. Transpose them to all strings and positions. The rhythms in each measure are generated from a single pick attack. Don't take the "-1" indicators too literally—just stay in the ballpark and concentrate on (literally) pumping out those rhythms.

Ex. 6.48a   **Ex. 6.48b**

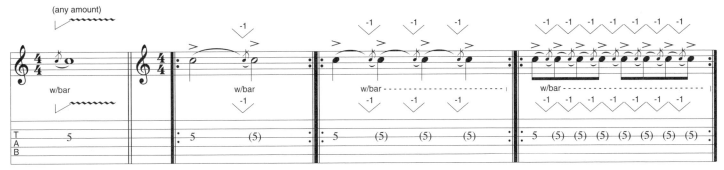

Ex. 6.48b (continued)

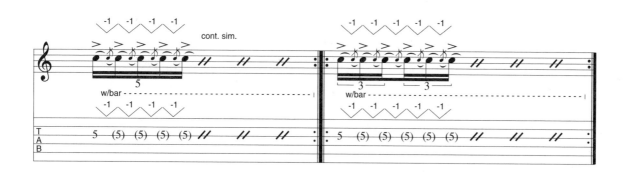

This "bar-picking" technique can serve you both rhythmically and melodically. **Ex. 6.49a** and **6.49b** generate similar eighth-note and eighth-note-triplet motifs from a single picked or hammered attack while incorporating hammer-ons and pull-offs. Don't hold on to the bar—use rhythmic karate chops.

Ex. 6.49a   **Ex. 6.49b**

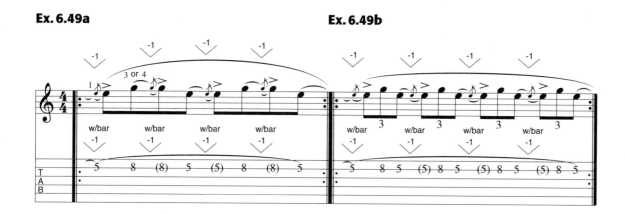

The bar can be used to bend to specific pitches. Accuracy really counts now, so lighten up your touch to articulate the half-step bends in **Ex 6.50a**. Try anchoring your fingers on the pickguard and playing the bar with your thumb. The bar no longer triggers the downbeat, so reinforce your time with a strong pinky-hammer. Since it now reflects specific bent pitches, we can drop those messy bar symbols from the standard notation, but "B"s and "R"s are added to indicate bar-bends and releases.

The bar can be adjusted to pull upward and raise pitches. This allows a smoother, more even vibrato. It also makes it possible to extract more melodies from any single note.

In **Ex. 6.50b**, three pitches are extrapolated from one attacked note. The bar notation adds "+" and "−" symbols between staves to indicate upward or downward bends. **Ex. 6.50c** shows the same motif applied to a high-G harmonic, and **Ex 6.50d** transposes the melodic activity to the key of G major.

Ex. 6.50a

Ex. 6.50b

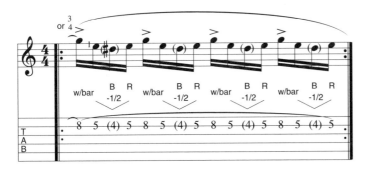

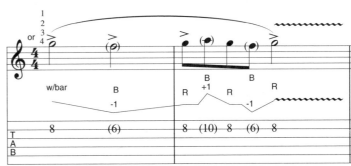

Ex. 6.50c

Ex. 6.50d

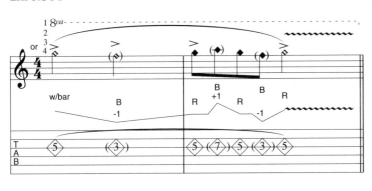

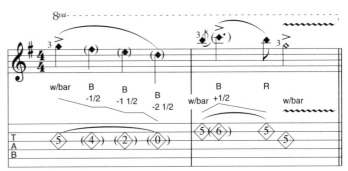

We've barely scratched the surface of this magic wand's potential. With the availability of mechanical devices such as the vibrato tailpiece—not to mention the glut of electronic effects on the market—the guitar has become chameleon-like and can no longer be limited to its previous musical roles.

Improvisation

Most of us have had the experience
of our jaw dropping while listening to our favorite players instantaneously generate
endless streams of cool musical ideas. The masters of improvisation play themselves in
and out of musical corners and always seem to land on their feet—even when the tempos and chord changes are flying. These great players appear to invent ideas out of the
blue, but do they actually create all those spur-of-the-moment sounds out of thin air?
Not at all.

"Create" is the wrong term. Musicians don't create—we *compose*. Composition is the
art of organizing musical elements to our liking, while improvisation is the instanta-
neous reorganization of previously learned musical ideas into new combinations. In
other words, improvisation is spontaneous composition. An improvised line can be
sparked by something learned last week, kindled with a scale exercise practiced ten
years ago, and ignited with a lick heard on the radio this morning.

The greatest improvisers are excellent listeners who develop their ears and musician-
ship to the highest levels. Improvisational ability depends on the breadth of players' musical vocabulary and their capacity to instantly recall and reorganize any part of it. Your
objective is to build a huge musical vocabulary by memorizing as many lines and permutations as possible and gaining the harmonic awareness to manipulate them infinitely.

People are natural-born improvisers. Consider this: Every time you speak without
reading or quoting, you are improvising. People become skilled users of their language
by learning to manipulate words to convey ideas, but can't claim creation of the words
themselves. Words are learned by example and repetition and reorganized as needed.
Music is a language, too—many languages, actually—and the same process we use
when we talk occurs during musical improvisation.

In the midst of a conversation, you'll occasionally encounter an obstacle which causes a lull. You can either draw on your additional knowledge of the subject matter, or—if you've run out of ideas—bail out and change the subject altogether. Naturally, those with greater understanding of a subject will stick with the subject longer than those without. The masters of musical improvisation are like great conversationalists. Their solos tell a complete story, hold our attention every step of the way, and leave us wanting more. There are great improvisers in all styles of music, and while personal taste will favor some over others, improvisational concepts are more or less the same, regardless of genre. Breaking down stylistic barriers universalizes the many languages of music.

Some claim that musical improvisation can't be taught and must be experienced. Fair enough, but then this must apply to all professions. People leave school armed with the knowledge and tools of any trade only to find many "rules" bent or broken in real-life applications. So to fit in, they improvise.

Approach musical improvisation as if you were learning a new language: one word at a time. It's hard to pinpoint the exact moment we first learned any particular word, even though it is now a permanent part of our vocabulary and we have no problem summoning it for conversational use.

Before we learned to speak, we tried to imitate others. Instinctively, after many failed attempts, we eventually uttered our first spoken sounds: raw, unmolded, and potentially characteristic of any world dialect—produced without any conscious memory of speech patterns and language. These sounds were easily dismissed as meaningless baby-babble, but in reality we were improvising—seeing what happened when we combined this scream with that whoop, or that gurgle with this squeak. There were no rules or restrictions—yet. Have you ever seen an infant stop abruptly in the middle of a screaming fit, suddenly amazed and delighted by the unplanned sound that just came out of its mouth? You'll see the same look on musicians' faces when they surprise themselves with a new combination of musical ideas in mid-flight.

Without direction, guidelines, and rules, we would not progress. We'd remain in a childlike state and face difficulties dealing with the real world. So we learn by example and repetition. We *copy*. Copying from recordings by your favorite players is an invaluable experience. To sound like your favorite players and understand how they think, you must copy their melodic lines and gain insight into how and why a certain line was used in a given situation. After many repetitions, a line becomes ingrained in your motor memory and is yours to manipulate at will. Your ability to manipulate the line in any musical territory depends on your ears and the depth of your knowledge of musical theory and stylistic genres.

Improvisational skills can be taught, but not all at once. They must be accumulated in small pieces and digested slowly. We add melodic lines, chords, and concepts to our musical vocabularies much the same way we've always added words to our spoken vocabularies: one at a time. Just as we learned how a word is spelled, written, and used, we can learn how a scale or chord is spelled, written, and used. Then, we move on to the next one. Do this faithfully and—slowly but surely—you will build a strong musical vocabulary. Learn one lick per day, and the cumulative result quickly becomes obvious. If you play in a band, put new lines and concepts into use immediately. Any on-the-job training opportunity should be used to its full advantage.

LEARNING FROM RECORDINGS

The most valuable source of inspiration and knowledge for any serious student is the wealth of recordings by music's greatest improvisers. As we've said, to sound like any given player, you must learn their lines. The way to achieve this is to listen repeatedly to a short segment of a line and transcribe it, either to paper or directly to your instrument.

Transcribing from compact discs is best, but you can also work from hard disk, tape, or even good old vinyl LPs. Here are a few tips:

- Learn lines one beat at a time by zeroing in on what is played on each beat.
- Sometimes it is easier to start at the end of a line and work your way backwards— one beat at a time—to its starting point.
- Employ ear-training concepts to identify intervallic motion as you listen from note to note, and from beat to beat.
- Learn to identify special left- and right-hand techniques.
- In guitar music, you can learn to hear the subtle variation in timbre when the same note is played on different strings. This helps locate the exact position in which a line was conceived.

- Analyze the harmonic background behind the line and determine how the line functions over it.

- Very fast lines can be re-recorded and played back at half-speed.

- Equalization can be used to highlight guitar parts buried in a thick mix. Try boosting upper-midrange frequencies (between 2kHz and 4kHz). Conversely, you can cut bass and treble frequencies that tend to mask guitars. Listening at a very low volume can also help.

- Once you learn a line, play along with the original recording. Try to blend in and match tone, dynamics, and phrasing.

- Listen to other players on other instruments—such as saxophone or piano—and copy their phrasing or harmonic concepts.

Of course, all of this takes time, patience, and a genuine love for the music. But, as with all musical study, the effect is cumulative. The more you do it, the easier it gets.

FORMING MELODIC LINES ON THE FINGERBOARD

We've discussed and practiced scales and chords to death. Now it's time to put them into application and compose your own custom-tailored lines. Let's focus first on building lines to fit individual chords.

Melodic lines can be constructed by following these five steps:

- Choose a chord sound to describe melodically. We'll begin simply with a *Dm* chord.

- Determine the chord's relative scales via key centers and other scale possibilities, and choose one. **Ex. 7.1a** shows seven scales with the potential to describe *Dm*. We'll choose *D* Aeolian, also known as the *D* natural minor scale.

Ex. 7.1a

- Dm = IIm in C (D Dorian mode)
- Dm = IIIm B♭ (D Phrygian mode)
- Dm = VIm in F (D Aeolian mode)
- Or use: D blues, D pentatonic minor, D harmonic minor, D melodic minor

---

- Choose a fingerboard position and outline the arpeggio of the chosen chord within the appropriate scale pattern (**Ex. 7.1b**). Each chord tone is a potential target, or ending note, for the line.

Ex. 7.1b

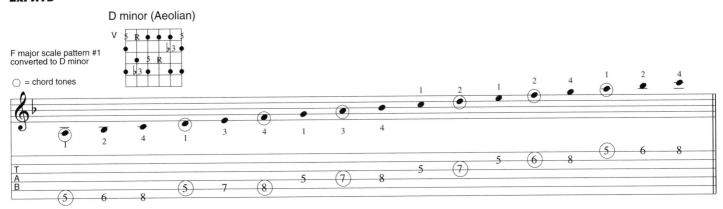

- Determine how many notes the line will contain and their rhythmic values. Choose one of the previously outlined chord tones as the last note, or point of arrival. For **Ex 7.1c**, we'll keep it simple with eight eighth-notes and a target *D* (third string, 7th fret).

Ex. 7.1c

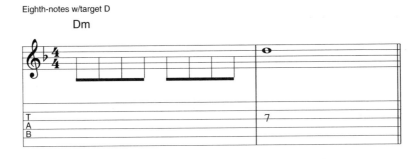

- Choose any notes in the pattern for the first eight notes. As long as you hit the target, the resulting line will describe *Dm*. It will also describe other diatonically related chord sounds if you change the target to correspond (see "Diatonic Substitutions," page 225). The entire line can be substituted to create altered chord sounds (see "Altered Chords," page 95). Chromatic tones can be imported from outside the scale pattern and used as passing tones between chord tones and scale tones. **Ex. 7.1d** demonstrates four possible *Dm* lines spawned by this formula.

Ex. 7.1d

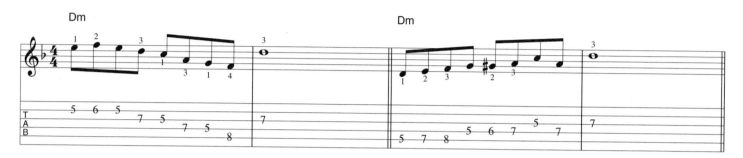

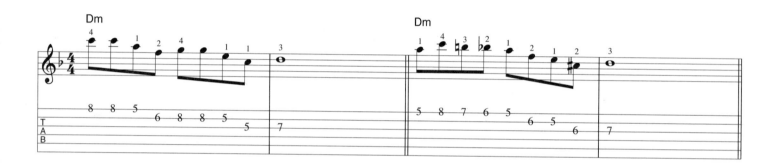

Generally, a line will sound closer to the original chord when chord tones fall on downbeats and other scale and passing tones fall on upbeats—especially when ascending or descending with consecutive scale tones. Don't hesitate to repeat notes or feel it is necessary to use all the notes in the scale at once. Try to develop a sense of how each part of a scale behaves melodically (active or static) in various harmonic territories.

Experiment and surprise yourself. Compose dozens of lines that describe your favorite pet chord sounds. Memorize the lines you like and discard the rest. Develop strong opinions about what works and what doesn't, and your own stylistic voice will begin to emerge. As a student of improvisation, you must research, collect, and catalog a sizable vocabulary of melodic lines and explore all of their rhythmic and melodic permutations.

For some inspiring lines, check out these books: Pat Martino's *Linear Impressions*; Joe Diorio's *21st-Century Intervallic Designs, Fusion,* and *Guitar Solos*; Don Mock's *Hot Licks*; and Les Wise's *Be-bop Bible* and *Inner Jazz*.

DIATONIC SUBSTITUTIONS

Any melodic line designed to fit one chord can be substituted to fit other chords. Diatonically related substitutions bring the chord to the line—with no transposition necessary—while non-diatonic subs transpose the line to fit the chord. First, we'll focus on diatonic subs.

Ex. 7.2

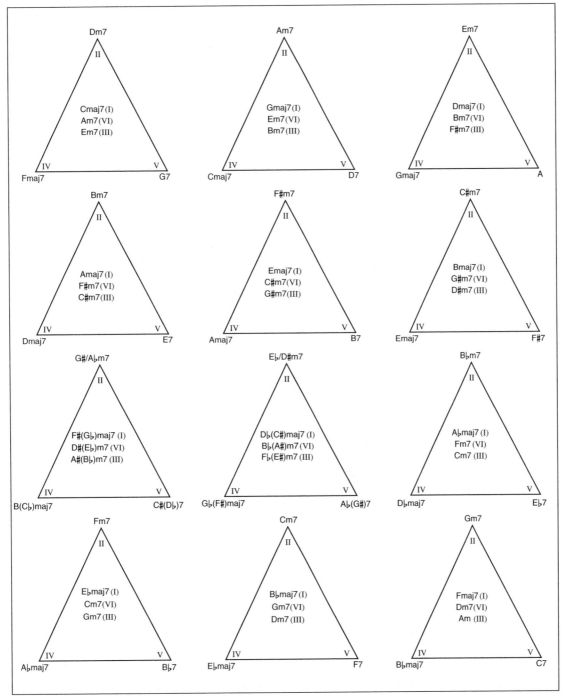

In any major key—or relative key or mode—there are three substitutions that cover the three basic chord categories: major, minor, and dominant. These form a "substitution triangle" which can be illustrated with the IIm7, IVmaj7, and V7 chords at the three points and the tonic (Imaj7), relative minor (VIm7), and secondary relative minor (IIIm7) in the center. The VIIm7♭5 chord is omitted but can be grouped with the V7 chord (V7+VIIm7♭5=V9). Any melodic line originally designed to describe one chord inside or on the points of the triangle is totally interchangeable with any other chord found in or outside the same triangle. When necessary, simply alter the target note to fit the sub. So if your line was formulated to fit *Dm7*, it will also fit *Cmaj7, Em7, Fmaj7, G7, Am7,* and *Bm7♭5*, plus any of their diatonic embellishments and extensions (6th, 9th, 11th, and 13th chords) or triadic reductions (*C, Em, F,* and so on). This concept also applies to any relative "reduced" scale, such as pentatonic and blues scales.

Consider the mind-boggling implications: *Every melodic line in your musical vocabulary is interchangeable!* Pentatonic minor and blues lines can fit over major-7th chords, major-7th lines over dominant or minor chords, minor-7th lines over—well, anything. A few new lines can generate endless melodic possibilities.

Ex. 7.2 (previous page) displays all twelve major-key substitution triangles. Use them to determine potential substitutions or to locate key centers at a glance.

IMPROVISING OVER CHORD PROGRESSIONS

To improvise single-note lines over a group of moving chords, you need a strong melodic vocabulary, a working knowledge of key centers, and an understanding of melodic and harmonic tension and release. With considerable practice, this information will give you the chops to solo over any chord progression.

HOW TO FIND KEY CENTERS

To determine a key center, examine each chord in a given progression and list the major or minor keys to which it belongs. In any major key, minor-7th chords have three different key-center possibilities, major-7th chords have two, and dominant-7th and minor-7th-♭5 chords each have one. Let's locate the major key centers for the progression in **Ex. 7.3** by analyzing each chord individually.

Ex. 7.3

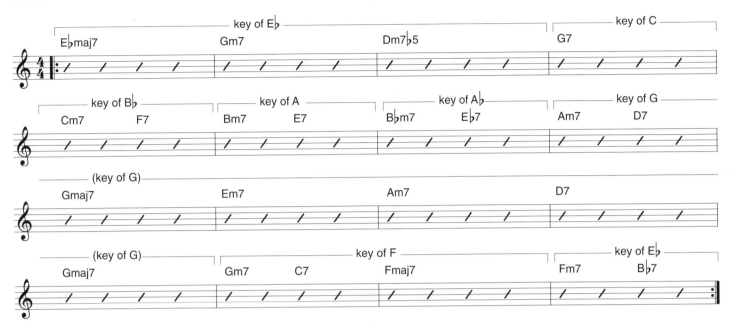

- *E♭maj7* is found in two different keys:

  *E♭maj7=*Imaj7 in *E♭*

  *E♭maj7=*IVmaj7 in *B♭*

- *Gm7* is found in three different keys:

  *Gm7=*IIm7 in *F.*

  *Gm7=*IIIm7 in *E♭*

  *Gm7=*VIm7 in *B♭*

- *Dm7♭5* is found in only one key:

  *Dm7♭5=*VIIm7♭5 in *E♭*

- *G7* is also found in only one key:

  *G7=*V7 in *C*

The key center for the first three bars is *E♭* because *E♭maj7, Gm7,* and *Dm7♭5* are all common to that key. In bar 4, the key center shifts to *C*, the only choice for *G7.*

Each of the next four bars is in a different key center. This can be determined imme- diately, since any dominant-7th chord has only one possible major key center. Here, each descending V7 chord is preceded by its IIm7 to form a string of chromatic IIm7-V7 movements and corresponding key centers—*Cm7-F7=*IIm7-V7 in the key of *B♭,*

2 2 7

Bm7-E7=IIm7-V7 in *A*, *Bbm7-Ebm7*=IIm7-V7 in *Ab*, and *Am7-D7*=IIm7-V7 in *G*. Each measure represents a key change but is not notated as such. It's up to the improviser to extract this data from the harmonic information contained in a progression.

Learning to spot V7 chords in a progression will cut down the process-of-elimination phase when hunting key centers. For example, you could do a chord-by-chord analysis of bars 9-12 (*Gmaj7*=Imaj7 in *G* or IVmaj7 in *C*, and so on) or simply use the V7 chord in bar 12 to determine the *G* major key center.

The *G* major key center carries over into bar 13 before dropping a whole-step to cover the IIm7-V7-Imaj7 movement in bars 14 and 15. The IIm7-V7 in the final measure boomerangs us back to the key of *Eb*.

When learning a new chord progression, write it out and bracket its key centers as shown in Ex. 7.3. Use V7 chords for quick key spotting.

Apply all of the above to minor and modal key centers.

Key-center playing allows all correct-sounding notes over the entire fingerboard to become instantly available to an improviser in any harmonic situation—almost. Yes, there is a catch.

MELODIC AND HARMONIC TENSION AND RELEASE

Melodic and harmonic tension is like breathing—a force that propels a line or chord progression forward (inhale) towards a point of arrival, release, or resolution (exhale). Without the forward momentum generated by melodic and harmonic tension, music tends to sound placid and repetitive. Conversely, constant tension can make music cacophonous. To maintain interest, most music requires a balance of tension and release. (The thrash-metal and new-age genres prove interest in both extremes.)

Every chord in a progression functions as either a tension or resolution point in its harmonic scheme. Generally, major and minor chord types serve as resolution points while dominant-7th chords generate tension. This is because the two key tones in a dominant-7th chord—the 3 and b7—correspond with the two points of unrest in any major scale—the 7 and 4. In a *G7* chord, for example, the 3 and b7 are *B* and *F*—the 7 and 4 of the *C* major scale.

There are two types of tension—"natural" and "altered"—and each is derived and used differently. True to their name, the natural tensions—7, 9 (2), 11 (4), and 13 (6)—cause less melodic and harmonic unrest because they are present in any major key. Use key centers to locate natural tensions. Altered tensions—♭5 (♯11), ♯5, ♭9, and ♯9—are not present in dominant chords relative to major keys, but can be found in some diatonic major and minor chords, including extended harmonies. Most notable are the diatonic VIIm7♭5, IIIm7♭9, and IVmaj7♯11 chords found in any harmonized major-scale system. (More altered major and minor chords—including minor/major-7th and major-7th-♯5 types—can be found in harmonized harmonic- or melodic-minor scale systems.)

There is a saying among jazz players: "If you can't hear the chord changes in your solo—without accompaniment—you ain't making it happen!" To make it happen, you must recognize the tension and release points in a chord progression, play altered tensions on the tension points, and provide resolution to strong chord tones at release or static points.

And so the aforementioned catch is revealed: While key-center playing provides endless melodic possibilities using all of the "correct" notes, and is great for generating resolution-point melodies, it also limits an improviser to playing only the milder, natural tensions over those restless dominant chords. The result? A potentially boring and tiresome experience for both player and listener.

There are two ways to create altered tension:

1. Derive lines from separate scales customized to fit every possible chord sound as it arises (**Ex. 7.4**). Technically, this works but is extremely impractical when chords are moving rapidly.

Ex. 7.4

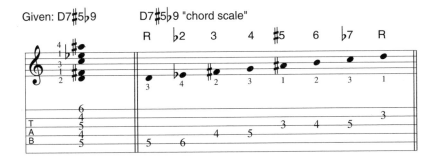

2. Learn to create altered tension and release by manipulating and substituting already familiar line forms. (Now we're talking!)

Since melodic and harmonic tensions are most applicable to dominant chord types, we'll focus on them. There are two categories of dominant chords: "functioning" and "non-functioning" (or "static").

STATIC DOMINANT CHORDS

When a single dominant tonality provides harmony for an extended period of time—as in much funk, rock, and blues music—it falls in the static category. Static dominant chords are commonly embellished with natural tensions (9, 11, 13) or the #9 (**Ex. 7.5**).

Ex. 7.5

IMPROVISING OVER STATIC DOMINANT CHORDS

Use key centers and diatonic substitutions to improvise over static dominant chords. You can substitute ideas from any point on the substitution triangle. In **Ex. 7.6**, *E* mixolydian is the obvious for *E7*, but you can also play any *Bm7* or *Dmaj7* line, as long as you target *E7* chord tones. Apply the same concept to static major and minor chords using modal key centers and diatonic subs.

Ex. 7.6

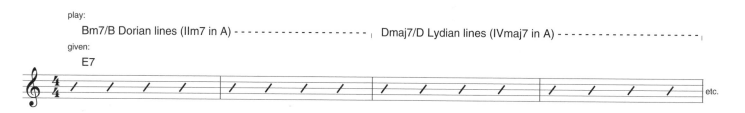

To temporarily introduce tension to a static harmonic climate, you can "sub the sub" by playing diatonic lines in substitute keys a minor or major second, minor third, or flatted fifth higher or lower (**Ex. 7.7**).

Ex. 7.7

FUNCTIONING DOMINANT CHORDS

A dominant chord gains "functional" status when it becomes part of a moving chord progression. Functioning dominant chords are commonly embellished with natural diatonic extensions and/or altered tensions (**Ex. 7.8**).

Ex. 7.8

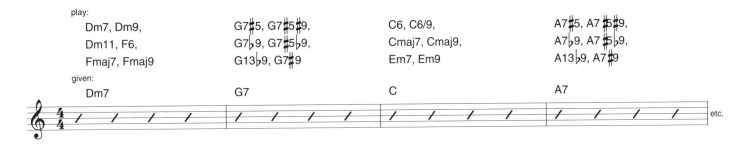

IMPROVISING OVER FUNCTIONING DOMINANT CHORDS

To improvise over functioning dominant chords, play altered tensions. To create altered tension, use the major scale one half-step above, or a minor scale—natural, Dorian, or especially melodic minor—one half-step above or one whole-step below any dominant chord. **Ex. 7.9** demonstrates how each of these scales provides all four alterations (except for *F* melodic minor, which omits the ♭5 and ♯5), as well as the ♭7 of *G7*. (Notice that the *A♭* major and *F* minor scales have a relative major/minor root relationship.) This empowers you to improvise over altered dominant chords using familiar line forms in totally new ways. To resolve, switch back to key-center substitutions and target chord tones. No cumbersome customized scales needed—just pure, unadulterated melodic line form! The revelation of this powerful tool is practically the punch line of this book—the part that could change your musical life. Exploit these substitution techniques, and you'll quickly gain access to exciting sounds that have previously taken players years or decades to master.

Ex. 7.9

Ex. 7.10 provides a handy reference chart that links the scales in Ex. 7.9 to a common 4-bar progression containing two functioning dominant seventh chords—the V7 (*G7*) and the VI7 (*A7*).

Ex. 7.10

release	tension	release	tension
play: Dm7, Fmaj7 lines (Cmajor key center)	Fm7, F melodic minor A♭maj7, A♭melodic minor } lines	Cmaj7, Am7, Em7, Dm7 lines (C major key center)	Gm7, G melodic minor B♭maj7, B♭melodic minor } lines
given: Dm7(IIm7)	G7alt(V7alt)	Cmaj7(Imaj7)	A7alt(VI7alt)

You can mix alterations at will—they all serve the same function. Feel free to play a ♭9 and/or ♭5 over a chord containing a ♯9 and/or ♯5. Just keep an ear open for clashes with the song's melody, which should always have first consideration. Now go back to the progression in Ex. 7.3, apply altered-tension subs, and discover your inner jazzbo.

IMPROVISING OVER II-V-I PROGRESSIONS

The most common harmonized root progression in popular music—II-V-I—is a textbook example of the tension/release concept in action. To form melodic lines over any major II-V-I progression, follow these steps:

- Begin with a Dorian, natural minor, or melodic minor–based line or motif that describes the sound of the IIm7 chord (**Ex. 7.11a**, bar 1, next page).
- Transpose the same motif up a minor third (one-and-a-half steps), and play it over the V7 chord to produce altered tensions (**Ex. 7.11a**, bar 2).
- Transpose the same motif up an additional major third (two whole-steps) and play it over the Imaj7 resolution (**Ex. 7.11a**, bar 3).

This three-step formula can work miracles, but transposing the exact same line or motif to three different positions quickly becomes obvious and predictable. The solution? Permute the transpositions. This smoothes out voice-leading between chord changes, allows you to stay in one position, and disguises the fact that you're playing the same motif. **Ex 7.11b** demonstrates two possible permutations of the original motif we used in Ex 7.11a.

Ex. 7.11a

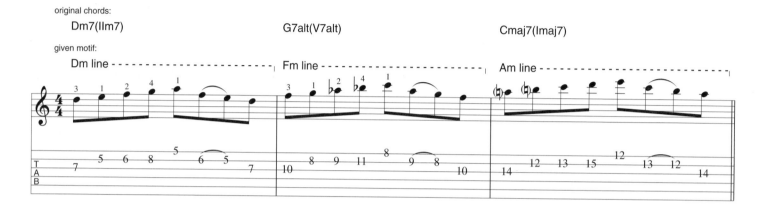

Ex. 7.11b

Ex. 7.12a adapts a *Dm7* motif to *F* melodic minor for the V7 chord in bar 2, and converts back to *A* minor for bar 3. **Ex. 7.12b** starts with the same IIm7 motif, then permutes the *F* Melodic minor and *Am7* lines in bars 2 and 3.

Ex 7.12c permutes all three measures and adapts the V7 motif in bar 2 to *A♭maj7*. **Ex. 7.12d** features additional permutations of the IIm7 and Imaj7 motifs, and the permuted V7 motif converted to *A♭* melodic minor. Every line in Examples 7.12a–7.12d originates from the first *Dm7* motif.

For minor IIm7♭5-V7alt-Im7 progressions, play major IIm7-V7alt-Imaj7 ideas a minor third higher (i.e., play *Dm7-G7alt-Cmaj7* lines over *Bm7♭5-E7alt-Am7*). Retarget whenever necessary.

Ex. 7.12a

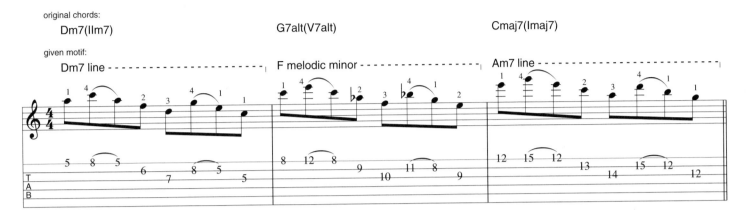

Ex. 7.12b

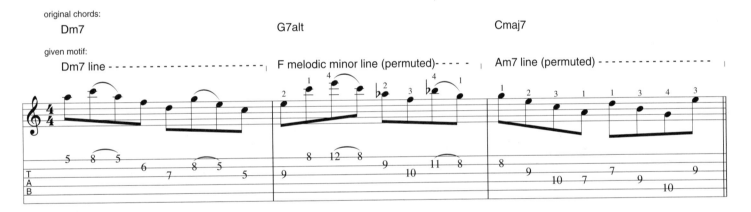

Ex. 7.12c

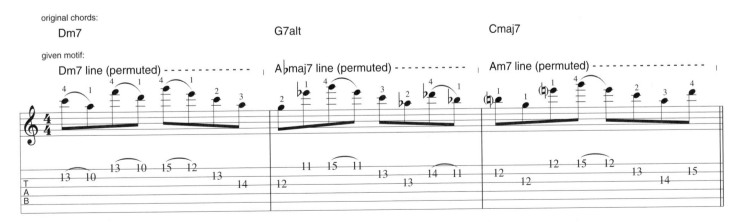

Ex. 7.12d

The chart in **Ex. 7.13** displays six formulas for creating altered tension and resolution in major or minor II–V–I progressions. Refer to it as often as necessary.

Ex. 7.13

Function:	Release	Tension	Release
Given harmony:	Dm7 (IIm7) Bm7♭5 (IIm7♭5)	G7alt (V7alt) E7alt (V7alt)	Cmaj7 (Imaj7) Am7 (Im7)
Play: (motifs, lines, scales, arpeggios)	D minor	F minor or F melodic minor	C major or A minor
	D minor	A♭ minor or A♭ melodic minor*	C major or A minor
	D minor	A♭ major	C major or A minor
	F major	F minor or F melodic minor	C major or A minor
	F major	A♭ major	C major or A minor
	F major	B major7**	C major or A minor

* A♭m6 = D♭9 = (♭5 substitution for G7)
** Relative major of A♭ (G#) minor

SIX WAYS TO A TONIC (REPRISE)

Though the chart appears in another part of the book (see Chapter 5, Ex. 5.38), I'd like to re-emphasize its importance in light of all this improvisational mumbo-jumbo. To reiterate: If you encounter an out-of-the-ordinary chord progression and don't know how to approach it improvisationally, it is likely to contain one of these six cadences disguised by embellishments, alterations, slash-chord symbols, or other devices. If not, its root motion is probably based on some intervallic cycle or sequence.

Analyze every chord progression you can find and practice improvising over them. Remember that *all* substitution concepts are applicable to *all* scales, arpeggios, motifs, lines, and chords. Gluing these together with left- and right-hand techniques, and rhythmic motifs, displacements, and permutations, aligns all the elements of music into one powerful system that becomes yours to manipulate physically, mentally, and emotionally.

PARTING THOUGHTS

In closing, I'd like to note that these rules of improvisation—and any rules of music, for that matter—are by no means compulsory. They just happen to work. You could live your life by them, or challenge, dispute, and shatter them until few remain intact. Music has one bottom line: If it sounds good to you, it *is* good. Developing strong musical opinions is as important as honing your chops.

Think of how recipes evolve. The first few times you cook any dish, you follow the written recipe literally. Soon, you are adding your own personal touches. Eventually, it becomes second nature—something you do by taste and feel. Finally, you hand it down to someone else and the cycle is complete. I hope you have followed suit and transformed many of the recipes in this book into your own creations.

If you take only one thing away from *The Guitar Cookbook*, let it be the awareness and understanding of the common ingredients all music shares.

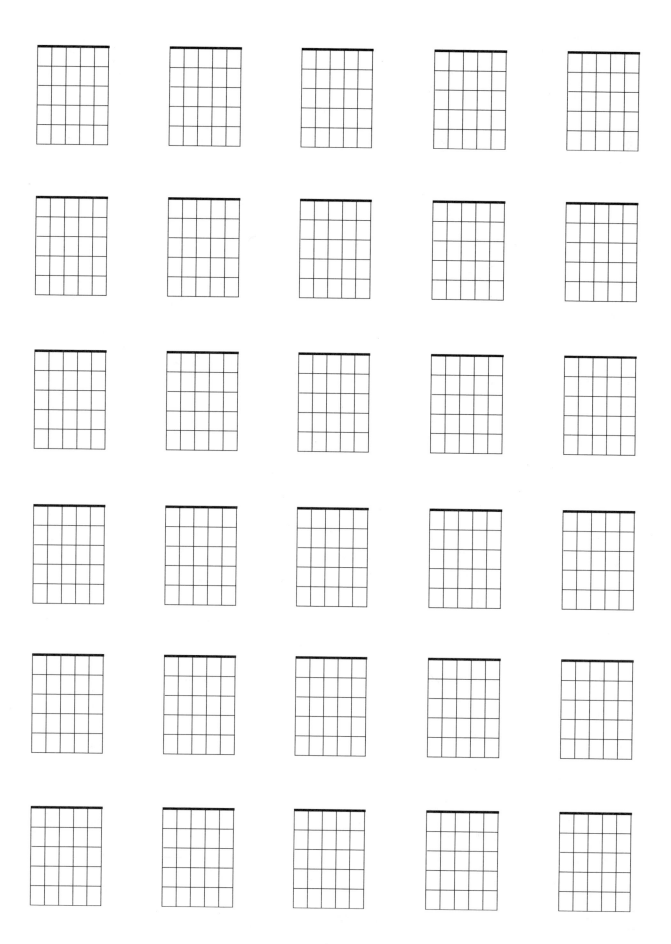

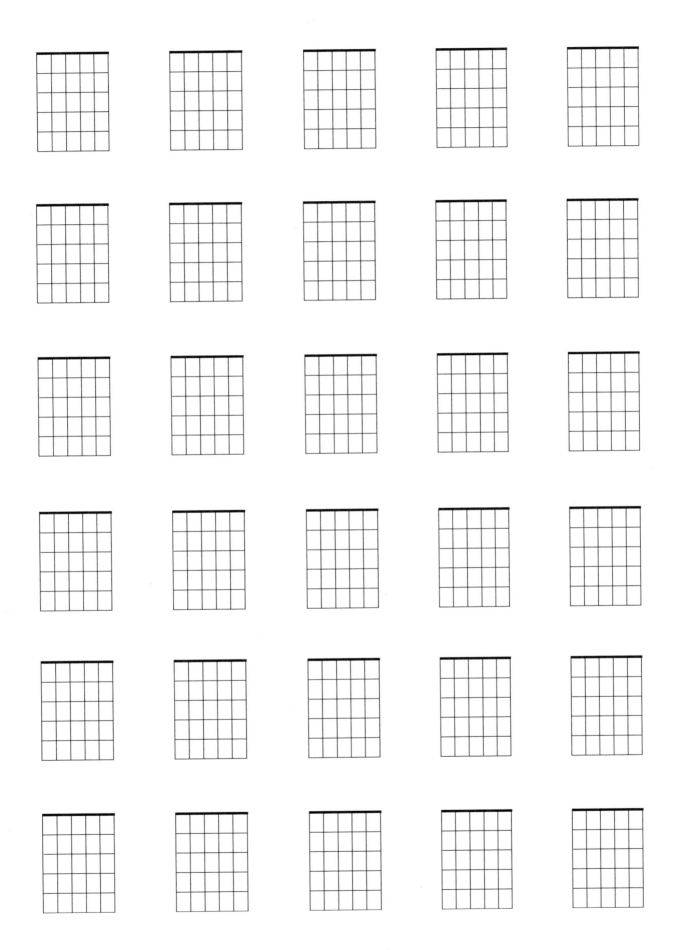

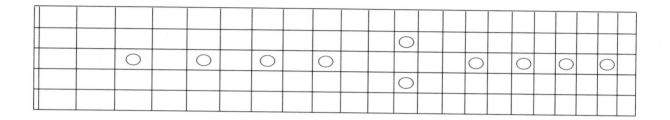

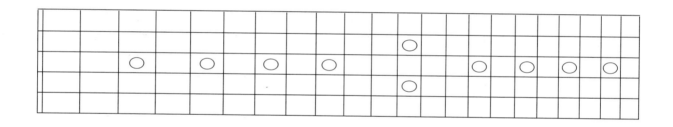

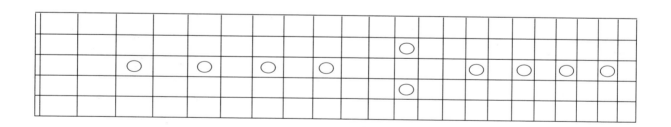

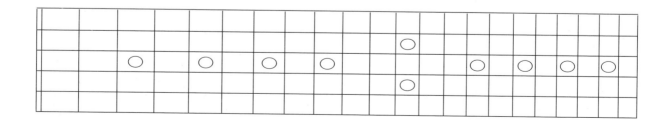

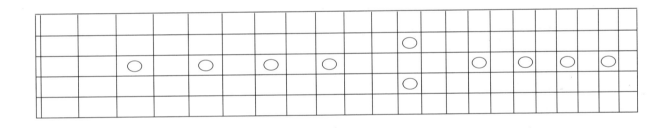

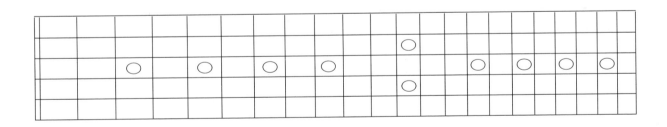

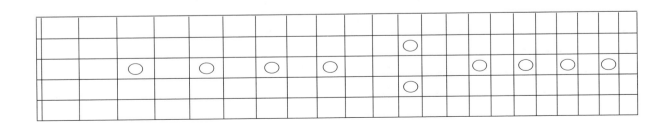

Acknowledgments

Profuse inspirational and existential thanks goes to:

- Every musician I've ever played with.
- All of the great teachers who shared their wisdom with me.
- All of the students who tolerated my attempts to emulate my teachers.
- My extended Gress-olini and Arnold families.
- My extended G.I.T. family (class of '79!).
- Todd Rundgren, Tony Levin, and their fans for dream fulfillment, gainful employment, and generous hospitality.
- Cover artist extraordinaire Mary Fleener.

My short list of personal heroes has to include: Jeff Beck, Eric Clapton, Jimi Hendrix, Todd Rundgren, the Beatles, Frank Zappa, Howard Roberts, Tommy Tedesco, Vincent Bell, Joe Diorio, Don Mock, Pat Martino, Jan Hammer, the Mahavishnu Orchestra, Miles Davis, Charlie Parker, John Coltrane, Eddie Sauter, Quincy Jones, Stan Kenton, Johnny Richards, George Russell, Les Paul, B.B. King, Jimmy Page, Adrian Belew, Tony Levin, Joe Satriani, Steve Vai, Jaco Pastorius, Herbie Hancock, Les Baxter, Martin Denny, Arthur Lyman, Jerry Goldsmith, Lalo Schifrin, John Ferenzik, Andy Johnson, the Nastasee brothers, Mike Ninno, Tass Filipos, Chuck's Lights, Harvey Pekar, Lynda Barry, and Herb Alpert & the Tijuana Brass. Thanks for the perspiration!

Special thanks to: The fab folks at Backbeat Books: Matt Kelsey, Richard Johnston, Dorothy Cox, Nancy Tabor, Nina Lesowitz, Julie Herrod-Lumsden, Jay Kahn, and Gary Montalvo, plus Adam Levy for bravery in copyediting, and Charylu Roberts for early pre-production layouts.

Finally, an insane debt of gratitude goes to Liz and Chris Ledgerwood for their excellence in music typesetting above and beyond the call of duty.

Visit Jesse's website at **www.jessegress.com**.